CW00546460

THE ABC OF BRITISH RAILWAYS LOCOMOTIVES

EDITED BY A. F. COOK

PART 1 - Nos. 1-9999
WESTERN REGION
STEAM LOCOMOTIVES

LONDON :

Ian Allan Ltd

NOTES ON THE USE OF THIS BOOK

1. This booklet lists British Railways locomotives numbered between 1 and 9999 in service at January 31st, 1951. This range of numbers covers Western Region (ex-G.W.R.) engines with the following exceptions :

   (i) Diesel and gas turbine locomotives, which are dealt with in the ABC OF BRITISH RAILWAYS LOCOMOTIVES NOS. 10000-39999.

   (ii) British Railways Class " WD " 2-8-0 locomotives in service on the Western Region. These are listed in the ABC OF BRITISH RAILWAYS LOCOMOTIVES Part 4—Nos. 60000-90999.

2. With the exception of Diesel locomotives, Western Region locomotives retain their original Great Western numbers.

3. This book is divided into three parts :—

   (a) An alphabetical list of classes, with dimensions and sub-divisions, and summary of locomotives in the class.

   (b) A numerical list of locomotives showing the class of each, and the name, if any.

   (c) A table of dimensions.

4. The aim of the book is that 1 (a) above shall provide a ready reference to particulars of individual locomotives in a class : and that 1 (b) shall be used for observation purposes.

5. The following notes are a guide to the system of reference marks and other details given in the lists of dimensions shown for each class in the alphabetical list of classes.

   (a) In the lists of dimensions " Su " indicates a superheated locomotive, and " SS " indicates that some locomotives of the class are superheated.

   (b) Locomotives are fitted with two inside cylinders, slide valves and Stephenson link motion, except where otherwise shown, e.g. (O) indicates outside cylinders and "P.V." piston valves.

   (c) The date on which a design of locomotive first appeared is indicated by " Introduced." If the oldest surviving locomotive was built at a later date, that also is indicated.

6. All locomotives are of G.W.R. origin, except where otherwise shown.

7. The following is a list of abbreviations used to indicate the pre-grouping owners of certain Western Region locomotives :

AD	Alexandra (Newport and South Wales) Docks & Railway.	CMDP	Cleobury Mortimer and Ditton Priors Light Railway.
BR	Barry Railway.	LMM	Llanelly & Mynydd Mawr Railway.
BM	Brecon and Merthyr Railway.		
BPGV	Burry Port & Gwendraeth Valley Railway.	MSWJ	Midland and South Western Junction Railway.
Cam.R.	Cambrian Railways.	PM	Powlesland & Mason (Contractor).
Car.R.	Cardiff Railway.		

WESTERN REGION LOCOMOTIVE RUNNING SHEDS AND SHED CODES

Depot No.	Depot	Depot No.	Depot	Depot No.	Depot
81A	OLD OAK COMMON	84A	WOLVERHAMPTON (Stafford Rd.)	86J	Aberdare
81B	Slough	84B	Oxley	86K	Abergavenny
	Aylesbury	84C	Banbury		Tredegar
	Marlow	84D	Leamington	87A	NEATH
	Watlington	84E	Tyseley		Glyn Neath
81C	Southall		Stratford on-Avon		Neath (N. & B.)
	Staines	84F	Stourbridge	87B	Duffryn Yard
81D	Reading	84G	Shrewsbury	87C	Danygraig
	Basingstoke		Ludlow	87D	Swansea East Dock
	Henley-on-T.		Trench	87E	Landore
81E	Didcot		Coalport	87F	Llanelly
	Wallingford		Clee Hill		Burry Port
	Winchester		Craven Arms		Pantyfnynon
81F	Oxford		Knighton	87G	Carmarthen
	Abingdon		Builth Road		Newcastle Emlyn
	Fairford	84H	Wellington	87H	Neyland
82A	BRISTOL (Bath Road)		Crewe		Cardigan
	Bath		Much Wenlock		Milford Haven
	Wells	84J	Croes Newydd		Pembroke Dock
	Weston-super-Mare		Bala		Whitland
	Yatton		Trawsfynydd	87J	Goodwick
82B	Bristol (S.P.M.)		Penmaenpool	87K	Swansea Victoria
82C	Swindon	84K	Chester		Carmarthen
	Andover	85A	Worcester		Llandovery
	Chippenham		Evesham		Upper Bank
	Malmesbury		Kingham		Gurnes
82D	Westbury	85B	Gloucester	88A	CARDIFF CATHAYS
	Frome		Brimscombe		Radyr
	Salisbury		Chalford	88B	Cardiff East Dock
82E	Yeovil		Cheltenham	88C	Barry
82F	Weymouth		Cirencester	88D	Merthyr
	Bridport		Lydney		Dowlais C.
83A	NEWTON ABBOT		Tetbury		Rhymney
	Ashburton	85C	Hereford		Cae Harris
	Kingsbridge		Kington	88E	Abercynon
83B	Taunton		Ledbury	88F	Treherbert
	Barnstaple		Leominster		Ferndale
	Bridgwater		Ross		Pwllyrhebog
	Minehead	85D	Kidderminster	89A	OSWESTRY
83C	Exeter	86A	NEWPORT (Ebbw Jc.)		Llanfyllin
	Tiverton Jcn.	86B	Newport Pill		Llanidloes
83D	Laira	86C	Cardiff (Canton)		Moat Lane
	Launceston	86D	Llantrisant		Welshpool
	Princetown	86E	Severn Tunnel Jcn.		Whitchurch
83E	St. Blazey	86F	Tondu	89B	Brecon
	Bodmin		Bridgend		Builth Wells
	Moorswater	86G	Pontypool Road	89C	Machynlleth
83F	Truro		Pontrilas		Aberayron
83G	Penzance		Branches Fork		Aberystwyth
	Helston	86H	Aberbeeg		Portmadoc
	St. Ives				Pwllheli

SUMMARY OF WESTERN REGION STEAM LOCOMOTIVE CLASSES

WITH HISTORICAL NOTES AND DIMENSIONS

In this list the classes are arranged by wheel arrangement in the following order : 4-6-0, 4-4-0, 2-8-0, 2-6-0, 2-4-0, 0-6-0, 2-8-2T, 2-8-0T, 2-6-2T, 0-6-2T, 0-6-0T, 0-4-2T, 0-4-0T. Codes in small bold type at the head of each class denote B.R. power classification.

4-6-0 6MT 1000 Class "County"

Introduced 1945 : Hawksworth design
Weights : Loco. 76 tons 17 cwt.
         Tender 49 tons 0 cwt.
Pressure : 280 lb. Su.
Cyls. : (O) 18½″×30″
Driving Wheels : 6′ 3″
T.E. : 32,580 lb.
P.V.

1000–29   Total 30

4-6-0 4P 2900 Class "Saint"

Introduced 1903 : Churchward design, developed from No. 2900 (originally No. 100, introduced 1902), earlier locomotives subsequently fitted with new boilers and superheaters, remainder built as such (oldest survivor 2981, built 1905 as 4-4-2).
Weights : Loco. 72 tons 0 cwt.
         Tender 40 tons 0 cwt.
Pressure : 225 lb. Su.
Cyls. : (O) 18½″×30″
Driving Wheels : 6′ 8½″
T.E. : 24,395 lb.
P.V.

2906/12/20/6/7/31–4/6–8/40/4/5/
7–54/81

                                Total 24

4-6-0 5P 4000 Class "Star"

Introduced 1907 : Churchward design, developed from No. 4000 (originally No. 40, introduced 1906 as a 4-4-2), earlier locomotives subsequently fitted with new boilers and superheaters, remainder built as such.
Weights : Loco. 75 tons 12 cwt.
         Tender 46 tons 14 cwt.
Pressure : 225 lb. Su.
Cyls. : (4) 15″×26″
Driving Wheels : 6′ 8½″
T.E : 27,800 lb.
Inside Walschaerts gear and rocking shafts, P.V.

4003/7/15/8/20–3/8/31/3–6/8/40–
4/6–50/2–62   Total 36

4-6-0 6P 4073 Class "Castle"

Introduced 1923 : Collett design, developed from "Star" (4000/16/32/7, 5083-92 converted from "Star," 111 from 4-6-2).
Weights : Loco. 79 tons 17 cwt.
         Tender 46 tons 14 cwt.
Pressure : 225 lb. Su.
Cyls. : (4) 16″×26″
Driving Wheels : 6′ 8½″
T.E. : 31,625 lb.
Inside Walschaerts gear and rocking shafts, P.V.

111, 4000/16/32/7/73–99, 5000–
99, 7000–37   Total 170

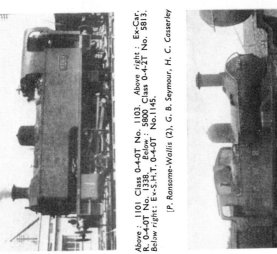

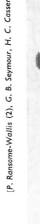

Above : 1101 Class 0-4-0T No. 1103. *Above right* : Ex-Car.
R. 0-4-0T No. 1338. *Below* : 5800 Class 0-4-2T No. 5813.
Below right : Ex-S.H.T. 0-4-0T No.1145.

[P. Ransome-Wallis (2), G. B. Seymour, H. C. Casserley

Above : 850 Class 0-6-0PT No. 2004 (with open cab)   [J. Davenport

Below : 850 Class 0-6-0PT No. 2012 (with closed-in cab) [F. W. Day

Above : 2021 Class 0-6-0PT No. 2089 (with open cab)

Below : 2021 Class 0-6-0PT No. 2115 (with closed-in cab)

[H. C. Casserley

Above : 5700 Class 0-6-0PT No. 9749 (with modified cab)

Below : 6400 Class 0-6-0PT No. 6411   [R. E. Vincent, D. M. Rowse

Above : 5700 Class 0-6-0PT No. 7718   [R. H. G. Simpson

Below : 1600 Class 0-6-0PT No. 1627   [H. C. Casserley

Facing Page. *Top left*: Ex-Car. R. 0-6-2T No. 155. *Top right*:
Ex-R.R. R1 Class 0-6-2T (reboilered) No. 40. *Bottom left*: Ex-
R.R. AP Class 0-6-2T (rebuilt) No. 79. *Bottom right*: Ex-R.R.
A1 Class 0-6-2T No. 67
[*R. Pocklington, F. W. Day* (2), *P. Ransome-Wallis*

This Page. *Top left*: Ex-B. & M. 0-6-2T No. 425. *Top right*: Re-
boilered ex-B. & M. 0-6-2T No. 435. *Bottom left*: Ex-T.V.
A Class 0-5-2T No. 372. *Bottom right*: Ex-T.V. O4 Class 0-6-2T
No. 204.
[*P. Ransome-Wallis* (2), *F. W. Day, A. Delicata*

Top left : Ex-B.P.G.V. 0-6-0ST No. 2192 Ashburnham.   *Top right* : Ex-L.M.M. 0-6-0T No. 803.   *Bottom left* : Ex-B.P.G.V. 0-6-0T No. 2167.
Bottom right : Ex-A.D. 0-6-0T No. 666.   P. Ransome-Wallis (2), A. Delicata
[J. N. Westwood, P. Ransome-Wallis (2), A. Delicata

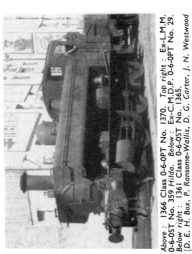

Above: 1366 Class 0-6-0PT No. 1370. Top right: Ex-L.M.M.
0-6-0ST No. 359 Hilda. Below: Ex-C.M.D.P. 0-6-0PT No. 29.
Below right: 1361 Class 0-6-0ST No. 1365.
[D. E. H. Box, P. Ransome-Wallis, D. G. Carter, J. N. Westwood

Above : 6000 C
4-6-0 No. 6024
Edward I.

Left : 4073 C
4-6-0 No. 5011
tagel Castle.

Below : 1000 C
4-6-0 No.1013 Co
of Dorset.

[B. Canning,
    P. Ransome-Wa
    B. A. Butt

4-6-0 5MT 4900 Class
" Hall "

*Introduced 1924 : Collett rebuild with 6' driving wheels of " Saint " (built 1907).

†Introduced 1928 : Modified design for new construction, with higher-pitched boiler, modified footplating and detail differences.

Weights : Loco. { 72 tons 10 cwt.*
{ 75 tons 0 cwt.†
Tender 46 tons 14 cwt.

Pressure : 225 lb. Su.
Cyls. : (O) 18½″ × 30″
Driving Wheels : 6' 0″
T.E. : 27,275 lb.

*4900
†4901–10/2–99, 5900–99, 6900–58   **Total 258**

4-6-0 7P 6000 Class
" King "

Introduced 1927 : Collett design.
Weights : Loco. 89 tons 0 cwt.
Tender 46 tons 14 cwt.

Pressure : 250 lb. Su.
Cyls. : (4) 16¼″ × 28″
Driving Wheels : 6' 6″
T.E. : 40,285 lb.
Inside Walschaerts gear and rocking shafts, P.V.

6000–29   **Total 30**

4-6-0 5MT 6800 Class
" Grange "

Introduced 1936 : Collett design, variation of " Hall " with smaller wheels, incorporating certain parts of withdrawn 4300 2-6-0 locos.
Weights : Loco. 74 tons 0 cwt.
Tender 40 tons 0 cwt.

Pressure : 225 lb. Su.
Cyls. : (O) 18½″ × 30″
Driving Wheels : 5' 8″
T.E. : 28,875 lb.
P.V.

6800–79   **Total 80**

4-6-0 5MT 6959 Class
" Modified Hall "

Introduced 1944 : Hawksworth development of " Hall," with larger superheater, " one-piece " main frames and plate framed bogie.
Weights : Engine 75 tons 16 cwt.
Tender 46 tons 14 cwt.

Pressure : 225 lb. Su.
Cyls. : (O) 18½″ × 30″
Driving Wheels : 6' 0″
T.E. : 27,275 lb.
P.V.

6959–99, 7900–29   **Total 71**

4-6-0 5MT 7800 Class
" Manor "

Introduced 1938 : Collett design for secondary lines, incorporating certain parts of withdrawn 4300 2-6-0 locos.
Weights : Loco. 68 tons 18 cwt.
Tender 40 tons 0 cwt.

Pressure : 225 lb. Su.
Cyls. : (O) 18″ × 30″
Driving Wheels : 5' 8″
T.E. : 27,340 lb.
P.V.

7800–29   **Total 30**

4-4-0 2P 3252 Class
" Duke "

Introduced 1895 : Dean design, some later fitted with new boilers and superheaters.
Weights : Loco. 47 tons 6 cwt.
Tender 34 tons 5 cwt., etc.

Pressure : 180 lb. SS.
Cyls. : 18″ × 26″
Driving Wheels : 5' 8″
T.E. : 18,955 lb.

9084/9   **Total 2**

4-4-0 3P 3300 Class
" Bulldog "

Introduced 1898 : Dean design, later
   fitted with new boilers and super-
   heaters (oldest survivor built 1903).
Weights : Loco. 51 tons 16 cwt.
             Tender 40 tons 0 cwt.
Pressure : 200 lb. Su.
Cyls. : 18" × 26"
Driving Wheels : 5' 8"
T.E. : 21,060 lb.

3377, 3444/7/9/51/3/4

Total 7

4-4-0 2P 9000 Class

Introduced 1936 : Collett rebuild, in-
   corporating " Duke " type boiler and
   " Bulldog " frames, for light lines.
Weights : Loco. 49 tons 0 cwt.
             Tender 40 tons 0 cwt.
Pressure : 180 lb. SS.
Cyls. : 18" × 26"
Driving Wheels : 5' 8"
T.E. : 18,955 lb.

9000—5/8—18/20—8   **Total 26**

2-8-0 8F 2800 Class

*Introduced 1903 : Churchward design,
   earlier locos. subsequently fitted with
   new boilers and superheaters.
†Introduced 1938 : Collett locos., with
   side window cabs and detail altera-
   tions.
Weights : Loco. {75 tons 10 cwt.*
                {76 tons 5 cwt.†
             Tender 40 tons 0 cwt.
Pressure : 225 lb. Su.
Cyls. : 18½" × 30"
Driving Wheels : 4' 7½"
T.E. : 35,380 lb.
P.V.

*2800—2883
†2884—99, 3800—66

Total 167

2-8-0 7F R.O.D. Class

Introduced 1911 : Robinson G.C. design
   (L.N.E.R. O4), built from 1917 for
   Railway Operating Division, R.E.,
   taken into G.W. stock from 1919, and
   subsequently fitted with G.W. boiler
   mountings and details.
Weights : Loco. 73 tons 11 cwt.
             Tender 47 tons 14 cwt.
Pressure : 185 lb. Su.
Cyls. : (O) 21" × 26"
Driving Wheels : 4' 8"
T.E. : 32,200 lb.
P.V.

3010—2/4—8/20/2—6/8/9/31—4/6/8
   40—4/7/8

Total 29

2-8-0 7F 4700 Class

Introduced 1919 : Churchward mixed
   traffic design (4700 built with smaller
   boiler and later rebuilt).
Weights : Loco. 82 tons 0 cwt.
             Tender 46 tons 14 cwt.
Pressure : 225 lb. Su.
Cyls. : (O) 19" × 30"
Driving Wheels : 5' 8"
T.E. : 30,460 lb.
P.V.

4700—8

Total 9

2-6-0 4MT 4300 Class

*Introduced 1911 : Churchward design.
†Introduced 1925 : Locos. with detail
   alterations affecting weight.
‡Introduced 1932 : Locos. with side
   window cabs and detail alterations.
Weights : Loco. {62 tons 0 cwt.*
                {64 tons 0 cwt.†
                {65 tons 6 cwt.‡
             Tender 40 tons 0 cwt.
Pressure : 200 lb. Su.
Cyls. : (O) 18½" × 30"
Driving Wheels : 5' 8"
T.E. : 25,670 lb.
P.V.

*4303/18/26/37/58/75/7/81, 5300/
   3/5—7/9—19/21—8/30—9/41/4—8/
   50/1/3/5—62/4/5/7—72/5—82/4—6/
   8/90—9, 6300—14/6—99, 7305—21
†7300—4
‡9300—19

Total 230

14

2-4-0   1MT   MSWJ

Introduced 1894 : Dubs design for M.S.W.J., reboilered by G.W.
Weights : Loco.   35 tons 5 cwt.
           Tender 30 tons 5 cwt.
Pressure : 165 lb.
Cyls. : 17″ × 24″
Driving Wheels : 5′ 6″
T.E. : 13,400 lb.

1334–6   **Total 3**

0-6-0   3MT   2251 Class

Introduced 1930 : Collett design.
Weights : Loco.   43 tons 8 cwt.
           Tender { 36 tons 15 cwt.
                   { 47 tons 6 cwt.
           (ex-R.O.D. tender from 3000 Class 2-8-0)
Pressure : 200 lb. Su.
Cyls. : 17½″ × 24″
Driving Wheels : 5′ 2″
T.E. : 20,155 lb.

2200–99, 3200–19   **Total 120**

0-6-0   2MT   2301 Class

Introduced 1883 : Dean design, later fitted with superheaters (oldest survivor built 1884).
Weights : Loco.   36 tons 16 cwt.
           Tender 34 tons 5 cwt.
Pressure : 180 lb. Su.
Cycls. : { 17″ × 24″
         { 17½″ × 24″
Driving Wheels : 5′ 2″
T.E. : { 17,120 lb.
      { 18,140 lb.

2322/3/7/39/40/3/9/50/1/4/85,2401/
7–9/11/4/26/31/44/5/9/52/8/60/2/
8/74/82–4, 2513/5/6/32/4/7/8/41/
3/51/6/68/72/3/8/9
                       Total 47

0-6-0   2MT   Cam.

Introduced 1903 : Jones Cambrian "89" class, reboilered by G.W. from 1924.
Weights : Loco.   38 tons 17 cwt.
           Tender 31 tons 13 cwt.
Pressure : 160 lb. SS.
Cyls. : 18″ × 26″
Driving Wheels : 5′ 1½″
T.E. : 18,625 lb.

844/9/55/64/73/87/92–6
                       Total 11

2-8-2T   8F   7200 Class

Introduced 1934 : Collett rebuild with extended bunker and trailing wheels of Churchward 4200 class 2-8-0T.
Weight : 92 tons 12 cwt.
Pressure : 200 lb. Su.
Cyls. : (O) 19″ × 30″
Driving Wheels : 4′ 7½″
T.E. : 33,170 lb.
P.V.

7200–53
                       Total 54

2-8-0T   { 7F* / 8F† }   4200 Class

*Introduced 1910 : Churchward design.
‡Introduced 1923 : 5205 class, with enlarged cyls. and detail alterations.
Weight { 81 tons 12 cwt.*
        { 82 tons 2 cwt.†
Pressure : 200 lb. Su.
Cyls. : { (O) 18½″ × 30″*
       { (O) 19″ × 30″†
Driving Wheels : 4′ 7½″
T.E. : { 31,450 lb.*
      { 33,170 lb.†
P.V.

*4200/1/3/6–8/11–5/7/8/21–33/5–
8/41–3/6–8/50–99, 5200–4
†5205–64   **Total 151**

2-6-2T   4MT   3100 Class

Introduced 1938 : Collett rebuild with higher pressure and smaller wheels of Churchward 3150 class (introduced 1906).
Weight : 81 tons 9 cwt.
Pressure : 225 lb. Su.
Cyls. : (O) 18½″ × 30″
Driving Wheels : 5′ 3″
T.E. : 31,170 lb.
P.V.

3100–4
                       Total 5

2-6-2T   4MT   3150 Class

Introduced 1906 : Churchward design, developed from original 3100 class, but with larger boiler, subsequently fitted with superheaters.
Weight : 81 tons 12 cwt.
Pressure : 200 lb. Su.
Cyls. : (O) 18½″ × 30″
Driving Wheels : 5′ 8″
T.E. : 25,670 lb.
P.V.

3150/1/3/7/60/1/3/4/7/70–2/4/6/7/
80/3/5–8/90   **Total 22**

2-6-2T 3MT 4400 Class

Introduced 1904 : Churchward design for light branches, subsequently fitted with superheaters.
Weight : 56 tons 13 cwt.
Pressure : 180 lb. Su.
Cyls. : (O) 17" × 24"
Driving Wheels : 4' 1½"
T.E. : 21,440 lb.
P.V.

4400/1/3–10 **Total 10**

2-6-2T 4MT 4500 Class

*Introduced 1906 : Churchward design for light branches, developed from 4400 class with larger wheels, earlier locos. subsequently fitted with superheaters.
†Introduced 1927 : 4575 class, with detail alterations and increased weight.
Weights {57 tons 0 cwt.*
{61 tons 0 cwt.†
Pressure : 200 lb. Su.
Cyls. : (O) 17" × 24"
Driving Wheels : 4' 7½"
T.E. : 21,250 lb.
P.V.

*4500–2/4–12/4–27/9/30/2–42/4–74
†4575–99, 5500–74 **Total 170**

2-6-2T 4MT
5100 & 6100 Classes

*5100 class. Introduced 1928 : Collett rebuild with detail alterations and increased weight of Churchward 3100 class (introduced 1903 and subsequently fitted with superheaters).
†5101 class. Introduced 1929 : Modified design for new construction.
‡6100 class. Introduced 1931 : Locos. for London suburban area with increased boiler pressure.
Weights {75 tons 10 cwt.*
{78 tons 9 cwt.†‡
Pressure {200 lb. Su.*†
{225 lb. Su.‡
Cyls. : (O) 18" × 30"
Driving Wheels : 5' 8"
T.E. {24,300 lb.*†
{27,340 lb.‡
P.V.

*5112/3/25/9/32/4/6–44/7/8
†4100–79, 5101–10/50–99
‡6100–69
Total 227

2-6-2T 4MT 8100 Class

Introduced 1938 : Collett rebuild with higher pressure and smaller wheels of Churchward locos. in 5100 class.
Weight : 76 tons 11 cwt.
Pressure : 225 lb. Su.
Cyls. : (O) 18" × 30"
Driving Wheels : 5' 6"
T.E. : 28,165 lb.
P.V.

8100–9 **Total 10**

2-6-2T 4MT AD

Introduced 1920 : Hawthorn Leslie design for A.D. Railway.
Weight : 65 tons 0 cwt.
Pressure : 160 lb.
Cyls. : (O) 19" × 26"
Driving Wheels : 4' 7"
T.E. : 23,210 lb.

1205 **Total 1**

2-6-2T Unclass. V of R

*Introduced 1902 : Davies and Metcalfe design for V. of R.
†Introduced 1923 : G.W. development of V. of R. design.
Weight : 25 tons 0 cwt.
Pressure : 165 lb.
Cyls. : (O) {11" × 17"*
{11½" × 17"†
Driving Wheels : 2' 6"
T.E. {9,615 lb.*
{10,510 lb.†
*9
† 7/8 **Total 3**

0-6-2T 5MT 5600 Class

*Introduced 1924 : Collett design for service in Welsh valleys.
†Introduced 1927 : Locos. with detail alterations.
Weight : {68 tons 12 cwt.*
{69 tons 7 cwt.†
Pressure : 200 lb. Su.
Cyls. : 18" × 26"
Driving Wheels : 4' 7½"
T.E. : 25,800 lb.
P.V.

*5600–99
†6600–99 **Total 200**

0-6-2T 3F Barry Rly.

*Introduced 1890 : Hosgood Barry Railway " B1 " class.
†Introduced 1924 : Reboilered by G.W.R.
Weights {55 tons 3 cwt.*
{53 tons 9 cwt.†
Pressure {160 lb.*
{150 lb.†
Cyls. : 17½″ × 26″
Driving Wheels : 4′ 3″
T.E. {20,825 lb.*
{19,525 lb.†

*276
†240/63/7/70/1/4   **Total 7**

0-6-2T 4F B & M

Introduced 1909 : Dunbar design for B. & M. Fitted with ex-Rhymney boiler by G.W.R.
Weight : 66 tons 19 cwt.
Pressure : 175 lb.
Cyls. : 18½″ × 26″
Driving Wheels : 4′ 6″
T.E. : 24,520 lb.

425   **Total 1**

3F

*Introduced 1926 : Dunbar design for B. & M., reboilered by G.W. with taper boiler (introduced 1915).
†Reboilered by G.W.R. with ex-Rhymney boiler.
Weight : 59 tons 5 cwt.
Pressure {175 lb. Su.*
{175 lb.†
Cyls. : 18″ × 26″
Driving Wheels : 5′ 0″
T.E. : 20,885 lb.

*431–5
†436   **Total 6**

0-6-2T 4F Cardiff Rly.

Introduced 1928 : G.W. rebuild with taper boiler of Ree Cardiff Railway design, introduced 1908.
Weight : 66 tons 12 cwt.
Pressure : 175 lb. Su.
Cyls. : 18″ × 26″
Driving Wheels : 4′ 6½″
T.E. : 22,990 lb.

155   **Total 1**

0-6-2T 4F Rhymney Rly.

Introduced 1904 : Jenkins and Robert Stephenson Rhymney " M " class (survivor built 1905).
Weight : 62 tons 11 cwt.
Pressure : 175 lb.   Cyls. : 18½″ × 26″
Driving Wheels : 4′ 6″
T.E. : 24,510 lb.

33   **Total 1**

4F

*Introduced 1921 : Hurry Riches Rhymney " R1 " class, development of " R." (Introduced 1907.)
†Introduced 1926 : Reboilered by G.W. with superheated taper boiler (earliest survivor rebuilt 1929).
Weights {66 tons 0 cwt.*
{62 tons 10 cwt.†
Pressure {175 lb.*
{200 lb. Su.†
Cyls. : 18½″ × 26″
Driving Wheels : 4′ 6″
T.E. {24,520 lb.*
{28,015 lb.†

*35–8, 41–3
†31/9, 40/4   **Total 11**

4F

*Introduced 1910 : Hurry Riches Rhymney " A " class, rebuilt by G.W. from round top to Belpaire boiler.
†Introduced 1914 : Class " A1," built with Belpaire boiler.
‡§Introduced 1929 : Reboilered by G.W. with superheated taper boiler.
Weights {64 tons 3 cwt.*†
{63 tons 0 cwt.‡§
Pressure {175 lb.*†
{175 lb.‡§
Cyls. {18″ × 26″*†‡
{18½″ × 26″§
Driving Wheels : 4′ 4½″
T.E. {23,870 lb.*†‡
{25,210 lb §

*57, 72/3   †65/7/8
‡56/8–60/3/6/9, 70/5   §55
                                    Total 16

17

3P

*Introduced 1926 : G.W. rebuild with superheated taper boiler of Hurry Riches Rhymney " P " class.

†Introduced 1928 : Rebuild of Rhymney " AP " class (superheated development of " P," introduced 1921), No. 76 originally " P," but later rebuilt with larger tanks to conform to " AP."

Weights {58 tons 19 cwt.*
{63 tons 0 cwt.†
Pressure : 175 lb. Su.
Cyls. {18″ × 26″*
{18½″ × 26″†
Driving Wheels : 5′ 0″
T.E. {20,885 lb.*
{21,700 lb.†

*82/3   †77–81   **Total 7**

0-6-2T   4F   TV

Introduced 1924 : G.W. rebuild with superheated taper boiler of Hurry Riches T.V " O4 " class (introduced 1907).

Weight : 61 tons 0 cwt.
Pressure : 175 lb. Su.
Cyls. : 17½″ × 26″
Driving Wheels : 4′ 6½″
T.E. : 21,730 lb.

203–5/7–11/5–20/36/78/9/82/4/5/90/2/3/5/9   **Total 25**

4P

Introduced 1924 : G.W. rebuild with superheated taper boiler of Cameron T.V. " A " class (introduced 1914). Two sizes of cylinder.

Weight : 65 tons 14 cwt
Pressure {175 lb. Su.*
{200 lb. Su.†
Cyls. {18½″ × 26″*
{17½″ × 26″†
Driving Wheels : 5′ 3″
T.E. {21,000 lb.*
{21,480 lb.†

*307–9/22/35/7/44/9/52/60/1/6/70–2/80/7/8
†303–6/12/6/43/5–8/51/6/7/62/4/5/7/8/73–9/81–6/9–91/3/4/7–9   **Total 58**

0-6-0T   2F   850 Class

*Introduced 1874 : Dean & G. Armstrong saddletank (survivor built 1883).

†Introduced 1910 : Rebuilt with pannier tanks (oldest survivor built 1875). No. 992 originally built with boiler having dome on firebox and Ramsbottom safety valves thereon.

Weight : 36 tons 3 cwt.
Pressure : 165 lb.
Cyls. : 16″ × 24″
Driving Wheels : 4′ 1½″
T.E. : 17,410 lb.

*1925
†992, 1903/17/35/41/3/57/64/7/8/91/3/6, 2001/2/4/8/10–2/4/6/7   **Total 24**

0-6-0ST   0F   1361 Class

Introduced 1910 : Churchward design for dock shunting.
Weight : 35 tons 4 cwt.
Pressure : 150 lb.
Cyls. : (O) 16″ × 20″
Driving Wheels : 3′ 8″
T.E. : 14,835 lb.

1361–5   **Total 5**

0-6-0PT   1F   1366 Class

Introduced 1934 : Collett development of 1361 class, with pannier tanks.
Weight : 35 tons 15 cwt
Pressure : 165 lb.
Cyls. : (O) 16″ × 20″
Driving Wheels : 3′ 8″
T.E. : 16,320 lb.

1366–71   **Total 6**

0-6-0T   4F   1500 Class

Introduced 1949 : Hawksworth short-wheelbase heavy shunting design.
Weight : 58 tons 4 cwt.
Pressure : 200 lb.
Cyls. : (O) 17½″ × 24″
Driving Wheels : 4′ 7½″
T.E. : 22,515 lb.
Walschaerts gear, P.V.

1500–9   **Total 10**

0-6-0PT   2F   1501 Class

Introduced 1872 : Dean & G. Armstrong saddle tanks, rebuilt with pannier tanks from 1910 (oldest survivor built 1879).

Weight : 42 tons 17 cwt.
Pressure : 165 lb.
Cyls. : 17" × 24"
Driving Wheels : 4' 7½"
T.E. : 17,525 lb.

1542   **Total 1**

0-6-0PT   2F   1600 Class

Introduced 1949 : Hawksworth light
    branch line and shunting design.
Weight : 41 tons 12 cwt.
Pressure : 165 lb.
Cyls. : 16½" × 24
Driving Wheels : 4' 1½"
T.E. : 18,515 lb.

1600–49
**N.B.—Locos. of this class are still
    being delivered.**

0-6-0PT   3F   1854 Class

Introduced 1890 : Dean design, rebuilt
    with pannier tanks from 1909.
Weight : 46 tons 13 cwt.
Pressure : 180 lb.
Cyls. : 17" × 24"
Driving Wheels : 4' 7½"
T.E. : 19,120 lb.

907, 1861   **Total 2**

0-6-0T   2F
2021 & 2181 Classes

*2021 class. Introduced 1897 : Dean
    saddletank, subsequently rebuilt with
    pannier tanks. Nos. 2101 onwards
    built with domeless Belpaire boilers,
    interchanged later throughout the
    class.
†2181 class. Introduced 1939 : 2021
    class modified with increased brake
    power for heavy gradients.
Weight : 39 tons 15 cwt.
Pressure : 165 lb.
Cyls. : 16½" × 24"
Driving Wheels : 4' 1½"
T.E. : 18,515 lb.

*2021/3/5–7/30–5/8/40/2–4/8/50/1
/3/4/6/60/1/3/6–70/2/3/5/6/9–83
/5/6/8/9/90/2–5/7–9, 2100/1/4/6–
9/11/2/5/7/21–3/7/9/31/4–6/8/40/
4/6–8/50–2/4/6/9/60

†2181–3/5–8/90

        Totals : 2021 Class 84
                    2181 Class 8

0-6-0PT   1P   5400 Class

Introduced 1931 : Collett design for
    light passenger work, push-and-pull
    fitted.
Weight : 46 tons 12 cwt.
Pressure : 165 lb.
Cyls. : 16½" × 24"
Driving Wheels : 5' 2"
T.E. : 14,780 lb.

5400–24

               Total 25

0-6-0PT   4F   5700 Class

*Introduced 1929 : Collett design for
    shunting and light goods work,
    developed from 2721 class.
†Introduced 1930 : Locos. with steam
    brake and no A.T.C. fittings, for
    shunting only.
‡Introduced 1933 : Locos. with con-
    densing gear for working over L.T.E.
    Metropolitan line.
§Introduced 1933 : Locos. with detail
    alterations, modified cab (except
    8700) and increased weight.
**Introduced 1948 : Steam brake locos.
    with increased weight.
Weights   { 47 tons 10 cwt.*†
         { 50 tons 15 cwt.‡
         { 49 tons 0 cwt. §**
Pressure : 200 lb.
Cyls : 17½" × 24"
Driving Wheels : 4' 7½"
T.E. : 22,515 lb.

*5700–99, 7700–99, 8701–49

†6700–49

‡9700–10

§3600–3799, 4600–99, 8700/50–
    99, 9600–82, 9711–99

6750–79   **Total 863

0-6-0PT   2P*   2F†
6400 & 7400 Classes

*6400 class. Introduced 1932 : Collett
    design for light passenger work,
    variation of 5400 class with smaller
    wheels.

*7400 class. Introduced 1936 : Non-push-and-pull fitted locos.
Weights $\begin{cases} 45 \text{ tons } 12 \text{ cwt.}* \\ 45 \text{ tons } 9 \text{ cwt.}† \end{cases}$
Pressure : 180 lb.
Cyls. : $16\frac{1}{2}'' \times 24''$
Driving Wheels : 4' $7\frac{1}{2}''$
T.E. : 18,010 lb.

*6400–39

†7400–49

Totals : 6400 Class 40
7400 Class 50

0-6-0PT   4F   9400 Class

*Introduced 1947 : Hawksworth taper-boiler design for heavy shunting.
†Introduced 1949 : Locos. with non-superheated boilers.
Weight : 55 tons 7 cwt.
Pressure : 200 lb. SS.
Cyls. : $17\frac{1}{2}'' \times 24''$
Driving Wheels : 4' $7\frac{1}{2}''$
T.E. : 22,515 lb.

*9400–9

†8400–99, 9410–99

N.B.—Locos. of this class are still being delivered.

0-6-0T   3F   AD

Introduced 1917 : Kerr Stuart design for Railway Operating Division, R.E., purchased by A.D. Railway 1919.
Weight : 50 tons 0 cwt.
Pressure : 160 lb.
Cyls. : (O) $17'' \times 24''$
Driving Wheels : 4' 0''
T.E. : 19,650 lb.

666/7   Total 2

0-6-0T   IF   BPGV

Intoduced 1906 : Avonside design for B.P.G.V.
Weight : 38 tons 0 cwt.
Pressure : 170 lb.
Cyls. : (O) $15'' \times 22''$
Driving Wheels : 3' 6''
T.E. : 17,030 lb.

2196   Total 1

0F

Introduced 1909 : Hudswell Clarke design for B.P.G.V.
Weight : 36 tons 8 cwt.
Pressure : 160 lb.
Cyls. : (O) $15'' \times 22''$
Driving Wheels : 3' 9''
T.E. : 14,960 lb.

2197   Total 1

IF

Introduced 1910 : Hudswell Clarke design for B.P.G.V., rebuilt by G.W.R.
Weight : 37 tons 15 cwt.
Pressure : 165 lb.
Cyls : (O) $15'' \times 22''$
Driving Wheels : 3' 9''
T.E. : 15,430 lb.

2198   Total 1

2F

*Introduced 1912 : Hudswell Clarke design for B.P.G.V.
†Rebuilt by G.W.R.
Weight : 37 tons 15 cwt.
Pressure : 160 lb.
Cyls : (O) $16'' \times 24''$
Driving Wheels : 3' 9''
T.E. : 18,570 lb.

*2166

†2162/5/7/8   Total 5

0-6-0ST   IF   BPGV

Introduced 1907 : Avonside design for B.P.G.V., rebuilt by G.W.R.
Weight : 38 tons 5 cwt.
Pressure : 165 lb.
Cyls. : (O) $15'' \times 22''$
Driving Wheels : 3' 6''
T.E. : 16,530 lb.

2176   Total 1

IF

Introduced 1900 : R. A. Carr design for B.P.G.V.
Weight : 41 tons 18 cwt.
Pressure : 140 lb.
Cyls. : (O) $16'' \times 24''$
Driving Wheels : 3' 8''
T.E. : 16,615 lb.

2192   Total 1

0F

Introduced 1901 : R. A. Carr design for
   B.P.G.V.
Weight : 35 tons 12 cwt.
Pressure : 140 lb.
Cyls. : (O) 15″ × 22″
Driving Wheels : 3′ 6″
T.E. : 14,025 lb.

2193   **Total 1**

0F

Introduced 1903 : Eager design for
   B.P.G.V.
Weight : 31 tons 7 cwt
Pressure : 150 lb.
Cyls. : (O) 15″ × 20″
Driving Wheels : 3′ 6″
T.E. : 13,660 lb.

2194/5   **Total 2**

0-6-0PT   4F   Cardiff Rly.

Introduced 1920 : Hope and Hudswell
   Clarke design for Cardiff Railway,
   reboilered by G.W. and fitted with
   pannier tanks.
Weight : 45 tons 6 cwt.
Pressure : 165 lb.
Cyls. : 18″ × 24″
Driving Wheels : 4′ 1¾″
T.E. : 22,030 lb.

681–4   **Total 4**

0-6-0PT   2F   CMDP

Introduced 1905 : M. Wardle saddle
   tank for C.M.D.P., reboilered by
   G.W. and fitted with pannier tanks.
Weight : 39 tons 18 cwt.
Pressure : 160 lb.
Cyls. : (O) 16″ × 22″
Driving Wheels : 3′ 6″
T.E. : 18,235 lb.

28/9   **Total 2**

0-6-0T   2F   LMM

Introduced 1911 : Hudswell Clarke
   design for L.M.M., reboilered by G.W.
Weight : 40 tons 12 cwt.
Pressure : 160 lb.
Cyls. : 16″ × 24″
Driving Wheels : 4′ 0″
T.E. : 17,410 lb.

803   **Total 1**

0-6-0ST   1F   LMM

Introduced 1912 : Hudswell Clarke
   design for L.M.M., reboilered by
   G.W. (survivor built 1917).
Weight : 34 tons 9 cwt.
Pressure : 160 lb.
Cyls. : (O) 15″ × 22″
Driving Wheels : 3′ 7½″
T.E. : 15,475 lb.

359   **Total 1**

0-6-0T   4F   Rhymney Rly.

Introduced 1930 : Hurry Riches
   Rhymney " S " class (introduced
   1908), rebuilt by G.W. with taper
   boiler.
Weight : 54 tons 8 cwt.
Pressure : 175 lb.
Cyls. : 18″ × 26″
Driving Wheels : 4′ 4½″
T.E. : 23,870 lb.

93–6   **Total 4**

4F

Introduced 1920 : Hurry Riches
   Rhymney " S1 " class.
Weight : 56 tons 8 cwt.
Pressure : 175 lb.
Cyls. $\begin{cases} 18″ \times 26″* \\ 18\frac{1}{2}″ \times 26″\dagger \end{cases}$
Driving Wheels : 4′ 4½″
T.E. $\begin{cases} 23,870 \text{ lb.*} \\ 25,210 \text{ lb.}\dagger \end{cases}$

*91/2   †90   **Total 3**

0-6-0ST   1F   SHT

Introduced 1912 : Peckett design for
   S.H.T.
Weight : 38 tons 10 cwt.
Pressure : 160 lb.
Cyls. : 16″ × 22″
Driving Wheels : 3′ 10″
T.E. : 16,650 lb.

1147   **Total 1**

0-6-0T   1F   TV

Introduced 1884 : Hurry Riches T.V.
   " H " class with steeply tapered
   boiler for Pwllyrhebog incline, sub-
   sequently rebuilt twice.
Weight : 44 tons 15 cwt.
Pressure : 140 lb.
Cyls. : 17½″ × 26″
Driving Wheels : 5′ 3″
T.E. : 15,040 lb.

193–5   **Total 3**

0-6-0T   0F   **WCP**

Introduced 1911 : Marsh rebuild of
Stroudley L.B.S.C. A1, purchased
W.C.P. 1925, acquired by G.W. 1940
(loco. built 1877, rebuilt to A1X 1919).
Weight : 28 tons 5 cwt.
Pressure : 150 lb.
Cyls. : 12″ × 20″
Driving Wheels : 4′ 0″   T.E. : 7,650 lb.

5   **Total 1**

0-6-0T   Unclass.   **W & L**

Introduced 1902 : Beyer Peacock
design for W. & L. section, Cam.
Railways.
Weight : 19 tons 18 cwt.
Gauge : 2′ 6¼″
Pressure : 150 lb.
Cyls. : (O) 11¼″ × 16″
Driving Wheels : 2′ 9″
T.E. : 8,175 lb.

822/3   **Total 2**

0-4-2T   1P
1400 & 5800 Classes

•1400 class introduced 1932 : Collett
design for light branch work (ori-
ginally designated 4800 class).
†5800 class introduced 1933 : Non push-
and-pull fitted locos.
Weight : 41 tons 6 cwt.
Pressure : 165 lb.
Cyls. : 16″ × 24″
Driving Wheels : 5′ 2″
T.E. : 13,900 lb.

*1400–74 †5800–19   Total 95

0-4-0T   3F   **1101 Class**

Introduced 1926 : Avonside Engine Co.
design to G.W. requirements for
dock shunting.
Weight : 38 tons 4 cwt.
Pressure : 170 lb.
Cyls. : (O) 16″ × 24″
Driving Wheels : 3′ 9½″
T.E. : 19,510 lb.
Walschaerts gear.

1101–6   **Total 6**

0-4-0ST   0F   **Car.R**

Introduced 1898 : Kitson design for
Car.R.
Weight : 25 tons 10 cwt.
Pressure : 160 lb.
Cyls. : (O) 14″ × 21″
Driving Wheels : 3′ 2½″
T.E. : 14,540 lb.
Hawthorn Kitson valve gear.

1338   **Total 1**

0-4-0ST   0F   **P & M**

Introduced 1907 : Peckett design for
P. & M. (oldest survivor built 1912).
Weight : 33 tons 10 cwt.
Pressure : 150 lb.
Cyls. : (O) 15″ × 21″
Driving Wheels : 3′ 7″   T.E. : 14,010 lb.

1150–2   **Total 3**

Introduced 1903 : Hawthorn Leslie
design for P. & M., reboilered by
G.W.R.
Weight : 26 tons 13 cwt.
Pressure : 120 lb.
Cyls. : (O) 14″ × 20″
Driving Wheels : 3′ 6″   T.E. : 9,520 lb.

1153   **Total 1**

0-4-0ST   0F   **SHT**

Introduced 1905 : Barclay design for
S.H.T.
Weight : 28 tons 0 cwt.
Pressure : 160 lb.
Cyls. : (O) 14″ × 22″
Driving Wheels : 3′ 5″   T.E. : 14,305 lb.

1140   **Total 1**

Introduced 1906 : Peckett design for
S.H.T. (similar to 1150-2).
Weight : 33 tons 10 cwt.
Pressure : 150 lb.
Cyls. : (O) 15″ × 21″
Driving Wheels : 3′ 7″
T.E. : 14,010 lb

1141/3/5   **Total 3**

Introduced 1909 : Hawthorn Leslie
design for S.H.T.
Weight : 26 tons 17 cwt.
Pressure : 150 lb.
Cyls. : (O) 14″ × 22″
Driving Wheels : 3′ 6″
T.E. : 13,090 lb.

1144   **Total 1**

Introduced 1911 : Hudswell Clarke
design for S.H.T.
Weight : 28 tons 15 cwt
Pressure : 160 lb.
Cyls. : (O) 15″ × 22″
Driving Wheels : 3′ 4″
T.E. : 16,830 lb.

1142   **Total 1**

0-4-0ST   Unclass.   **YTW**

Introduced 1900 : Peckett design
supplied to Ystalyfera Tin Works.
Weight : 23 tons 0 cwt.
Pressure : 146 lb.
Cyls. : (O) 14½″ × 22″
Driving Wheels : 3′ 2″
T.E : 13,000 lb.

1   **Total 1**

NUMERICAL LIST OF WESTERN REGION
STEAM LOCOMOTIVES

Locomotives are of G.W. origin except where indicated by initials.

1 Hercules 0–4–0 YTW	78 0–6–2T RR
5 Portishead 0–6–0 WCP	79 0–6–2T RR
7 2–6–2T V of R	80 0–6–2T RR
8 2–6–2T V of R	81 0–6–2T RR
9 2–6–2T V of R	82 0–6–2T RR
28 0–6–0T CMDP	83 0–6–2T RR
29 0–6–0T CMDP	90 0–6–0T RR
31 0–6–2T RR	91 0–6–0T RR
33 0–6–2T RR	92 0–6–0T RR
35 0–6–2T RR	93 0–6–0T RR
36 0–6–2T RR	94 0–6–0T RR
37 0–6–2T RR	95 0–6–0T RR
38 0–6–2T RR	96 0–6–0T RR
39 0–6–2T RR	111 Viscount Churchill
40 0–6–2T RR	4–6–0 4073 Class
41 0–6–2T RR	155 0–6–2T Car.R.
42 0–6–2T RR	193 0–6–0T TV
43 0–6–2T RR	194 0–6–0T TV
44 0–6–2T RR	195 0–6–0T TV
55 0–6–2T RR	203 0–6–2T TV
56 0–6–2T RR	204 0–6–2T TV
57 0–6–2T RR	205 0–6–2T TV
58 0–6–2T RR	207 0–6–2T TV
59 0–6–2T RR	208 0–6–2T TV
60 0–6–2T RR	209 0–6–2T TV
63 0–6–2T RR	210 0–6–2T TV
65 0–6–2T RR	211 0–6–2T TV
66 0–6–2T RR	215 0–6–2T TV
67 0–6–2T RR	216 0–6–2T TV
68 0–6–2T RR	217 0–6–2T TV
69 0–6–2T RR	218 0–6–2T TV
70 0–6–2T RR	219 0–6–2T TV
72 0–6–2T RR	220 0–6–2T TV
73 0–6–2T RR	236 0–6–2T TV
75 0–6–2T RR	240 0–6–2T BR
77 0–6–2T RR	263 0–6–2T BR

267	0–6–2T BR	370	0–6–2T TV
270	0–6–2T BR	371	0–6–2T TV
271	0–6–2T BR	372	0–6–2T TV
274	0–6–2T BR	373	0–6–2T TV
276	0–6–2T BR	374	0–6–2T TV
278	0–6–2T TV	375	0–6–2T TV
279	0–6–2T TV	376	0–6–2T TV
282	0–6–2T TV	377	0–6–2T TV
284	0–6–2T TV	378	0–6–2T TV
285	0–6–2T TV	379	0–6–2T TV
290	0–6–2T TV	380	0–6–2T TV
292	0–6–2T TV	381	0–6–2T TV
293	0–6–2T TV	382	0–6–2T TV
295	0–6–2T TV	383	0–6–2T TV
299	0–6–2T TV	384	0–6–2T TV
303	0–6–2T TV	385	0–6–2T TV
304	0–6–2T TV	386	0–6–2T TV
305	0–6–2T TV	387	0–6–2T TV
306	0–6–2T TV	388	0–6–2T TV
307	0–6–2T TV	389	0–6–2T TV
308	0–6–2T TV	390	0–6–2T TV
309	0–6–2T TV	391	0–6–2T TV
312	0–6–2T TV	393	0–6–2T TV
316	0–6–2T TV	394	0–6–2T TV
322	0–6–2T TV	397	0–6–2T TV
335	0–6–2T TV	398	0–6–2T TV
337	0–6–2T TV	399	0–6–2T TV
343	0–6–2T TV	425	0–6–2T BM
344	0–6–2T TV	431	0–6–2T BM
345	0–6–2T TV	432	0–6–2T BM
346	0–6–2T TV	433	0–6–2T BM
347	0–6–2T TV	434	0–6–2T BM
348	0–6–2T TV	435	0–6–2T BM
349	0–6–2T TV	436	0–6–2T BM
351	0–6–2T TV	666	0–6–0T AD
352	0–6–2T TV	667	0–6–0T AD
356	0–6–2T TV	681	0–6–0T Car.R.
357	0–6–2T TV	682	0–6–0T Car.R.
359	Hilda	683	0–6–0T Car.R.
	0–6–0T LMM	684	0–6–0T Car.R.
360	0–6–2T TV	803	0–6–0T LMM
361	0–6–2T TV	822	The Earl 0–6–0T W. & L.
362	0–6–2T TV	823	Countess 0–6–0T W. & L.
364	0–6–2T TV	844	0–6–0 Cam.R.
365	0–6–2T TV	849	0–6–0 Cam.R.
366	0–6–2T TV	855	0–6–0 Cam.R.
367	0–6–2T TV	864	0–6–0 Cam.R.
368	0–6–2T TV	873	0–6–0 Cam.R.

887 0–6–0 Cam.R.	1101 0–4–0T 1101 Class
892 0–6–0 Cam.R.	1102 0–4–0T 1101 Class
893 0–6–0 Cam.R.	1103 0–4–0T 1101 Class
894 0–6–0 Cam.R.	1104 0–4–0T 1101 Class
895 0–6–0 Cam.R.	1105 0–4–0T 1101 Class
896 0–6–0 Cam.R.	1106 0–4–0T 1101 Class
907 0–6–0T 1854 Class	1140 0–4–0T SHT
992 0–6–0T 850 Class	1141 0–4–0T SHT
	1142 0–4–0T SHT
	1143 0–4–0T SHT

4-6-0   1000 Class
"County"

1144 0–4–0T SHT
1145 0–4–0T SHT
1147 0–6–0ST SHT
1150 0–4–0T PM
1151 0–4–0T PM
1152 0–4–0T PM
1153 0–4–0T PM
1205 2–6–2T AD
1334 2–4–0 MSWJ
1335 2–4–0 MSWJ
1336 2–4–0 MSWJ
1338 0–4–0T Car.R.

1000 County of Middlesex
1001 County of Bucks
1002 County of Berks
1003 County of Wilts
1004 County of Somerset
1005 County of Devon
1006 County of Cornwall
1007 County of Brecknock
1008 County of Cardigan
1009 County of Carmarthen
1010 County of Carnarvon
1011 County of Chester
1012 County of Denbigh
1013 County of Dorset
1014 County of Glamorgan
1015 County of Gloucester
1016 County of Hants
1017 County of Hereford
1018 County of Leicester
1019 County of Merioneth
1020 County of Monmouth
1021 County of Montgomery
1022 County of Northampton
1023 County of Oxford
1024 County of Pembroke
1025 County of Radnor
1026 County of Salop
1027 County of Stafford
1028 County of Warwick
1029 County of Worcester

0-6-0T   1361 Class

1361	1363	1365
1362	1364	

0-6-0T   1366 Class

1366	1368	1370
1367	1369	1371

0-4-2T   1400 Class

1400	1402	1404	1406
1401	1403	1405	1407

25

1408	1425	1442	1459
1409	1426	1443	1460
1410	1427	1444	1461
1411	1428	1445	1462
1412	1429	1446	1463
1413	1430	1447	1464
1414	1431	1448	1465
1415	1432	1449	1466
1416	1433	1450	1467
1417	1434	1451	1468
1418	1435	1452	1469
1419	1436	1453	1470
1420	1437	1454	1471
1421	1438	1455	1472
1422	1439	1456	1473
1423	1440	1457	1474
1424	1441	1458	

0-6-0T   1500 Class

1500	1503	1506	1509
1501	1504	1507	
1502	1505	1508	

1542 0-6-0T 1501 Class

0-6-0T   1600 Class

1600	1613	1626	1639
1601	1614	1627	1640
1602	1615	1628	1641
1603	1616	1629	1642
1604	1617	1630	1643
1605	1618	1631	1644
1606	1619	1632	1645
1607	1620	1633	1646
1608	1621	1634	1647
1609	1622	1635	1648
1610	1623	1636	1649
1611	1624	1637	
1612	1625	1638	

1861 0-6-0T 1854 Class

0-6-0T   850 Class

1903	1957	1996	2011
1917	1964	2001	2012
1925	1967	2002	2014
1935	1968	2004	2016
1941	1991	2008	2017
1943	1993	2010	

0-6-0T   2021 Class

2021	2056	2089	2122
2023	2060	2090	2123
2025	2061	2092	2127
2026	2063	2093	2129
2027	2066	2094	2131
2030	2067	2095	2134
2031	2068	2097	2135
2032	2069	2098	2136
2033	2070	2099	2138
2034	2072	2100	2140
2035	2073	2101	2144
2038	2075	2104	2146
2040	2076	2106	2147
2042	2079	2107	2148
2043	2080	2108	2150
2044	2081	2109	2151
2048	2082	2111	2152
2050	2083	2112	2154
2051	2085	2115	2156
2053	2086	2117	2159
2054	2088	2121	2160

0-6-0T   BPGV Rly.

2162	2166	2167	2168
2165			

0-6-0ST   BPGV Rly.

2176

0-6-0T   2181 Class

2181	2183	2186	2188
2182	2185	2187	2190

0-6-0ST   BPGV Rly.

2192 Ashburnham
2193 Burry Port
2194 Kidwelly
2195

0-6-0T   BPGV Rly.

2196 Gwendraeth
2197 Pioneer
2198

0-6-0   2251 Class

2200	2225	2250	2275
2201	2226	2251	2276
2202	2227	2252	2277
2203	2228	2253	2278
2204	2229	2254	2279
2205	2230	2255	2280
2206	2231	2256	2281
2207	2232	2257	2282
2208	2233	2258	2283
2209	2234	2259	2284
2210	2235	2260	2285
2211	2236	2261	2286
2212	2237	2262	2287
2213	2238	2263	2288
2214	2239	2264	2289
2215	2240	2265	2290
2216	2241	2266	2291
2217	2242	2267	2292
2218	2243	2268	2293
2219	2244	2269	2294
2220	2245	2270	2295
2221	2246	2271	2296
2222	2247	2272	2297
2223	2248	2273	2298
2224	2249	2274	2299

0-6-0   2301 Class

2322	2349	2407	2431
2323	2350	2408	2444
2327	2351	2409	2445
2339	2354	2411	2449
2340	2385	2414	2452
2343	2401	2426	2458

2460	2484	2537	2568
2462	2513	2538	2572
2468	2515	2541	2573
2474	2516	2543	2578
2482	2532	2551	2579
2483	2534	2556	

2-8-0   2800 Class

2800	2825	2850	2875
2801	2826	2851	2876
2802	2827	2852	2877
2803	2828	2853	2878
2804	2829	2854	2879
2805	2830	2855	2880
2806	2831	2856	2881
2807	2832	2857	2882
2808	2833	2858	2883
2809	2834	2859	2884
2810	2835	2860	2885
2811	2836	2861	2886
2812	2837	2862	2887
2813	2838	2863	2888
2814	2839	2864	2889
2815	2840	2865	2890
2816	2841	2866	2891
2817	2842	2867	2892
2818	2843	2868	2893
2819	2844	2869	2894
2820	2845	2870	2895
2821	2846	2871	2896
2822	2847	2872	2897
2823	2848	2873	2898
2824	2849	2874	2899

For full details of

B.R. CLASS "WD" 2-8-0s

running on the Western Region,

see the

A.B.C. OF B.R. LOCOMOTIVES

PT. IV. Nos. 60000-90999

4-6-0　　　2900 Class
" Saint "

2906 Lady of Lynn
2912 Saint Ambrose
2920 Saint David
2926 Saint Nicholas
2927 Saint Patrick
2931 Arlington Court
2932 Ashton Court
2933 Bibury Court
2934 Butleigh Court
2936 Cefntilla Court
2937 Clevedon Court
2938 Corsham Court
2940 Dorney Court
2944 Highnam Court
2945 Hillingdon Court
2947 Madresfield Court
2948 Stackpole Court
2949 Stanford Court
2950 Taplow Court
2951 Tawstock Court
2952 Twineham Court
2953 Titley Court
2954 Tockenham Court
2981 Ivanhoe

2-8-0　　　R.O.D. Class

3010	3020	3029	3040
3011	3022	3031	3041
3012	3023	3032	3042
3014	3024	3033	3043
3015	3025	3034	3044
3016	3026	3036	3047
3017	3028	3038	3048
3018			

2-6-2T　　　3100 Class

3100	3102	3103	3104
3101			

2-6-2T　　　3150 Class

3150	3163	3174	3186
3151	3164	3176	3187
3153	3167	3177	3188
3157	3170	3180	3190
3160	3171	3183	
3161	3172	3185	

0-6-0　　　2251 Class

3200	3205	3210	3215
3201	3206	3211	3216
3202	3207	3212	3217
3203	3208	3213	3218
3204	3209	3214	3219

0-6-0T　　　9400 Class

Numbers Allocated 3400–9

4-4-0　　　3300 Class
" Bulldog "

3377
3444 Cormorant
3447 Jackdaw
3449 Nightingale
3451 Pelican
3453 Seagull
3454 Skylark

0-6-0T　　　5700 Class

3600	3608	3616	3624
3601	3609	3617	3625
3602	3610	3618	3626
3603	3611	3619	3627
3604	3612	3620	3628
3605	3613	3621	3629
3606	3614	3622	3630
3607	3615	3623	3631

3632	3674	3716	3758	3812	3826	3840	3854
3633	3675	3717	3759	3813	3827	3841	3855
3634	3676	3718	3760	3814	3828	3842	3856
3635	3677	3719	3761	3815	3829	3843	3857
3636	3678	3720	3762	3816	3830	3844	3858
3637	3679	3721	3763	3817	3831	3845	3859
3638	3680	3722	3764	3818	3832	3846	3860
3639	3681	3723	3765	3819	3833	3847	3861
3640	3682	3724	3766	3820	3834	3848	3862
3641	3683	3725	3767	3821	3835	3849	3863
3642	3684	3726	3768	3822	3836	3850	3864
3643	3685	3727	3769	3823	3837	3851	3865
3644	3686	3728	3770	3824	3838	3852	3866
3645	3687	3729	3771	3825	3839	3853	
3646	3688	3730	3772				
3647	3689	3731	3773				
3648	3690	3732	3774				
3649	3691	3733	3775				
3650	3692	3734	3776				
3651	3693	3735	3777				
3652	3694	3736	3778				
3653	3695	3737	3779				
3654	3696	3738	3780				
3655	3697	3739	3781				
3656	3698	3740	3782				
3657	3699	3741	3783				
3658	3700	3742	3784				
3659	3701	3743	3785				
3660	3702	3744	3786				
3661	3703	3745	3787				
3662	3704	3746	3788				
3663	3705	3747	3789				
3664	3706	3748	3790				
3665	3707	3749	3791				
3666	3708	3750	3792				
3667	3709	3751	3793				
3668	3710	3752	3794				
3669	3711	3753	3795				
3670	3712	3754	3796				
3671	3713	3755	3797				
3672	3714	3756	3798				
3673	3715	3757	3799				

4-6-0 4073 Class "Castle"

4000 North Star

4-6-0 4000 Class "Star"

4003 Lode Star
4007 Swallowfield Park
4015 Knight of St. John

4-6-0 4073 Class "Castle"

4016 The Somerset Light Infantry (Prince Albert's)

4-6-0 4000 Class "Star"

4018 Knight of the Grand Cross
4020 Knight Commander
4021 British Monarch
4022
4023
4028
4031 Queen Mary

2-8-0 2800 Class

3800	3803	3806	3809
3801	3804	3807	3810
3802	3805	3808	3811

4-6-0 4073 Class "Castle"

4032 Queen Alexandra

29

4-6-0 4000 Class
"Star"

4033 Queen Victoria
4034 Queen Adelaide
4035 Queen Charlotte
4036 Queen Elizabeth

4-6-0 4073 Class
"Castle"

4037 The South Wales Borderers

4-6-0 4000 Class
"Star"

4038 Queen Berengaria
4040 Queen Boadicea
4041 Prince of Wales
4042 Prince Albert
4043 Prince Henry
4044 Prince George
4046 Princess Mary
4047 Princess Louise
4048 Princess Victoria
4049 Princess Maud
4050 Princess Alice
4052 Princess Beatrice
4053 Princess Alexandra
4054 Princess Charlotte
4055 Princess Sophia
4056 Princess Margaret
4057 Princess Elizabeth
4058 Princess Augusta
4059 Princess Patricia
4060 Princess Eugenie
4061 Glastonbury Abbey
4062 Malmesbury Abbey

4-6-0 4073 Class
"Castle"

4073 Caerphilly Castle
4074 Caldicot Castle
4075 Cardiff Castle
4076 Carmarthen Castle
4077 Chepstow Castle
4078 Pembroke Castle
4079 Pendennis Castle
4080 Powderham Castle
4081 Warwick Castle
4082 Windsor Castle
4083 Abbotsbury Castle
4084 Aberystwyth Castle
4085 Berkeley Castle
4086 Builth Castle
4087 Cardigan Castle
4088 Dartmouth Castle
4089 Donnington Castle
4090 Dorchester Castle
4091 Dudley Castle
4092 Dunraven Castle
4093 Dunster Castle
4094 Dynevor Castle
4095 Harlech Castle
4096 Highclere Castle
4097 Kenilworth Castle
4098 Kidwelly Castle
4099 Kilgerran Castle

2-6-2T 5100 Class

4100	4120	4140	4160
4101	4121	4141	4161
4102	4122	4142	4162
4103	4123	4143	4163
4104	4124	4144	4164
4105	4125	4145	4165
4106	4126	4146	4166
4107	4127	4147	4167
4108	4128	4148	4168
4109	4129	4149	4169
4110	4130	4150	4170
4111	4131	4151	4171
4112	4132	4152	4172
4113	4133	4153	4173
4114	4134	4154	4174
4115	4135	4155	4175
4116	4136	4156	4176
4117	4137	4157	4177
4118	4138	4158	4178
4119	4139	4159	4179

2-8-0T   4200 Class

4200	4230	4258	4280
4201	4231	4259	4281
4203	4232	4260	4282
4206	4233	4261	4283
4207	4235	4262	4284
4208	4236	4263	4285
4211	4237	4264	4286
4212	4238	4265	4287
4213	4241	4266	4288
4214	4242	4267	4289
4215	4243	4268	4290
4217	4246	4269	4291
4218	4247	4270	4292
4221	4248	4271	4293
4222	4250	4272	4294
4223	4251	4273	4295
4224	4252	4274	4296
4225	4253	4275	4297
4226	4254	4276	4298
4227	4255	4277	4299
4228	4256	4278	
4229	4257	4279	

2-6-0   4300 Class

4303	4326	4358	4377
4318	4337	4375	4381

2-6-2T   4400 Class

4400	4404	4407	4410
4401	4405	4408	
4403	4406	4409	

2-6-2T   4500 Class

4500	4511	4522	4534
4501	4512	4523	4535
4502	4514	4524	4536
4504	4515	4525	4537
4505	4516	4526	4538
4506	4517	4527	4539
4507	4518	4529	4540
4508	4519	4530	4541
4509	4520	4532	4542
4510	4521	4533	4544

4545	4559	4573	4587
4546	4560	4574	4588
4547	4561	4575	4589
4548	4562	4576	4590
4549	4563	4577	4591
4550	4564	4578	4592
4551	4565	4579	4593
4552	4566	4580	4594
4553	4567	4581	4595
4554	4568	4582	4596
4555	4569	4583	4597
4556	4570	4584	4598
4557	4571	4585	4599
4558	4572	4586	

0-6-0T   5700 Class

4600	4625	4650	4675
4601	4626	4651	4676
4602	4627	4652	4677
4603	4628	4653	4678
4604	4629	4654	4679
4605	4630	4655	4680
4606	4631	4656	4681
4607	4632	4657	4682
4608	4633	4658	4683
4609	4634	4659	4684
4610	4635	4660	4685
4611	4636	4661	4686
4612	4637	4662	4687
4613	4638	4663	4688
4614	4639	4664	4689
4615	4640	4665	4690
4616	4641	4666	4691
4617	4642	4667	4692
4618	4643	4668	4693
4619	4644	4669	4694
4620	4645	4670	4695
4621	4646	4671	4696
4622	4647	4672	4697
4623	4648	4673	4698
4624	4649	4674	4699

2-8-0   4700 Class

4700	4703	4705	4707
4701	4704	4706	4708
4702			

31

4-6-0   4900 Class
" Hall "

4900 Saint Martin
4901 Adderley Hall
4902 Aldenham Hall
4903 Astley Hall
4904 Binnegar Hall
4905 Barton Hall
4906 Bradfield Hall
4907 Broughton Hall
4908 Broome Hall
4909 Blakesley Hall
4910 Blaisdon Hall
4912 Berrington Hall
4913 Baglan Hall
4914 Cranmore Hall
4915 Condover Hall
4916 Crumlin Hall
4917 Crosswood Hall
4918 Dartington Hall
4919 Donnington Hall
4920 Dumbleton Hall
4921 Eaton Hall
4922 Enville Hall
4923 Evenley Hall
4924 Eydon Hall
4925 Eynsham Hall
4926 Fairleigh Hall
4927 Farnborough Hall
4928 Gatacre Hall
4929 Goytrey Hall
4930 Hagley Hall
4931 Hanbury Hall
4932 Hatherton Hall
4933 Himley Hall
4934 Hindlip Hall
4935 Ketley Hall
4936 Kinlet Hall
4937 Lanelay Hall
4938 Liddington Hall
4939 Littleton Hall
4940 Ludford Hall
4941 Llangedwyn Hall
4942 Maindy Hall
4943 Marrington Hall
4944 Middleton Hall
4945 Milligan Hall
4946 Moseley Hall
4947 Nanhoran Hall
4948 Northwick Hall
4949 Packwood Hall
4950 Patshull Hall
4951 Pendeford Hall
4952 Peplow Hall
4953 Pitchford Hall
4954 Plaish Hall
4955 Plaspower Hall
4956 Plowden Hall
4957 Postlip Hall
4958 Priory Hall
4959 Purley Hall
4960 Pyle Hall
4961 Pyrland Hall
4962 Ragley Hall
4963 Rignall Hall
4964 Rodwell Hall
4965 Rood Ashton Hall
4966 Shakenhurst Hall
4967 Shirenewton Hall
4968 Shotton Hall
4969 Shrugborough Hall
4970 Sketty Hall
4971 Stanway Hall
4972 Saint Brides Hall
4973 Sweeney Hall
4974 Talgarth Hall
4975 Umberslade Hall
4976 Warfield Hall
4977 Watcombe Hall
4978 Westwood Hall
4979 Wootton Hall
4980 Wrottesley Hall
4981 Abberley Hall
4982 Acton Hall
4983 Albert Hall
4984 Albrighton Hall
4985 Allesley Hall
4986 Aston Hall
4987 Brockley Hall
4988 Bulwell Hall
4989 Cherwell Hall
4990 Clifton Hall
4991 Cobham Hall
4992 Crosby Hall
4993 Dalton Hall

4994 Downton Hall
4995 Easton Hall
4996 Eden Hall
4997 Elton Hall
4998 Eyton Hall
4999 Gopsal Hall

4-6-0   4073 Class
" Castle "

5000 Launceston Castle
5001 Llandovery Castle
5002 Ludlow Castle
5003 Lulworth Castle
5004 Llanstephan Castle
5005 Manorbier Castle
5006 Tregenna Castle
5007 Rougemont Castle
5008 Raglan Castle
5009 Shrewsbury Castle
5010 Restormel Castle
5011 Tintagel Castle
5012 Berry Pomeroy Castle
5013 Abergavenny Castle
5014 Goodrich Castle
5015 Kingswear Castle
5016 Montgomery Castle
5017 St. Donats Castle
5018 St. Mawes Castle
5019 Treago Castle
5020 Trematon Castle
5021 Whittington Castle
5022 Wigmore Castle
5023 Brecon Castle
5024 Carew Castle
5025 Chirk Castle
5026 Criccieth Castle
5027 Farleigh Castle
5028 Llantilio Castle
5029 Nunney Castle
5030 Shirburn Castle
5031 Totnes Castle
5032 Usk Castle
5033 Broughton Castle
5034 Corfe Castle
5035 Coity Castle
5036 Lyonshall Castle
5037 Monmouth Castle

5038 Morlais Castle
5039 Rhuddlan Castle
5040 Stokesay Castle
5041 Tiverton Castle
5042 Winchester Castle
5043 Earl of Mount Edgcumbe
5044 Earl of Dunraven
5045 Earl of Dudley
5046 Earl of Cawdor
5047 Earl of Dartmouth
5048 Earl of Devon
5049 Earl of Plymouth
5050 Earl of St. Germans
5051 Earl of Bathurst
5052 Earl of Radnor
5053 Earl of Cairns
5054 Earl of Ducie
5055 Earl of Eldon
5056 Earl of Powis
5057 Earl of Waldegrave
5058 Earl of Clancarty
5059 Earl St. Aldwyn
5060 Earl of Berkeley
5061 Earl of Birkenhead
5062 Earl of Shaftesbury
5063 Earl Baldwin
5064 Bishop's Castle
5065 Newport Castle
5066 Wardour Castle
5067 St. Fagans Castle
5068 Beverston Castle
5069 Isambard Kingdom Brunel
5070 Sir Daniel Gooch
5071 Spitfire
5072 Hurricane
5073 Blenheim
5074 Hampden
5075 Wellington
5076 Gladiator
5077 Fairey Battle
5078 Beaufort
5079 Lysander
5080 Defiant
5081 Lockheed Hudson
5082 Swordfish
5083 Bath Abbey
5084 Reading Abbey
5085 Evesham Abbey

5086 Viscount Horne
5087 Tintern Abbey
5088 Llanthony Abbey
5089 Westminster Abbey
5090 Neath Abbey
5091 Cleeve Abbey
5092 Tresco Abbey
5093 Upton Castle
5094 Tretower Castle
5095 Barbury Castle
5096 Bridgwater Castle
5097 Sarum Castle
5098 Clifford Castle
5099 Compton Castle

5228	5238	5247	5256
5229	5239	5248	5257
5230	5240	5249	5258
5231	5241	5250	5259
5232	5242	5251	5260
5233	5243	5252	5261
5234	5244	5253	5262
5235	5245	5254	5263
5236	5246	5255	5264
5237			

2-6-2T   5100 Class

5101	5140	5163	5183
5102	5141	5164	5184
5103	5142	5165	5185
5104	5143	5166	5186
5105	5144	5167	5187
5106	5147	5168	5188
5107	5148	5169	5189
5108	5150	5170	5190
5109	5151	5171	5191
5110	5152	5172	5192
5112	5153	5173	5193
5113	5154	5174	5194
5125	5155	5175	5195
5129	5156	5176	5196
5132	5157	5177	5197
5134	5158	5178	5198
5136	5159	5179	5199
5137	5160	5180	
5138	5161	5181	
5139	5162	5182	

2-8-0T   4200 Class

5200	5207	5214	5221
5201	5208	5215	5222
5202	5209	5216	5223
5203	5210	5217	5224
5204	5211	5218	5225
5205	5212	5219	5226
5206	5213	5220	5227

2-6-0   4300 Class

5300	5326	5353	5379
5303	5327	5355	5380
5305	5328	5356	5381
5306	5330	5357	5382
5307	5331	5358	5384
5309	5332	5359	5385
5310	5333	5360	5386
5311	5334	5361	5388
5312	5335	5362	5390
5313	5336	5364	5391
5314	5337	5365	5392
5315	5338	5367	5393
5316	5339	5368	5394
5317	5341	5369	5395
5318	5344	5370	5396
5319	5345	5371	5397
5321	5346	5372	5398
5322	5347	5375	5399
5323	5348	5376	
5324	5350	5377	
5325	5351	5378	

0-6-0T   5400 Class

5400	5407	5414	5421
5401	5408	5415	5422
5402	5409	5416	5423
5403	5410	5417	5424
5404	5411	5418	
5405	5412	5419	
5406	5413	5420	

2 6-2T   4500 Class

5500	5502	5504	5506
5501	5503	5505	5507

5508	5525	5542	5559	5708	5731	5754	5777
5509	5526	5543	5560	5709	5732	5755	5778
5510	5527	5544	5561	5710	5733	5756	5779
5511	5528	5545	5562	5711	5734	5757	5780
5512	5529	5546	5563	5712	5735	5758	5781
5513	5530	5547	5564	5713	5736	5759	5782
5514	5531	5548	5565	5714	5737	5760	5783
5515	5532	5549	5566	5715	5738	5761	5784
5516	5533	5550	5567	5716	5739	5762	5785
5517	5534	5551	5568	5717	5740	5763	5786
5518	5535	5552	5569	5718	5741	5764	5787
5519	5536	5553	5570	5719	5742	5765	5788
5520	5537	5554	5571	5720	5743	5766	5789
5521	5538	5555	5572	5721	5744	5767	5790
5522	5539	5556	5573	5722	5745	5768	5791
5523	5540	5557	5574	5723	5746	5769	5792
5524	5541	5558		5724	5747	5770	5793
				5725	5748	5771	5794

0-6-2T   5600 Class

5600	5625	5650	5675	5726	5749	5772	5795
5601	5626	5651	5676	5727	5750	5773	5796
5602	5627	5652	5677	5728	5751	5774	5797
5603	5628	5653	5678	5729	5752	5775	5798
5604	5629	5654	5679	5730	5753	5776	5799
5605	5630	5655	5680				
5606	5631	5656	5681				

0-4-2T   1400 Class

5607	5632	5657	5682	5800	5805	5810	5815
5608	5633	5658	5683	5801	5806	5811	5816
5609	5634	5659	5684	5802	5807	5812	5817
5610	5635	5660	5685	5803	5808	5813	5818
5611	5636	5661	5686	5804	5809	5814	5819
5612	5637	5662	5687				
5613	5638	5663	5688				

4-6-0   4900 Class "Hall"

5614	5639	5664	5689	5900 Hinderton Hall
5615	5640	5665	5690	5901 Hazel Hall
5616	5641	5666	5691	5902 Howick Hall
5617	5642	5667	5692	5903 Keele Hall
5618	5643	5668	5693	5904 Kelham Hall
5619	5644	5669	5694	5905 Knowsley Hall
5620	5645	5670	5695	5906 Lawton Hall
5621	5646	5671	5696	5907 Marble Hall
5622	5647	5672	5697	5908 Moreton Hall
5623	5648	5673	5698	5909 Newton Hall
5624	5649	5674	5699	5910 Park Hall
				5911 Preston Hall

0-6-0T   5700 Class

5700	5702	5704	5706
5701	5703	5705	5707

35

5912	Queen's Hall	5960	Saint Edmund Hall
5913	Rushton Hall	5961	Toynbee Hall
5914	Ripon Hall	5962	Wantage Hall
5915	Trentham Hall	5963	Wimpole Hall
5916	Trinity Hall	5964	Wolseley Hall
5917	Westminster Hall	5965	Woollas Hall
5918	Walton Hall	5966	Ashford Hall
5919	Worsley Hall	5967	Bickmarsh Hall
5920	Wycliffe Hall	5968	Cory Hall
5921	Bingley Hall	5969	Honington Hall
5922	Caxton Hall	5970	Hengrave Hall
5923	Colston Hall	5971	Merevale Hall
5924	Dinton Hall	5972	Olton Hall
5925	Eastcote Hall	5973	Rolleston Hall
5926	Grotrian Hall	5974	Wallsworth Hall
5927	Guild Hall	5975	Winslow Hall
5928	Haddon Hall	5976	Ashwicke Hall
5929	Hanham Hall	5977	Beckford Hall
5930	Hannington Hall	5978	Bodinnick Hall
5931	Hatherley Hall	5979	Cruckton Hall
5932	Haydon Hall	5980	Dingley Hall
5933	Kingsway Hall	5981	Frensham Hall
5934	Kneller Hall	5982	Harrington Hall
5935	Norton Hall	5983	Henley Hall
5936	Oakley Hall	5984	Linden Hall
5937	Stanford Hall	5985	Mostyn Hall
5938	Stanley Hall	5986	Arbury Hall
5939	Tangley Hall	5987	Brocket Hall
5940	Whitbourne Hall	5988	Bostock Hall
5941	Campion Hall	5989	Cransley Hall
5942	Doldowlod Hall	5990	Dorford Hall
5943	Elmdon Hall	5991	Gresham Hall
5944	Ickenham Hall	5992	Horton Hall
5945	Leckhampton Hall	5993	Kirby Hall
5946	Marwell Hall	5994	Roydon Hall
5947	Saint Benet's Hall	5995	Wick Hall
5948	Siddington Hall	5996	Mytton Hall
5949	Trematon Hall	5997	Sparkford Hall
5950	Wardley Hall	5998	Trevor Hall
5951	Clyffe Hall	5999	Wollaton Hall
5952	Cogan Hall		
5953	Dunley Hall		
5954	Faendre Hall		
5955	Garth Hall		
5956	Horsley Hall		
5957	Hutton Hall		
5958	Knolton Hall		
5959	Mawley Hall		

4-6-0 **6000 Class**
" King "

6000	King George V
6001	King Edward VII
6002	King William IV

6003 King George IV			
6004 King George III			
6005 King George II			
6006 King George I			
6007 King William III			
6008 King James II			
6009 King Charles II			
6010 King Charles I			
6011 King James I			
6012 King Edward VI			
6013 King Henry VIII			
6014 King Henry VII			
6015 King Richard III			
6016 King Edward V			
6017 King Edward IV			
6018 King Henry VI			
6019 King Henry V			
6020 King Henry IV			
6021 King Richard II			
6022 King Edward III			
6023 King Edward II			
6024 King Edward I			
6025 King Henry III			
6026 King John			
6027 King Richard I			
6028 King George VI			
6029 King Edward VIII			

2-6-0   4300 Class

6300	6326	6351	6376
6301	6327	6352	6377
6302	6328	6353	6378
6303	6329	6354	6379
6304	6330	6355	6380
6305	6331	6356	6381
6306	6332	6357	6382
6307	6333	6358	6383
6308	6334	6359	6384
6309	6335	6360	6385
6310	6336	6361	6386
6311	6337	6362	6387
6312	6338	6363	6388
6313	6339	6364	6389
6314	6340	6365	6390
6316	6341	6366	6391
6317	6342	6367	6392
6318	6343	6368	6393
6319	6344	6369	6394
6320	6345	6370	6395
6321	6346	6371	6396
6322	6347	6372	6397
6323	6348	6373	6398
6324	6349	6374	6399
6325	6350	6375	

2-6-2T   6100 Class

6100	6118	6136	6153
6101	6119	6137	6154
6102	6120	6138	6155
6103	6121	6139	6156
6104	6122	6140	6157
6105	6123	6141	6158
6106	6124	6142	6159
6107	6125	6143	6160
6108	6126	6144	6161
6109	6127	6145	6162
6110	6128	6146	6163
6111	6129	6147	6164
6112	6130	6148	6165
6113	6131	6149	6166
6114	6132	6150	6167
6115	6133	6151	6168
6116	6134	6152	6169
6117	6135		

0-6-0T   6400 Class

6400	6410	6420	6430
6401	6411	6421	6431
6402	6412	6422	6432
6403	6413	6423	6433
6404	6414	6424	6434
6405	6415	6425	6435
6406	6416	6426	6436
6407	6417	6427	6437
6408	6418	6428	6438
6409	6419	6429	6439

0-6-2T   5600 Class

6600	6606	6612	6618
6601	6607	6613	6619
6602	6608	6614	6620
6603	6609	6615	6621
6604	6610	6616	6622
6605	6611	6617	6623

6624	6643	6662	6681
6625	6644	6663	6682
6626	6645	6664	6683
6627	6646	6665	6684
6628	6647	6666	6685
6629	6648	6667	6686
6630	6649	6668	6687
6631	6650	6669	6688
6632	6651	6670	6689
6633	6652	6671	6690
6634	6653	6672	6691
6635	6654	6673	6692
6636	6655	6674	6693
6637	6656	6675	6694
6638	6657	6676	6695
6639	6658	6677	6696
6640	6659	6678	6697
6641	6660	6679	6698
6642	6661	6680	6699

0-6-0T   5700 Class

6700	6720	6740	6760
6701	6721	6741	6761
6702	6722	6742	6762
6703	6723	6743	6763
6704	6724	6744	6764
6705	6725	6745	6765
6706	6726	6746	6766
6707	6727	6747	6767
6708	6728	6748	6768
6709	6729	6749	6769
6710	6730	6750	6770
6711	6731	6751	6771
6712	6732	6752	6772
6713	6733	6753	6773
6714	6734	6754	6774
6715	6735	6755	6775
6716	6736	6756	6776
6717	6737	6757	6777
6718	6738	6758	6778
6719	6739	6759	6779

4-6-0   6800 Class
" Grange "

6800 Arlington Grange
6801 Aylburton Grange
6802 Bampton Grange

6803 Bucklebury Grange
6804 Brockington Grange
6805 Broughton Grange
6806 Blackwell Grange
6807 Birchwood Grange
6808 Beenham Grange
6809 Burghclere Grange
6810 Blakemere Grange
6811 Cranbourne Grange
6812 Chesford Grange
6813 Eastbury Grange
6814 Enbourne Grange
6815 Frilford Grange
6816 Frankton Grange
6817 Gwenddwr Grange
6818 Hardwick Grange
6819 Highnam Grange
6820 Kingstone Grange
6821 Leaton Grange
6822 Manton Grange
6823 Oakley Grange
6824 Ashley Grange
6825 Llanvair Grange
6826 Nannerth Grange
6927 Llanfrechfa Grange
6828 Trellech Grange
6829 Burmington Grange
6830 Buckenhill Grange
6831 Bearley Grange
6832 Brockton Grange
6833 Calcot Grange
6834 Dummer Grange
6835 Eastham Grange
6836 Estevarney Grange
6837 Forthampton Grange
6838 Goodmoor Grange
6839 Hewell Grange
6840 Hazeley Grange
6841 Marlas Grange
6842 Nunhold Grange
6843 Poulton Grange
6844 Penhydd Grange
6845 Paviland Grange
6846 Ruckley Grange
6847 Tidmarsh Grange
6848 Toddington Grange
6849 Walton Grange
6850 Cleeve Grange

6851 Hurst Grange
6852 Headbourne Grange
6853 Morehampton Grange
6854 Roundhill Grange
6855 Saighton Grange
6856 Stowe Grange
6857 Tudor Grange
6858 Woolston Grange
6859 Yiewsley Grange
6860 Aberporth Grange
6861 Crynant Grange
6862 Derwent Grange
6863 Dolhywel Grange
6864 Dymock Grange
6865 Hopton Grange
6866 Morfa Grange
6867 Peterston Grange
6868 Penrhos Grange
6869 Resolven Grange
6870 Bodicote Grange
6871 Bourton Grange
6872 Crawley Grange
6873 Caradoc Grange
6874 Haughton Grange
6875 Hindford Grange
6876 Kingsland Grange
6877 Llanfair Grange
6878 Longford Grange
6879 Overton Grange

4-6-0   4900 Class
" Hall "

6900 Abney Hall
6901 Arley Hall
6902 Butlers Hall
6903 Belmont Hall
6904 Charfield Hall
6905 Claughton Hall
6906 Chicheley Hall
6907 Davenham Hall
6908 Downham Hall
6909 Frewin Hall
6910 Gossington Hall
6911 Holker Hall
6912 Helmster Hall
6913 Levens Hall
6914 Langton Hall
6915 Mursley Hall

6916 Misterton Hall
6917 Oldlands Hall
6918 Sandon Hall
6919 Tylney Hall
6920 Barningham Hall
6921 Borwick Hall
6922 Burton Hall
6923 Croxteth Hall
6924 Grantley Hall
6925 Hackness Hall
6926 Holkham Hall
6927 Lilford Hall
6928 Underley Hall
6929 Whorlton Hall
6930 Aldersey Hall
6931 Aldborough Hall
6923 Burwarton Hall
6933 Birtles Hall
6934 Beachamwell Hall
6935 Browsholme Hall
6936 Breccles Hall
6937 Conyngham Hall
6938 Corndean Hall
6939 Calveley Hall
6940 Didlington Hall
6941 Fillongley Hall
6942 Eshton Hall
6943 Farnley Hall
6944 Fledborough Hall
6945 Glasfryn Hall
6946 Heatherden Hall
6947 Helmingham Hall
6948 Holbrooke Hall
6949 Haberfield Hall
6950 Kingsthorpe Hall
6951 Impney Hall
6952 Kimberley Hall
6953 Leighton Hall
6954 Lotherton Hall
6955 Lydcott Hall
6956 Mottram Hall
6957 Norcliffe Hall
6958 Oxburgh Hall

4-6-0   6959 Class
" Modified Hall "

6959 Peatling Hall
6960 Raveningham Hall

6961 Stedham Hall	7004 Eastner Castle
6962 Soughton Hall	7005 Lamphey Castle
6963 Throwley Hall	7006 Lydford Castle
6964 Thornbridge Hall	7007 Great Western
6965 Thirlestaine Hall	7008 Swansea Castle
6966 Witchingham Hall	7009 Athelney Castle
6967 Willesley Hall	7010 Avondale Castle
6968 Woodcock Hall	7011 Banbury Castle
6969 Wraysbury Hall	7012 Barry Castle
6970 Whaddon Hall	7013 Bristol Castle
6971 Athelhampton Hall	7014 Caerhays Castle
6972 Beningbrough Hall	7015 Carn Brea Castle
6973 Bricklehamtpon Hall	7016 Chester Castle
6974 Bryngwyn Hall	7017 G. J. Churchward
6975 Capesthorne Hall	7018 Drysllwyn Castle
6976 Graythwaite Hall	7019 Fowey Castle
6977 Grundisburgh Hall	7020 Gloucester Castle
6978 Haroldstone Hall	7021 Haverfordwest Castle
6979 Helperly Hall	7022 Hereford Castle
6980 Llanrumney Hall	7023 Penrice Castle
6981 Marbury Hall	7024 Powis Castle
6982 Melmerby Hall	7025 Sudeley Castle
6983 Otterington Hall	7026 Tenby Castle
6984 Owsden Hall	7027 Thornbury Castle
6985 Parwick Hall	7028 Cadbury Castle
6986 Rydal Hall	7029 Clun Castle
6987 Shervington Hall	7030 Cranbrook Castle
6988 Swithland Hall	7031 Cromwell's Castle
6989 Wightwick Hall	7032 Denbigh Castle
6990 Witherslack Hall	7033 Hartlebury Castle
6991 Acton Burnell Hall	7034 Ince Castle
6992 Arborfield Hall	7035 Ogmore Castle
6993 Arthog Hall	7036 Taunton Castle
6994 Baggrave Hall	7037 Swindon
6995 Benthall Hall	
6996 Blackwell Hall	
6997 Bryn-Ivor Hall	
6998 Burton Agnes Hall	
6999 Capel Dewi Hall	

4-6-0   7000 Class
" Castle "

7000 Viscount Portal
7001 Sir James Milne
7002 Devizes Castle
7003 Elmley Castle

2-8-2T   7200 Class

7200	7210	7220	7230
7201	7211	7221	7231
7202	7212	7222	7232
7203	7213	7223	7233
7204	7214	7224	7234
7205	7215	7225	7235
7206	7216	7226	7236
7207	7217	7227	7237
7208	7218	7228	7238
7209	7219	7229	7239

7240	7244	7248	7252
7241	7245	7249	7253
7242	7246	7250	
7243	7247	7251	

2-6-0   4300 Class

7300	7306	7312	7318
7301	7307	7313	7319
7302	7308	7314	7320
7303	7309	7315	7321
7304	7310	7316	
7305	7311	7317	

0-6-0T   7400 Class

7400	7413	7426	7438
7401	7414	7427	7439
7402	7415	7428	7440
7403	7416	7429	7441
7404	7417	7430	7442
7405	7418	7431	7443
7406	7419	7432	7444
7407	7420	7433	7445
7408	7421	7434	7446
7409	7422	7435	7447
7410	7423	7436	7448
7411	7424	7437	7449
7412	7425		

0-6-0T   5700 Class

7700	7718	7736	7754
7701	7719	7737	7755
7702	7720	7738	7756
7703	7721	7739	7757
7704	7722	7740	7758
7705	7723	7741	7759
7706	7724	7742	7760
7707	7725	7743	7761
7708	7726	7744	7762
7709	7727	7745	7763
7710	7728	7746	7764
7711	7729	7747	7765
7712	7730	7748	7766
7713	7731	7749	7767
7714	7732	7750	7768
7715	7733	7751	7769
7716	7734	7752	7770
7717	7735	7753	7771

7772	7779	7786	7793
7773	7780	7787	7794
7774	7781	7788	7795
7775	7782	7789	7796
7776	7783	7790	7797
7777	7784	7791	7798
7778	7785	7792	7799

4-6-0   7800 Class
" Manor "

7800 Torquay Manor
7801 Anthony Manor
7802 Bradley Manor
7803 Barcote Manor
7804 Baydon Manor
7805 Broome Manor
7806 Cockington Manor
7807 Compton Manor
7808 Cookham Manor
7809 Childrey Manor
7810 Draycott Manor
7811 Dunley Manor
7812 Erlestoke Manor
7813 Freshford Manor
7814 Fringford Manor
7815 Fritwell Manor
7816 Frilsham Manor
7817 Garsington Manor
7818 Granville Manor
7819 Hinton Manor
7820 Dinmore Manor
7821 Ditcheat Manor
7822 Foxcote Manor
7823 Hook Norton Manor
7824 Iford Manor
7825 Lechlade Manor
7826 Longworth Manor
7827 Lydham Manor
7828 Odney Manor
7829 Ramsbury Manor

4-6-0   6959 Class
" Modified Hall "

7900 St. Peter's Hall
7901 Dodington Hall
7902 Eaton Mascot Hall

7903 Foremarke Hall			
7904 Fountains Hall			
7905 Fowey Hall			
7906 Fron Hall			
7907 Hart Hall			
7908 Henshall Hall			
7909 Heveningham Hall			
7910 Hown Hall			
7911 Lady Margaret Hall			
7912 Little Linford Hall			
7913 Little Wyrley Hall			
7914 Lleweni Hall			
7915 Mere Hall			
7916 Mobberley Hall			
7917 North Aston Hall			
7918 Rhose Wood Hall			
7919 Runter Hall			
7920 Coney Hall			
7921 Edstone Hall			
7922 Salford Hall			
7923 Speke Hall			
7924 Thornycroft Hall			
7925 Westol Hall			
7926 Willey Hall			
7927 Willington Hall			
7928 Wolf Hall			
7929 Wyke Hall			

2-6-2T 8100 Class

8100	8103	8106	8108
8101	8104	8107	8109
8102	8105		

0-6-0T 9400 Class

8400	8413	8426	8439
8401	8414	8427	8440
8402	8415	8428	8441
8403	8416	8429	8442
8404	8417	8430	8443
8405	8418	8431	8444
8406	8419	8432	8445
8407	8420	8433	8446
8408	8421	8434	8447
8409	8422	8435	8448
8410	8423	8436	8449
8411	8424	8437	8450
8412	8425	8438	8451

8452	8464	8476	8488
8453	8465	8477	8489
8454	8466	8478	8490
8455	8467	8479	8491
8456	8468	8480	8492
8457	8469	8481	8493
8458	8470	8482	8494
8459	8471	8483	8495
8460	8472	8484	8496
8461	8473	8485	8497
8462	8474	8486	8498
8463	8475	8487	8499

0-6-0T 5700 Class

8700	8725	8750	8775
8701	8726	8751	8776
8702	8727	8752	8777
8703	8728	8753	8778
8704	8729	8754	8779
8705	8730	8755	8780
8706	8731	8756	8781
8707	8732	8757	8782
8708	8733	8758	8783
8709	8734	8759	8784
8710	8735	8760	8785
8711	8736	8761	8786
8712	8737	8762	8787
8713	8738	8763	8788
8714	8739	8764	8789
8715	8740	8765	8790
8716	8741	8766	8791
8717	8742	8767	8792
8718	8743	8768	8793
8719	8744	8769	8794
8720	8745	8770	8795
8721	8746	8771	8796
8722	8747	8772	8797
8723	8748	8773	8798
8724	8749	8774	8799

4-4-0 9000 Class

9000	9009	9016	9024
9001	9010	9017	9025
9002	9011	9018	9026
9003	9012	9020	9027
9004	8013	9021	9028
9005	9014	9022	
9008	9015	9023	

42

4-4-0   3252 Class
" Duke "

9084 Isle of Jersey
9089

2-6-0   4300 Class

9300	9305	9310	9315
9301	9306	9311	9316
9302	9307	9312	9317
9303	9308	9313	9318
9304	9309	9314	9319

0-6-0T   9400 Class

9400	9425	9450	9475
9401	9426	9451	9476
9402	9427	9452	9477
9403	9428	9453	9478
9404	9429	9454	9479
9405	9430	9455	9480
9406	9431	9456	9481
9407	9432	9457	9482
9408	9433	9458	9483
9409	9434	9459	9484
9410	9435	9460	9485
9411	9436	9461	9486
9412	9437	9462	9487
9413	9438	9463	9488
9414	9439	9464	9489
9415	9440	9465	9490
9416	9441	9466	9491
9417	9442	9467	9492
9418	9443	9468	9493
9419	9444	9469	9494
9420	9445	9470	9495
9421	9446	9471	9496
9422	9447	9472	9497
9423	9448	9473	9498
9424	9449	9474	9499

0-6-0T   5700 Class

9600	9646	9709	9755
9601	9647	9710	9756
9602	9648	9711	9757
9603	9649	9712	9758
9604	9650	9713	9759
9605	9651	9714	9760
9606	9652	9715	9761
9607	9653	9716	9762
9608	9654	9717	9763
9609	9655	9718	9764
9610	9656	9719	9765
9611	9657	9720	9766
9612	9658	9721	9767
9613	9659	9722	9768
9614	9660	9723	9769
9615	9661	9724	9770
9616	9662	9725	9771
9617	9663	9726	9772
9618	9664	9727	9773
9619	9665	9728	9774
9620	9666	9729	9775
9621	9667	9730	9776
9622	9668	9731	9777
9623	9669	9732	9778
9624	9670	9733	9779
9625	9671	9734	9780
9626	9672	9735	9781
9627	9673	9736	9782
9628	9674	9737	9783
9629	9675	9738	9784
9630	9676	9739	9785
9631	9677	9740	9786
9632	9678	9741	9787
9633	9679	9742	9788
9634	9680	9743	9789
9635	9681	9744	9790
9636	9682	9745	9791
9637	9700	9746	9792
9638	9701	9747	9793
9639	9702	9748	9794
9640	9703	9749	9795
9641	9704	9750	9796
9642	9705	9751	9797
9643	9706	9752	9798
9644	9707	9753	9799
9645	9708	9754	

STREAM-LINED DIESEL RAIL-CARS

Car No.	Date	Engines	Total b.h.p.	Seats	Car No.	Date	Engines	Total b.h.p.	Seats
1	1934	1	121	69	18§	1937	2	242	70
2-4*	1934	2	242	44	19-21/3-32	1940	2	210	48
5-7	1935	2	242	70	33	1941	2	210	48
8, 9	1936	2	242	70	34‡	1941	2	210	—
10-12†	1936	2	242	63	35-36‖	1941	4	420	104
13-16	1936	2	242	70	22-38‖	1942	4	420	104
17‡	1936	2	242						

* Buffet and lavatory facilities.
† Lavatory facilities.
‡ Parcels cars.
§ Experimentally geared to haul trailer car, became prototype of subsequent designs.

‖ Twin-coach units with buffet and lavatory facilities. Adjoining statistics apply per 2-car unit. When new, some of these units worked as 3-car rakes by the addition of an ordinary 70 ft. corridor coach.

1	6	12	17	22	27	32	38
2	7	13	18	23	28	33	
3	8	14	19	24	29	34	
4	10	15	20	25	30	35	
5	11	16	21	26	31	36	

SERVICE LOCOS

Petrol

0-4-0 : 15, 23, 24, 26 and 27
Total 5

Top to bottom : 4900 Class 4-6-0 No. 4920 *Dumbleton Hall* ;   6959 Class 4-6-0 No. 7924 *Thornycroft Hall* ;   2900 Class 4-6-0 No. 2936 *Cefntilla Court.*

[*M. W. Earley, P. M. Alexander, R. E. Vincent.*

This Page. *Above :* 3300 Class 4-4-0 No. 3454 Skylark. *Above right* 3252 Class 4-4-0 No. 9084 Isle of Jersey. *Right :* 4000 Class 4-6-0 No. 4052 Princess Beatrice.
[M. W. Earley, J. N. Westwood, P. M. Alexander

Facing Page. *Top left :* 7800 Class 4-6-0 No. 7809 Childrey Manor. *Top right :* 6800 Class 4-6-0 No. 6829 Burmington Grange. *Bottom left :* 4300 Class 2-6-0 No. 6329. *Bottom right :* 4300 Class 2-6-0 No. 9319 (with side-window cab).
[P. Ransome-Wallis, R. E. Vincent (2), H. C. Casserley

Facing Page. *Top to bottom :* 4700 Class 2-8-0 No. 4702; 2800 Class 2-8-0 No. 3836 (with side-window cab) ; 2800 Class 2-8-0 No. 2844 ; ROD Class 2-8-0 No. 3044.
[D. G. Carpenter, H. C. Casserley, R. E. Vincent, A. Delicata

This Page. *Top to bottom :* 2301 Class 0-6-0 No. 2573; 2251 Class 0-6-0 No. 3212; Ex - M.S.W.J. 2 - 4 -0 No. 1336.
[A. Delicata, J. N. Westwood, R. E. Vincent

Facing Page. *Top left* : 7200 Class 2-8-2T No. 7216. *Top right* : 6100 Class 2-6-2T No. 6169. *Bottom left* : 4200 Class 2-8-0T No. 4225. *Bottom right* : 8100 Class 2-6-2T No. 8108.

[*P. Ransome-Wallis, W. Gilburt, A. Delicata, J. N. Westwood*

This Page. *Right* : 4500 Class 2-6-2T No. 4526. *Below* : 4400 Class 2-6-2T No. 4407. *Below right* : 4575 Class 2-6-2T No. 5551.

[*H. C. Casserley, P. Ransome-Wallis, D. M. Rowse*

Above : 1500 Class 0-6-0T No. 1505.   Above right : 3150 Class
2-6-2T No. 3154.   Below : 9400 Class 0-6-0T No. 8451.   Below
right : 5600 Class 0-6-2T No. 6682.

[C. R. L. Coles, T. A. Saunders, A. Delicata, F. F. Moss

PRINCIPAL DIMENSIONS OF WESTERN REGION LOCOMOTIVES

(Tractive Effort calculated to the nearest 5 lb.) Su = Superheated. SS = Some Superheated.

In the "Class" column, numbers in brackets refer to the lowest number in those classes which are not officially designated by a general class number.

Class	Designer	Original Owning Co. (if other than G.W.)	Building or Rebuilding Date	Weight of Loco. (T. Cwt.)	Boiler Pressure	Cylinders	Driving Wheels	Tractive Effort at 85% B.P.	Power Class	Route Restriction Colour
4-6-0										
1000	Hawksworth	—	1945-7	76 17	280 Su.	(0) 18¼ × 30	6' 3"	32,580	D	Red
2900	Churchward	—	1903-13	72 0	225 Su.	(0) 18½ × 30	6' 8½"	24,395	C	Red
4000	Churchward	—	1907-14	75 17	225 Su.	(4) 15 × 26	6' 8½"	27,800	D	Red
4073	Collett	—	1923-50	79 17	225 Su.	(4) 16 × 26	6' 8½"	31,625	D	Red
4900	{ Churchward (1907) / reb. Collett }	—	1924	{ 72 10 / 75 0 }	225 Su.	(0) 18½ × 30	6' 0"	27,275	D	Red
6000	Collett	—	1928-43	89 0	250 Su.	(4) 16¼ × 28	6' 6"	40,285	Special	Double Red
6800	Collett	—	1927-30	74 0	225 Su.	(0) 18½ × 30	5' 8"	28,875	D	Red
6959	Hawksworth	—	1936-50	75 16	225 Su.	(0) 18½ × 30	6' 0"	27,275	D	Red
7800	Collett	—	1938-50	68 18	225 Su.	(0) 18 × 30	5' 8"	27,340	D	Blue
4-4-0										
3252	{ Dean (1895) / reb. Collett }	—	{ 1895-7 / 1929 }	{ 47 6 / 49 0 }	180 SS.	18 × 26	5' 8"	18,955	B	Yellow
3300	Dean (1895-7)	—	1903-10	51 16	200 Su.	18 × 26	5' 8"	21,060	B	Blue
9000	reb. Collett	—	1936-9	49 0	180 SS.	18 × 26	5' 8"	18,955	B	Yellow
2-8-0										
2800	{ Churchward / Collett }	—	{ 1903-19 / 1938-42 }	{ 75 10 / 76 5 }	225 Su.	(0) 18½ × 30	4' 7½"	35,380	E	Blue
R.O.D.	Robinson (G.C.)	—	1917-9	73 11	185 Su.	(0) 21 × 26	4' 8"	32,200	D	Blue
4700	Churchward	—	1919-23	82 0	225 Su.	(0) 19 × 30	5' 8"	30,460	D	Red

Class	Designer	Original Owning Co. (if other than G.W.)	Building or Rebuilding Date	Weight of Loco.	Boiler Pressure	Cylinders	Driving Wheels	Tractive Effort at 85% B.P.	Power Class	Route Restriction Colour
				T. Cwt.						
2-6-0										
4300	{ Churchward { Collett	— —	1911–25 1932	{ 62 0 64 0 65 6	200 Su.	(0) 18½ × 30	5′ 8″	25,670	D	{ Blue { Red †
2-4-0										
(1334)	Dubs.	M.S.W.J.	1894	35 5	165	17 × 24	5′ 6″	13,400	A	—
0-6-0										
2251	Collett	—	1930–48	43 8	200 Su.	{ 17½ × 24	5′ 2″	20,155	B	Yellow
2301	Dean	—	1884–99	36 16	180 Su.	{ 17 × 24	5′ 2″	17,120	A	—
(844)	Jones, reb. G.W. from 1924	Cam	1903–18	38 17	160 SS.	{ 17½ × 24 18 × 26	5′ 1½″	{ 18,140 18,625	A	Yellow
2-8-2T										
7200	Churchward (1913–30) reb. Collett	—	1934–9	92 2	200 Su.	(0) 19 × 30	4′ 7½″	33,170	E	Red
2-8-0T										
4200	Churchward	—	1910–40	{ 81 12 82 2	200 Su.	{ (0) 18½ × 30 (0) 19 × 30	4′ 7½″	{ 31,450 33,170	E	Red
2-6-2T										
3100	Churchward (1907) reb. Collett	—	1938–9	81 9	225 Su.	(0) 18½ × 30	5′ 3″	31,170	E	Red
3150	Churchward	—	1906–8	81 12	200 Su.	(0) 18½ × 30	5′ 8″	25,670	D	Red
4400	Churchward	—	1904	56 15	180 Su.	(0) 17 × 24	4′ 1½″	21,440	C	—
4500	{ Churchward { Collett	— —	1906–24 1927–9	{ 57 0 61 0	200 Su.	(0) 17 × 24	4′ 7½″	21,250	C	Yellow
5100	{ Churchward (1905–6) reb. Collett { Collett	— —	1928–30 1929–49	{ 75 10 78 9	200 Su.	(0) 18 × 30	5′ 8″	24,300	D	Blue

Class	Designer	Railway	Date	Weight	Pressure	Cylinders	Wheel dia.	T.E.	Route	Colour
6100	Collett	—	1931-5	78 9	225 Su.	(O)18 × 30	5' 8"	27,340	D	Blue
8100	Churchward (1903-6) reb. Collett	—	1938-9	76 11	225 Su.	(O)18 × 30	5' 6"	28,165	D	Blue
(1205)	Hawthorn Leslie	A.D.	1920	65 0	160	(O)19 × 26	4' 7"	23,210	C	Yellow
2-6-2T										
(7)*	Davies & Metcalfe / Collett	V of R. / —	1902 / 1923	25 0	165	(O)11 × 17 / (O)11¼ × 17	2' 6"	9,615 / 10,510	—	—
0-6-2T										
5600	Collett	—	1924-6 / 1927-8	68 12 / 69 7	200 Su.	18 × 26	4' 7½"	25,800	D	Red
(240)	Hosgood / reb. G.W. from 1924	Barry	1890-1900	55 5 / 53 9	160 / 150	17½ × 26	4' 3"	20,825 / 19,525	B	—
(422)	Dunbar, reb. G.W.	B. & M.	1909-14	66 19	175	18½ × 26	4' 6"	24,520	D	Red
(431)	Dunbar, reb. G.W. / Ree, reb. G.W. from 1926	B. & M.	1915-20	59 5	175 Su.	18 × 26	5' 0"	20,885	B	Blue
(155)	Jenkins	Car.	1908	66 12	175 Su.	18 × 26	4' 6½"	22,990	D	Red
(33)	Hurry Riches	Rhym.	1905	62 11	175 Su.	18½ × 26	4' 6"	24,510	D	Red
(31)	Hurry Riches / Hurry Riches reb. G.W. from 1926	Rhym.	1921 / 1907-21	66 0 / 62 10	175 Su. / 200 Su.	18½ × 26 / 18½ × 26	4' 6" / 4' 6"	24,520 / 28,015	D	Red
(55)	Hurry Riches / reb. G.W. from 1926	Rhym.	1910-8	64 3	175	18 × 26	4' 4½"	23,870	C	Blue
(82)	Hurry Riches / reb. G.W. from 1929	Rhym.	1910-8 / 1909	63 0 / 58 19	175 Su.	18 × 26 / 18 × 26	4' 4½" / 5' 0"	23,870 / 25,210	C	Blue
(77)	Hurry Riches / reb. G.W. 1926	Rhym.	1909-21	63 0	175 Su.	18½ × 26	5' 0"	20,885	B	Blue
(203)	Hurry Riches / reb. G.W. from 1928	T.V.	1924-31	61 0	175 Su.	17½ × 26	4' 6½"	21,700 / 21,730	B	Blue
(303)	Cameron (1914)-21 / reb. G.W.	T.V	1924-48	65 14	175 Su. / 200 Su.	18½ × 26 / 17½ × 26	5' 3"	21,000 / 21,480	C	Red

† Nos. 9300-19.

* 1' 11¾" gauge.

0-6-0T

Class	Designer	Original Owning Co. (if other than G.W.)	Building or Rebuilding Date	Weight of Loco. T. Cwt.	Boiler Pressure	Cylinders	Driving Wheels	Tractive Effort at 85% B.P.	Power Class	Route Restriction Colour
850	Dean & Armstrong / Dean reb. Churchward	—	1883 / 1875–95	36 3	165	16 × 24	4' 1½"	17,410	—	—
1361	Churchward	—	1910	35 4	150	(0)16 × 20	3' 8"	14,835	—	—
1366	Churchward	—	1934	35 15	165	(0)16 × 20	3' 8"	16,320	—	—
1500	Hawksworth	—	1949	58 4	200	(0)17½ × 24	4' 7½"	22,515	C	Red
1501	Dean & Armstrong reb. Churchward	—	1879–96	42 17	165	17 × 24	4' 7½"	17,525	A	Yellow
1600	Hawksworth	—	1949–50	41 12	165	16½ × 24	4' 1½"	18,515	A	—
1854	Dean reb. Churchward	—	1890–5	46 13	180	17 × 24	4' 7½"	19,120	A	Blue
2021	Dean reb. Churchward	—	1897–1905	39 15	165	16½ × 24	4' 1½"	18,515	A	—
2181	Dean, mod. Collett	—	1939–40	46 12	165	16½ × 24	4' 1½"	18,515	—	Yellow
5400	Collett	—	1931–2	47 10	165	16½ × 24	5' 2"	14,780	A	Yellow
5700	Collett	—	1929–31 / 1933–49 / 1933 / 1932–7	50 15 / 49 6 / 45 12	200	17½ × 24	4' 7½"	22,515	C	Blue†
6400 & 7400	Collett	—	1936–50 / 1947–50	45 9	180	16½ × 24	4' 7½"	18,010	A	Yellow
9400	Hawksworth	—	1947–50	55 7	200 SS.	(0)17½ × 24	4' 7½"	22,515	C	Red
(666)	Kerr Stuart	A.-D.	1917	50 0	160	17 × 24	4' 0"	19,650	B	Blue
(2196)	Avonside	B.P.G.V.	1906–8	38 5	170	(0)15 × 22	3' 6"	17,030	A	—
(2175)	Avonside reb. G.W.	B.P.G.V.	1907	38 8	165	(0)15 × 22	3' 9"	16,530	—	—
(2197)	Hudswell Clarke	B.P.G.V.	1909	36 8	160	(0)15 × 22	3' 9"	14,960	—	—
(2198)	Hudswell Clarke reb. G.W.	—	1910	37 15	165	(0)15 × 22	3' 9"	15,430	—	—
(2162)	Hudswell Clarke	B.P.G.V.	1912–9	44 4 / 44 0	160	(0)16 × 24	3' 9"	18,570	A	Yellow

No.	Maker	Rly.	Date	Weight t	c	Press.	Cylinders	Dr. wheel	Weight	Class	Livery
(2192)	R. A. Carr	B.P.G.V.	1900	41	8	140	(0) 16 × 24	3′ 8″	16,615	A	Yellow
(2193)	R. A. Carr	B.P.G.V.	1901	35	12	140	(0) 15 × 22	3′ 6″	14,025	A	Yellow
(2194)	Eager	B.P.G.V.	1903–5	31	7	150	(0) 15 × 20	3′ 6″	13,660	—	—
(681)	Hope reb. G.W.	Car.	1920	45	6	165	(0) 18 × 24	4′ 1¾″	22,030	C	Yellow
(28)	M.Wardle reb.G.W.	C.M.D.P.	1905	39	18	160	16 × 24	4′ 0″	18,235	A	Yellow
(803)	Hudswell Clarke	L.M.M.	1911	40	12	160	(0) 16 × 24	4′ 0″	17,410	A	—
(359)	Hudswell Clarke	L.M.M.	1917	34	9	160	16 × 22	3′ 7½″	15,475	—	—
(93)	Hurry Riches reb. G.W.	Rhym.	1908	54	0	175	(0) 18 × 26	4′ 4½″	23,870	C	Red
(90)	Hurry Riches	Rhym.	1920	56	8	175	18 × 26	4′ 4½″	25,210	C	Red
(1146)	Peckett	S.H.T.	1912	38	10	160	18½ × 26	4′ 10″	16,650	A	—
(193)	Hurry Riches	T.V.	1884	44	15	140	17½ × 26	5′ 3″	15,040	A	Yellow
0-6-0T											
(5)	Stroudley (L.B.S.C.) (1877) reb. Marsh	W.C.P.	1919	28	5	150	12 × 20	4′ 0″	7,650	—	—
(822)*	Beyer Peacock	W. & L.	1902	19	18	150	(0) 11½ × 16	2′ 9″	8,175	—	—
0-4-2T 4100 & 5800	Collett	—	1932–6 / 1933	41	6	165	16 × 24	5′ 2″	13,900	—	—
0-4-0T											
1101	Avonside & Collett	Car.	1926	38	4	170	(0) 16 × 24	3′ 9½″	19,510	B	Red
(1338)	Kitson	P. & M.	1898	25	10	160	(0) 14 × 21	3′ 2½″	14,540	—	—
(1150)	Peckett	P. & M.	1912	30	13	120	(0) 15 × 20	3′ 7″	14,010	—	—
(153)	Hawthorn Leslie	S.H.T.	1903	26	13	120	(0) 14 × 22	3′ 6″	9,520	A	Yellow
(140)	Barclay	S.H.T.	1905	28	0	150	15 × 22	3′ 5″	14,305	—	—
(141)	Peckett	S.H.T.	1906	33	10	150	(0) 14 × 20	3′ 7″	14,010	—	—
(144)	Hawthorn Leslie	S.H.T.	1909	26	17	150	(0) 14 × 17	3′ 6″	13,090	—	Blue
(142)	Hudswell Clark	Y.T.W.	1911	28	15	160	15 × 22	3′ 4″	16,830	A	Yellow
(1)	Peckett		1900	23	0	140	(0) 14½ × 22	3′ 2″	13,000	—	Yellow

* 2′ 6½″ gauge.

THE ABC OF BRITISH RAILWAYS LOCOMOTIVES

EDITED BY A. F. COOK AND O. J. MORRIS

PART 2—Nos. 10000-39999 BRITISH RAILWAYS NON-STEAM AND S.R. STEAM LOCOMOTIVES

LONDON:

Ian Allan Ltd

THE NEW STANDARD B.R. CAB

To be fitted to all new B.R. designs

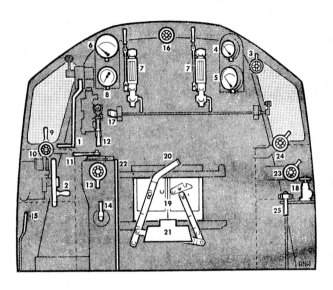

1. Regulator lever.	15. Cylinder drain cocks lever.
2. Reversing gear handle	16. Steam manifold cut-off valve.
3. Train heating supply valve.	17. Whistle control handle.
4. Train heating pressure gauge.	18. Coal slacking hose water cock.
5. Boiler pressure gauge.	19. Double firedoors.
6. Steam chest pressure gauge.	20. Firedoors operating lever
7. Boiler water level gauge.	21. Firehole half-door.
8. Vacuum brake gauge.	22. Anti-glare screen.
9. Small ejector steam supply valve.	23. Live steam injector steam supply valve.
10. Large ejector steam supply valve.	24. Exhaust steam injector steam supply valve.
11. Vacuum brake lever.	25. Injector water control.
12. Steam brake lever.	
13. Blower valve.	
14. Steam sanding valve.	

NEW STANDARD LOCOMOTIVES

FURTHER details have been released by the Railway Executive of the initial six standard locomotive designs, all two-cylinder, of which the first examples are expected to be in service by the spring of 1951. The principal aims are interchangeability of duties, maximum radius of action, and maximum mileage between repairs. The larger locomotives and all tenders will be fitted with roller bearings, and coupled axle-boxes will incorporate manganese liners to give better wearing capacity. The largest possible firegrate area will be provided in each design, to cope with the quality of fuel which has to be used in these days. As far as practicable, fittings and general details will be standardised.

There will first be two new mixed traffic Pacific types, a medium and a light. The 1951 batch of the former will be numbered 70000-24 ; of these 15 will be for the Eastern Region (G.E. Section) and 10 for the Western Region, their power being roughly comparable with that of " West Country " Pacifics, " Castle " and L.M.R. Class " 6 " 4-6-0s, and E.R. " V2 " 2-6-2s. The first light Pacifics will be numbered 72000-9, and are to be allocated to Scotland ; they are intended to undertake similar duties to those of the W.R. " Counties " and L.M.R. " 5XP " 4-6-0s, as well as the heavier tasks now given to Class " 5 " and " B1 " 4-6-0s, which may indicate such routes as the Highland main line. Both Pacifics, designed at Derby, will be built at Crewe.

Two types of mixed traffic 4-6-0s also will be built, a heavy and a light. Of the former, designed at Doncaster, 30 will be constructed at Derby, five for the Scottish and 25 for the London Midland Region, numbered 73000-29 ; of the latter, designed at Brighton and built at Swindon, there will at first be 20, numbered 75000-19, half each for the Western and London Midland Regions. The six new standard types are completed by 2-6-4 and 2-6-2 tank designs, the 2-6-4 designed at Brighton and built both there and at Derby, and the 2-6-2 designed and built at Swindon. Of the 2-6-4 tanks, 54 will be built, 21 for the Scottish, 20 for the London Midland, 10 for the Southern and 3 for the North Eastern Region ; they will be numbered 80000-53. Of the 2-6-2 tanks the order is for 20, half each for the Southern and Western Regions, numbered 82000-19.

Interesting reflections on this 159-locomotive programme are that none of the new engines are to be built at Doncaster or Darlington, and that only 15 of the engines are for the Eastern and 3 for the North Eastern Region, as compared with 20 for the Southern, 30 for the Western, 36 for the Scottish and 55 for the London Midland Regions.

GAS TURBINE LOCOMOTIVES

THE appearance on the Western Region of Britain's first gas turbine locomotive, No. 18000, is a reminder that the supremacy of steam on the railways is now to be challenged from yet another quarter. For a good many years past straight electric power has been a competitor, though this form of traction in Great Britain has had to depend on steam power for the generation of its electricity, and the high cost of its installation hitherto has been justified only on busy suburban passenger lines. Then there opened the era of the internal combustion engine on the railways, first with petrol-engined railcars in France.

But petrol is a very expensive fuel for railway operation, and it was not until the Germans had adapted for railway traction the diesel engine, which works with oil fuel of a considerably cruder and cheaper quality, that the internal combustion engine took its place as a really powerful rival of the steam locomotive. In the United States it has made such enormous strides that in no more than fifteen years all but 50 per cent. of the passenger services and the shunting, and nearly 40 per cent. of the long-distance freight working, have now been turned over from steam to diesel-electric traction. The Germans and Americans have both associated electricity with the diesel engine in developing this form of motive power ; diesel engines driving electric generators, which in their turn supply current to traction motors, provide a much more flexible method of transmission than any attempt to transmit 1,000 to 2,000 horsepower directly by gears, as is done in the much smaller and less powerful diesel-mechanical railcars of the Western Region.

And now, as I said at the beginning, steam has to face yet another competitor in the form of the gas turbine. This is not entirely steam's fault ; on the contrary, in recent years great strides have been made in improving the efficiency of the steam locomotive. The trouble lies largely with the high price and poor quality of present-day coal. Diesel oil is a far cheaper fuel, and the crude oil used in the gas turbine is much cheaper still. Indeed, the oil last-mentioned is one of the by-products from the manufacture of high grade fuels like petrol ; thus, the greater the scale on which petrol is refined, so much the more crude fuel, suitable for the gas turbine, becomes available. In the U.S.A. to-day it is a glut on the market, and has dropped to one-quarter of its wartime price. If, as the gas turbine experts hope, it becomes possible one day to work the gas turbine on a locomotive direct from pulverised coal, working costs might be cut still more.

4

Two years of concentrated research by the well-known engineering firm of Brown Boveri in Switzerland produced the first gas turbine locomotive, in 1941. Apart from a period when it was loaned to the French National Railways, this machine has since been putting in good service on the Swiss Federal Railways, mainly over the few remaining non-electrified branches in that country. Early in 1946, American locomotive designers took up the same idea, and it took them four years to perfect the first U.S.A. gas turbine locomotive. Their accumulated experience with diesel-electric locomotives proved helpful, and when the "Big Blow," as the first American example has been nicknamed, entered service on the Union Pacific Railroad, it was seen to have a strong outward resemblance to a modern diesel locomotive.

It has been tried successfully on all the principal U.P. main lines, over summits as high as Sherman Hill, 8,013 ft. above the sea, but has put in most of its time on the desert route between Salt Lake City and Los Angeles, over which it is in competition exclusively with diesels. No. 18000, the new Swiss-built gas turbine locomotive for the Western Region of British Railways, thus is the third of this type to take the rails ; and the fourth is likely to be the rather larger locomotive, No. 18100, now under construction for the W.R. by Metropolitan-Vickers. Both these latter are to be tried against the London Midland express passenger diesels, Nos. 10000 and 10001, which have been authorised for this purpose to work between Paddington and Plymouth.

How does a gas-turbine locomotive work ? The principle is that air is drawn through intakes to a compressor, where it is compressed to about 40 or 45 lb. per sq. in. The compressed air then passes through a heat exchanger, in which its temperature is raised to about 500 deg. F. Part of this heated air is then passed into a combustion chamber, into which the fuel oil, finely divided in the form of spray, is introduced and ignited, and the temperature of this part of the compressed air thus is raised to some 3,300 deg. F. while its volume is greatly increased. The remainder of the air, by-passing the combustion chamber, mixes with the expanded and highly heated air, and the resultant product, at a temperature of about 1,100 deg. F., reaches the turbine. After driving the turbine, the hot gases pass through the heat exchanger to heat the incoming air, before they are discharged through the locomotive roof.

The turbine of the new W.R. locomotive develops a total of 10,300 h.p., but of this no less than 7,800 h.p. is needed to drive the air compressor, so that less than one-quarter of the turbine's output, 2,500 h.p., is available for traction. This is used to drive an electric generator, through reduction gearing, and the current so produced is used, in its turn, through four traction motors to

5

drive the locomotive, the outer axles of each six-wheel bogie being motor-driven. The locomotive is thus of the A1A-A1A type. At 20 m.p.h. the tractive effort available is 33,000 lb., at 60 m.p.h. 13,000 lb., and at 90 m.p.h., the maximum rated continuous speed, 8,800 lb. In running order the locomotive weighs 113 tons, of which 75 tons rests on the four motor-driven axles and is available for adhesion ; it is 63 ft. long. Sufficient fuel can be carried for a run of 250 miles in normal loading conditions.

For starting up the gas turbine, a diesel engine of 150 h.p. is installed, which drives an auxiliary generator. To get the locomotive under way, the diesel engine first is started by means of a small auxiliary motor, fed with current from the locomotive's storage batteries. As the diesel engine and the auxiliary generator work up into speed the current so produced is used to start up the main generator. This in its turn starts the air compressor, which accelerates until the air is compressed to the stage when ignition becomes possible. The turbine itself now takes over, and accelerates from 1,300 to 3,500 r.p.m. Up to this point diesel fuel oil has been used, but it is now shut off, and the injection of crude oil begins. This sounds a rather complicated sequence, but actually no more than 4 minutes is needed to start up from cold. The driving control in the cab has eleven positions, each corresponding to a certain predetermined power output.

Various problems connected with the gas turbine locomotive remain yet to be solved. One is the length of time that the turbine blades will stand up to the impact of high pressure and highly heated gases without needing replacement or repair. The Americans estimate that their " Big Blow " will need overhaul three times as often as a diesel-electric locomotive of comparable power, but the former is much the simpler machine of the two, and should normally cost considerably less to build and to maintain. Moreover, the fuel needed for the diesel engine costs three times as much as the " Bunker C " oil used by the gas turbine. A minor trouble with the Union Pacific's " Big Blow " has been the locomotive's " scream " while warming up. " Within 50 feet of the locomotive, as she warms up," an American paper said recently, " all talk is drowned out. Though this is not so serious in a freight yard, six ' X-50s ' warming up in a downtown station would create bedlam."

BOILERS AND CABS

BRITISH Railways inherited some 20,000 locomotives, of which the most modern represented four schools of thought. It is interesting to compare the details of these four schools. To the foreigner they are all typically English, but inspection reveals many differences in practice. In this article, we will confine ourselves to a consideration of the differences in boilers and cab fittings.

The tapered boiler was standard on the G.W.R. for all but the smallest locomotives from early in the Churchward period. Through Maunsell it passed to the S.R., and later, through Stanier to the L.M.S.R., so that at nationalisation it was practically standard for all modern engines, except the smallest, of three groups. The L.N.E.R. adhered to the parallel boiler for all locomotives with narrow fireboxes, that is for all but the largest locomotives and the two " V4 " light 2-6-2s. The parallel boiler is heavier than a taper boiler with the same size of firebox, but is cheaper to construct. The 1948 Exchanges showed no superiority in efficiency in the G.W. and L.M.S. locomotives compared with their L.N.E. parallel-boiler counterparts, but it was rumoured that the L.N.E.R. found the L.M.S. taper boiler for the " 8F " 2-8-0 much more expensive to construct than its own " B1 " and " O1 " boiler, even when built in numbers.

There are differences in the method of arranging the taper. It is usual to have all the taper on the top, the bottom edge of the barrel being horizontal. The Southern Pacifics have the converse arrangement, which results, amongst other things, in the smokebox being sufficiently high to clear the steeply-inclined inside valves. On the L.N.E. locomotives and on the L.M.S. " Princess Coronation " Pacifics the taper is divided between top and bottom. The front ring of the barrel is often parallel, although this may not be readily apparent from the shape of the casing.

Combined with the L.N.E.R. preference for parallel boilers was their universal use of round top fireboxes. This type of firebox was also used on two notable Southern classes—the " King Arthurs " and " Schools "—but apart from this the Belpaire firebox has been used on all the standard types of the G.W.R., L.M.S.R. and S.R. For the M.o.S. Austerity locomotives, in the design of which maximum simplicity was sought, the round top firebox and parallel boiler were used, a significant fact considering that the designs were prepared under the direction of an L.M.S. engineer, and derived much inspiration from the L.M.S. " 8F."

The G.W. boilers have combined top feed and safety valves on the barrel, both these fittings being of Swindon design. Steam is

collected by an open pipe over the firebox, and controlled by a smokebox regulator. The L.M.S.R., following Stanier's early experiments with the Swindon arrangement, returned to the traditional British practice of dome regulator and safety valves on the firebox, but retained top feed valves set well forward on the barrel. The S.R. has top and under-water feed on different classes, but on the whole followed tradition. On the Bulleid Pacifics, however, the safety valves are at the front of the barrel, and sometimes deliver a column of water when the engine stops abruptly. Apart from experiments with multiple-valve smokebox regulators, L.N.E.R. practice was conventional, with under-water feed, dome-regulator and safety valves on the firebox.

In the application of superheaters there has been general conformity of practice except on the G.W.R. The Robinson type of equipment, originating on the G.C.R., was extensively used on the L.M.S.R. and L.N.E.R., and the S.R., after some years of experience with the Eastleigh pattern, introduced the Maunsell type, generally similar to the Robinson. The principal differences in these types is in the shape of the header, and in the method of fastening the elements. The number of elements is usually between 18 and 42, this representing the range between an 0-8-0 and a Pacific, and there is usually one element in each large tube, with two loops.

As in other respects, Swindon was distinctive in its superheater layout, and followed a general policy of using smaller superheaters than the other companies, the intention being to heat the steam just sufficiently to prevent condensation. The arrangement of the Swindon superheater is also different, as there are three elements in each large tube, but each element has only one loop. The more recent Swindon boilers have superheaters of more conventional proportions, and the subsidiary trials carried out on the W.R. after the 1948 exchanges, using Welsh coal, showed an advantage in efficiency to the "King" with enlarged superheater.

The superheater snifting valve is a conspicuous boiler mounting, and produces important differences in the boiler outlines of the four groups. In the early days of superheating, dampers, were provided to cover the ends of the flues, to reduce the force of the draught when steam was shut off. This lessened the risk of the elements being burned when no steam was circulating to cool them. The dampers were later superseded by snifting valves, which are held shut by steam pressure, but are lifted from their seats by air pressure when the pumping action of the pistons during coasting creates a partial vacuum in the steam pipes. This permits air to enter the superheater and leave by the exhaust, reducing also the risk of smokebox ashes being drawn into the blastpipe. Modern

heat-resisting steels have eliminated the risk of burned elements, and it is now usual to fit combined pressure-relief and anti-vacuum valves to the cylinders. The L.N.E.R. nevertheless continued the use of dome-shaped snifting valves behind the chimney, whilst on the L.M.S.R. similar valves are fitted to the steam chest (the " clicking " which they produce when bouncing on their seats is a characteristic sound of an L.M.S. locomotive coasting). On the S.R. Maunsell superheaters the snifting valves take the form of small vertical cylinders on each side of the smokebox below the chimney. Experiments on the S.R. have shown that the pressure in the superheater rarely falls sufficiently low for the snifting valves to perform their intended function, and they are being removed as locomotives pass through shops.

At the rear of the firebox, known to enginemen by the anomalous description of the " front," are the controls. Here also Swindon is distinctive, as it retains the right hand position of the driver, which was once general, but has now been largely superseded on modern locomotives by the more logical left hand position. The G.W. tapered boiler and wide cab give the driver a much wider view than on many other large locomotives, and the change to left hand drive has not been considered necessary.

The regulator handle may move across the firebox or fore-and-aft. The latter arrangement was standard for most locomotives on the L.N.E.R. under Gresley, although retained only for Pacifics since, and is also used on the S.R. Pacifics and " Leaders." It enables the driver to pull hard (if necessary) on the handle, without leaving his seat or twisting his body, but it requires a more complicated gland where the regulator rod enters the firebox.

The reversing wheel is normally arranged with the screw parallel to the boiler, so that the driver moves the handle across in front of him. In many cabs this cannot be done, except at the risk of bruised legs, unless the driver leaves his seat. The larger Gresley locomotives have a vertical reversing column, a more convenient arrangement, but one which involves an extra ball crank in the rodding. The only recent locomotives with power reverse are those of Mr. Bulleid. The difficulty of making small adjustments of cut-off, and of locking the gear in position whilst running, have been found to outweigh the advantages of power reverse.

On the L.M.R. steam brakes are standard on all modern locomotives. They are controlled from the vacuum brake by the old Midland type of brake handle, which is nearly vertical, and moves across the cab. Provision is not made for independent control of the locomotive brake, and a vacuum must be maintained even when working a non-fitted train. In Gresley days vacuum brakes on the locomotives were gradually adopted as standard on the

L.N.E.R., but on post-Gresley engines the steam brake is used, with separate control, in addition to the automatic operation from the vacuum train brake. On the S.R. there are both vacuum and steam brakes on different classes, with independent control of the steam brake, but on the W.R. vacuum on the locomotive is standard. The brake handle is similar to the L.M.S. type, with a separate control for the ejector. On the usual vacuum brake ejectors the brake handle rotates about a spindle crossways to the cab. The W.R. retains the motion-driven pump in place of a small ejector, although this fitting was formerly used on the L.M.S.R. and S.R.

The comfort of the engineman has improved greatly with the advent of side window cabs, extended cab roofs and side wind-screens, the latter being a notable detail which originated on the L.N.E.R. Another innovation used only on the L.N.E.R. was the bucket seat for the crew. Despite these improvements, many pre-nationalisation cabs give the impression that the designer has made a few concessions to the enginemen, rather than that their comfort and convenience have been the predominating factors in cab design.

CURRENT EVENTS ON THE SOUTHERN REGION

New construction of steam locomotives in S.R. shops has been confined to L.M.R. "4MT" 2-6-4 tank locomotives, which are replacing L.B.S.C. "I3" locomotives on certain duties. There remains one Pacific to be built, and despite the uncertainty which has surrounded its construction, this is likely to appear eventually as a standard "lightweight."

The experimental Diesel-mechanical shunting locomotive has been completed at Ashford, and the two express Diesel-electric locomotives are well in hand.

The last Stroudley "D1" 0-4-2 tank locomotives have been withdrawn from ordinary service, the two remaining locomotives of the class being used for stationary duties. The interesting 0-8-0 tank *Hecate*, which was acquired by the S.R. from the Kent and East Sussex Railway, has ended its career as shed shunter at Nine Elms. The last of the unrebuilt Billinton "C2" 0-6-0 locomotives has also been withdrawn.

NOTES ON THE USE OF THIS BOOK

1. The remainder of this book lists and describes British Railways locomotives numbered between 10000 and 39999 in service at November 15th, 1950. This range of numbers covers all British Railways internal combustion and electric locomotives and steam locomotives of the former Southern Railway, now Southern Region. For details of "4MT" 2-6-4 tanks and "WD" 2-8-0s operating on the S.R., the reader should consult Pts. 3 and 4 respectively of the *A.B.C. of British Railways Locomotives*.

2. The remaining pages provide, in the following order :
   (i) A list of British Railways Motive Power Depots with their code numbers (pages 13–16).
   (ii) A list of locomotives, in numerical order and showing against each its classification and the code of its home shed, which can be identified from (i) above (pages 25–33). Steam locomotives bear their appropriate shed code number on a small plate at the foot of the smokebox door. Locomotives not given a code number in this list were not in service at the time of compilation. In this list named locomotives are noted by an asterisk, and a full list of names will be found on pages 34–40.
   (iii) A summary list of the classes included in this range of numbers, beginning with B.R. internal combustion and electric locomotives (in which, pages 49–52, the classes are listed in the numerical order of the locomotives) and concluding with S.R. steam locomotives (in which, pages 53–64, the classes are listed in alphabetical order).

The aim of this booklet is that the numerical list shall be used for observation purposes, while the class summaries, which provide details of dimensions, sub-divisions within the class, etc., will provide more comprehensive information on individual engines.

3. The following notes are a guide to the system of reference marks and other details given in the lists of dimensions shown for each class in the alphabetical list of classes.

(a) In the lists of dimensions " Su " indicates a superheated locomotive.

(b) Locomotives are fitted with two inside cylinders, slide valves and Stephenson link motion, except where otherwise shown, e.g. (O) indicates outside cylinders and " P.V." piston valves.

(c) The letter " S " following a number indicates a Service Locomotive. On the S.R. (only) this marking appears on the locomotive.

(d) (W) before a number indicates an Isle of Wight locomotive. The " W " is no longer painted on the locomotives, but may still be seen on the bunker numberplate of some of them.

(e) The date on which a design of locomotive first appeared is indicated by " Introduced." If the oldest surviving locomotive was built at a later date, that also is indicated. Differences between sub-divisions of a class can be followed by tracing the appropriate reference mark throughout the details given for that class.

(f) The code given in smaller bold type at the head of each class, e.g. " 4MT " denotes its British Railways power classification.

4. In accordance with the usual British practice the wheel arrangement of Diesel and petrol locomotives are defined by the Whyte system (i.e., 0-6-6-0) and electric locomotives by the letter system (i.e., Co+Co). Service locomotives are not included in this section.

For full details of
BRITISH RAILWAYS CLASS
" WD " 2-8-0s
running on the Southern Region
see the
A.B.C. OF BRITISH RAILWAYS
LOCOMOTIVES PT. IV. Nos.
60000-90999

For full details of
BRITISH RAILWAYS CLASS
" 4MT " 2-6-4 TANKS
running on the Southern Region,
see the
A.B.C. OF BRITISH RAILWAYS
LOCOMOTIVES PT. III. Nos.
40000-59999

MOTIVE POWER DEPOTS AND CODES

LONDON MIDLAND REGION

1A	**Willesden**	12B	Carlisle (Canal)
1B	Camden	12C	Penrith
1C	Watford	12D	Workington
1D	Devons Road	12E	Moor Row
2A	**Rugby**	14A	**Cricklewood**
2B	Nuneaton	14B	Kentish Town
2C	Warwick	14C	St. Albans
2D	Coventry	15A	**Wellingboro**
3A	**Bescot**	15B	Kettering
3B	Bushbury	15C	Leicester
3C	Walsall	15D	Bedford
3D	Aston	16A	**Nottingham**
3E	Monument Lane	16C	Kirby
4A	**Bletchley**	16D	Mansfield
4B	Northampton	17A	**Derby**
5A	**Crewe North**	17B	Burton
5B	Crewe South	17C	Coalville
5C	Stafford	17D	Rowsley
5D	Stoke	18A	**Toton**
5E	Alsager	18B	Westhouses
5F	Uttoxeter	18C	Hasland
6A	**Chester**	18D	Staveley
6B	Mold Junction	19A	**Sheffield**
6C	Birkenhead	19B	Millhouses
6D	Chester (Northgate)	19C	Canklow
6E	Wrexham	20A	**Leeds** (Holbeck)
6F	Bidston	20B	Stourton
7A	**Llandudno Junction**	20C	Royston
7B	Bangor	20D	Normanton
7C	Holyhead	20E	Manningham
7D	Rhyl	21A	**Saltley**
8A	**Edge Hill**	21B	Bournville
8B	Warrington	21C	Bromsgrove
8C	Speke Junction	21D	Stratford-on-Avon
8D	Widnes	22A	**Bristol**
8E	Brunswick	22B	Gloucester
9A	**Longsight**	23A	**Skipton**
9B	Stockport	23B	Hellifield
9C	Macclesfield	23C	Lancaster
9D	Buxton	24A	**Accrington**
9E	Tra'ord Park	24B	Rose Grove
9F	Heaton Mersey	24C	Lostock Hall
9G	Northwich	24D	Lower Darwen
10A	**Springs Branch**	25A	**Wakefield**
10B	Preston	25B	Huddersfield
10C	Patricroft	25C	Goole
10D	Plodder Lane	25D	Mirfield
10E	Sutton Oak	25E	Sowerby Bridge
10F	Wigan (C.L.)	25F	Low Moor
11A	**Carnforth**	25G	Farnley Junction
11B	Barrow	26A	**Newton Heath**
11C	Oxenholme	26B	Agecroft
11D	Tebay	26C	Bolton
12A	**Carlisle** (Upperby)	26D	Bury

MOTIVE POWER DEPOTS AND CODES

26E	Bacup	27D	Wigan (Central)
26F	Lees	27E	Walton
26G	Belle Vue	27E	Southport
27A	**Bank Hall**	28A	**Blackpool**
27B	Aintree	28B	Fleetwood
27C	Southport		

EASTERN REGION

30A	**Stratford**	34E	Neasden
30B	Hertford East	35A	**New England**
30C	Bishops Stortford	35B	Grantham
30D	Southend (Victoria)	35C	Peterborough (ex L.M.S.)
30E	Colchester	36A	**Doncaster**
30F	Parkeston	36B	Mexborough
31A	**Cambridge**	36C	Frodingham
31B	March	36D	Barnsley
31C	Kings Lynn	36E	Retford
31D	South Lynn	37A	**Ardsley**
31E	Bury St. Edmunds	37B	Copley Hill
32A	**Norwich**	37C	Bradford
32B	Ipswich	38A	**Colwick**
32C	Lowestoft	38B	Annesley
32D	Yarmouth (South Town)	38C	Leicester
32E	Yarmouth (Vauxhall)	38D	Staveley
32F	Yarmouth (Beach)	38E	Woodford
32G	Melton Constable	39A	**Gorton**
32A	**Plaistow**	39B	Sheffield
33B	Tilbury	40A	**Lincoln**
33C	Shoeburyness	40B	Immingham
34A	**Kings Cross**	40C	Louth
34B	Hornsey	40D	Tuxford
34C	Hatfield	40E	Langwith
34D	Hitchin	40F	Boston

NORTH EASTERN REGION

50A	**York**	52A	**Gateshead**
	Normanton		Bowes Bridge
50B	Leeds (Neville Hill)	52B	Heaton
	Ilkley	52C	Blaydon
50C	Selby		Alston
50D	Starbeck		Hexham
	Pateley Bridge		Reedsmouth
50E	Scarborough	52D	Tweedmouth
50F	Malton		Alnmouth
	Pickering	52E	Percy Main
50G	Whitby	52F	North Blyth
51A	**Darlington**		South Blyth
	Middleton-in-Teasdale		Rothbury
51B	Newport	53A	**Hull** (Dairycoates)
51C	West Hartlepool	53B	Hull (Botanic Gardens)
51D	Middlesborough	53C	Hull (Springhead)
	Guisborough		Alexandra Dock
51E	Stockton	53D	Bridlington
51F	West Auckland	53E	Cudworth
	Wearhead	54A	**Sunderland**
51G	Haverton Hill		Durham
51H	Kirkby Stephen	54B	Tyne Dock
51J	Northallerton		Pelton Leve
	Leyburn	54C	Borough Gardens
51K	**Saltburn**	54D	Consett

MOTIVE POWER DEPOTS AND CODES

SCOTTISH REGION

60A	**Inverness**	64G	Hawick
60B	Aviemore	65A	**Eastfield**
60C	Helmsdale	65B	St. Rollox
60D	Wick	65C	Parkhead
60E	Forres	65D	Dawsholm
61A	**Kittybrewster**	65E	Kipps
61B	Ferryhill (Aberdeen)	65F	Grangemouth
61C	Keith	65G	Yoker
62A	**Thornton**	65H	Helensburgh
62B	Dundee (Tay Bridge)	65I	Balloch
62C	Dunfermline (Upper)	66A	**Polmadie**
63A	**Perth South**	66B	Motherwell
63B	Stirling	66C	Hamilton
63C	Forfar	66D	Greenock
63D	Fort William	67A	**Corkerhill**
63E	Oban	67B	Hurlford
64A	**St. Margaret's**	67C	Ayr
64B	Haymarket	67D	Ardrossan
64C	Dalry Road	68A	**Carlisle** (Kingmoor)
64D	Carstairs	68B	Dumfries
64E	Polmont	68C	Stranraer
64F	Bathgate	68D	Beattock

SOUTHERN REGION

70A	**Nine Elms**	73A	**Stewarts Lane**
70B	Feltham	73B	Bricklayer's Arms
70C	Guildford		New Cross Gate
70D	Basingstoke	73C	Hither Green
70E	Reading	73D	Gillingham
71A	**Eastleigh**	73E	Faversham
71B	Bournemouth	74A	**Ashford**
71C	Dorchester	74B	Ramsgate
71D	Fratton	74C	Dover
71E	Newport (I.O.W.)		Folkestone
71F	Ryde	74D	Tonbridge
71G	Bath (S. & D.)	74E	St. Leonards
71H	Templecombe	75A	**Brighton**
71I	Southampton		Newhaven
72A	**Exmouth Junction**	75B	Redhill
72B	Salisbury	75C	Norwood Junction
72C	Yeovil	75D	Horsham
72D	Plymouth	75E	Three Bridges
72E	Barnstaple Junction	75F	Tunbridge Wells
72F	Wadebridge	75G	Eastbourne

WESTERN REGION

81A	**Old Oak Common**	82E	Yeovil
81B	Slough	82F	Weymouth
91C	Southall	83A	**Newton Abbot**
81D	Reading	83B	Taunton
81E	Didcot	83C	Exeter
81F	Oxford	83D	Plymouth (Laira)
82A	**Bristol** (Bath Road)	83E	St. Blazey
82B	Bristol (St. Philip's Marsh)	83F	Truro
82C	Swindon	83G	Penzance
82D	Westbury	84A	**Wolverhampton** (Stafford Road)

MOTIVE POWER DEPOTS AND CODES

84B	Wolverhampton (Oxley)	86J	Aberdare
84C	Banbury	86K	Abergavenny
84D	Leamington	87A	**Neath**
84E	Tyseley	87B	Duffryn Yard
84F	Stourbridge	87C	Danygraig
84G	Shrewsbury	87D	Swansea East Dock
84H	Wellington	87E	Landore
84J	Croes Newydd	87F	Llanelly
84K	Chester	87G	Carmarthen
85A	**Worcester**	87H	Neyland
85B	Gloucester	87J	Goodwick
85C	Hereford	87K	Swansea Victoria
85D	Kidderminster	88A	**Cardiff** (Cathays)
86A	**Newport** (Ebbw. Jcn.)	88B	Cardiff East Dock
86B	Newport (Pill.)	88C	Barry
86C	Cardiff (Canton)	88D	Merthyr
86D	Llantrisant	88E	Abercynon
86E	Severn Tunnel Junction	88F	Treherbert
86F	Tondu	89A	**Oswestry**
86G	Pontypool Road	89B	Brecon
86H	Aberbeeg	89C	Machynlleth

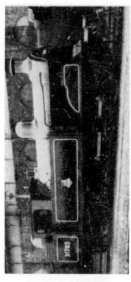

Left Upper: 0-4-4-0 Diesel Electric Locomotive No. 10800
Above: Class M7 0-4-4T No. 30133. Below: Class R1 0-4-4T No. 31703
Left Lower: Class H 0-4-4T No. 31182.
[L. Beard, W. Gilburt, H. C. Casserley, R. H. Tunstall.

This Page.

Top to bottom : Class U 2-6-0 No. 31804 (rebuilt from "River" 2-6-4T) ; Class U 2-6-0 No. 31628 (built new); Class U1 2-6-0 No. 31894.

[H. C. Casserley (2), C. C. B. Herbert.

Facing Page. *Top to bottom :* Class L11 4-4-0 No. 30442 ; Class T9 4-4-0 No. 30710 ; Class L12 4-4-0 No. 30423 ; Class S11 4-4-0 No. 30398.

[W. Gilburt, C. C. B. Herbert, W. Beckerlegge, F. W. Day.

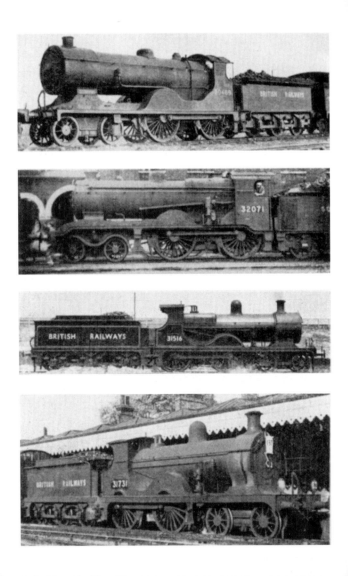

Class MN 4-6-2 No. 35017 *Belgian Marine*. [*P. Ransome-Wallis.*

Above : Class WC 4-6-2 No. 34005 *Barnstaple*. [*G. O. P. Pearce.*

Below : Class LN 4-6-0 No. 30856 *Lord St. Vincent*. [*W. Gilburt.*

BRITISH RAILWAYS
INTERNAL COMBUSTION LOCOMOTIVES
Nos. 10000-18000

WITH SHED ALLOCATIONS
(Correct to 2nd February, 1951)

No.	Shed	No.	Shed	No.	Shed	No.	Shed
Diesel Electric		12010	1A	12057	18A	15098	30B
Co+Co		12011	8C	12058	1A	15099	30B
London Midland		12012	8C	12059	21A		
10000	1A	12013	8C	12060	21A		
10001	1A	12014	8C	12061	21A	**Diesel Electric**	
		12015	8C	12062	21A	**0–6–0**	
		12016	8C	12063	14A	**Western**	
Diesel Mech.		12017	8C	12064	14A	15100	87C
4–8–4		12018	5B	12065	14A	15101	81A
London Midland		12019	1A	12066	14A	15102	81A
10100		12020	8C	12067	14A	15103	81A
		12021	1A	12068	14A	15104	81A
		12022	1A	12069	18A	15105	81A
Diesel Electric		12023	1A	12070	18A	15106	81A
I-Co+Co-I		12024	8C	12071	18A	15107	82B
Southern		12025	8C	12072	18A		
10201		12026	8C	12073	18A		
10202		12027	8C	12074	21A	**Diesel Electric**	
		12028	8C	12075	21A	**0–6–0**	
		12029	1A	12076	21A	**Southern**	
Diesel Electric		12030	1A	12077	21A	15201	75C
Bo+Bo		12031	1A	12078	5B	15202	75C
London Midland		12032	1A	12079	68A	15203	75C
10800	4A	12033	5B	12080	68A	15211	75C
		12034	5B	12081	68A	15212	75C
		12035	5B	12082	68A	15213	75C
Diesel Mech.		12036	5B	12083	68A	15214	75C
0–6–0		12037	5B	12084	12B	15215	75C
Southern		12038	18A	12085	12B	15216	75C
11001	75C	12039	21A	12086	12B	15217	75C
		12040	21A	12087	12B	15218	73C
		12041	21A			15219	73C
Diesel Electric		12042	21A			15220	73C
0–6–0		12043	21A	**Diesel Electric**		15221	73C
London Midland		12044	21A	**0–6–0**		15222	73C
12000	5B	12045	18A	**Eastern**		15223	73C
12001	5B	12046	18A	15000	31B	15224	73C
12002	5B	12047	18A	15001	31B	15225	73C
12003	8C	12048	18A	15002	31B	15226	73C
12004	1A	12049	5B	15003	31B		
12005	1A	12050	5B	15004	31B		
12006	18A	12051	5B			**Gas Turbine**	
12007	8C	12052	5B	**Petrol Electric**		**A-I-A-A-I-A**	
12008	8C	12053	5B	**0–4–0**		**Western**	
12009	1A	12054	5B	**Eastern**		18000	81A
		12055	5B	15097	51C		
		12056	18A				

25

BRITISH RAILWAYS
ELECTRIC LOCOMOTIVES
Nos. 20001-26510

WITH SHED ALLOCATIONS

No.	Shed	No.	Shed	No.	Shed	No.	Shed
Class CC		26010		26031		26052	
Co–Co		26011		26032		26053	
Southern		26012		26033		26054	
20001	Durnsford Rd.	26013		26034		26055	
20002	Durnsford Rd.	26014		26035		26056	
20003	Durnsford Rd.	26015		26036		26057	
		26016		26037			
		26017		26038		**Class ESI**	
Class EMI		26018		26039		**Bo—Bo**	
Bo—Bo		26019		26040		**North Eastern**	
Eastern		26020	39A	26041		26500	52B
26000†		26021		26042		26501	52B
26001	39A	26022		26043			
26002	39A	26023		26044			
26003	39A	26024		26045		**Class EBI**	
26004	39A	26025		26046		**Bo—Bo**	
26005	39A	26026		26047		**Eastern**	
26006	39A	26027		26048		26510	30A
26007	39A	26028		26049			
26008		26029		26050		†On loan to	
26009		26030		26051		Netherlands Rlys.	

BRITISH RAILWAYS LOCOMOTIVES
Nos. 30007-36005

WITH SHED ALLOCATIONS

No.	Class	Shed	No.	Class	Shed	No.	Class	Shed	No.	Class	Shed
30007	TI	72D	30032	M7	71A	30045	M7	71D	30058	M7	72C
30020	TI	71D	30033	M7	71A	30046	M7	72A	30059	M7	71B
30021	M7	70C	30034	M7	72A	30047	M7	75D	30060	M7	70C
30022	M7	70C	30035	M7	72D	30048	M7	71A	30061	U.S.A.	711
30023	M7	72B	30036	M7	72E	30049	M7	72A	30062	U.S.A.	711
30024	M7	72A	30037	M7	72D	30050	M7	71D	30063	U.S.A.	711
30025	M7	72A	30038	M7	70A	30051	M7	71B	30064	U.S.A.	711
30026	M7	70C	30039	M7	72A	30052	M7	71B	30065	U.S.A.	711
30027	M7	75D	30040	M7	71B	30053	M7	71D	30066	U.S.A.	711
30028	M7	71B	30041	M7	72B	30054	M7	71D	30067	U.S.A.	711
30029	M7	71A	30042	M7	72E	30055	M7	72A	30068	U.S.A.	711
30030	M7	72A	30043	M7	70B	30056	M7	70C	30069	U.S.A.	711
30031	M7	71A	30044	M7	72E	30057	M7	71B	30070	U.S.A.	711

No.	Class	Shed	No.	Class	Shed	No.	Class	Shed	No.	Class	Shed
30071	U.S.A.	711	30172	L11	71D	30286	T9	71A	30379	M7	71B
30072	U.S.A.	711	30173	L11	71A	30287	T9	71A	30384	K10	70C
30073	U.S.A.	711	30174	L11	70B	30288	T9	71A	30389	K10	72C
30074	U.S.A.	711	30175	L11	71A	30289	T9	71A	30395	S11	71D
30082	B4	71A	30177	O2	71C	30300	T9	72B	30396	S11	71D
30083	B4	74A	30179	O2	71C	30301	T9	72B	30397	S11	70D
30084	B4	72D	30182	O2	72D	30302	T9	72B	30398	S11	71D
30086*	B4	71B	30183	O2	72D	30303	T9	71D	30399	S11	71C
30087	B4	71B	30192	O2	72A	30304	T9	72B	30401	S11	70C
30088	B4	72D	30193	O2	72A	30305	T9	71D	30402	S11	70C
30089*	B4	71A	30197	O2	71C	30306	700	71A	30403	S11	71B
30093*	B4	71B	30199	O2	72A	30307	T9	71C	30404	S11	71B
30094	B4	72D	30200	O2	72F	30308	700	70C	30406	L11	70A
30096*	B4	71A	30203	O2	72F	30309	700	70B	30408	L11	72A
30102*	B4	72D	30204	O2	71B	30310	T9	71D	30409	L11	72A
30104	M7	71B	30207	O2	72D	30311	700	70C	30411	L11	71A
30105	M7	72A	30212	O2	71B	30312	700	72B	30413	L11	70A
30106	M7	71B	30213	O2	71A	30313	T9	71A	30414	L11	71A
30107	M7	72D	30216	O2	72D	30314	T9	71D	30415	L12	71C
30108	M7	70C	30221	O2	70A	30315	700	72B	30416	L12	71D
30109	M7	71A	30223	O2	71C	30316	700	71A	30417	L12	71D
30110	M7	70C	30224	O2	72A	30317	700	72B	30418	L12	71D
30111	M7	71B	30225	O2	71A	30318	M7	71B	30419	L12	71D
30112	M7	71B	30229	O2	71C	30319	M7	70A	30420	L12	71A
30113	T9	71D	30230	O2	72A	30320	M7	72A	30421	L12	71A
30114	T9	71D	30231	O2	71C	30321	T9	72E	30422	L12	71A
30115	T9	71D	30232	O2	72A	30322	M7	70A	30423	L12	71A
30116	T9	71C	30233	O2	71C	30323	M7	72A	30424	L12	71A
30117	T9	71C	30236	O2	72D	30324	M7	70C	30425	L12	71A
30118	T9	71D	30238	G6	70C	30325	700	70C	30426	L12	71A
30119	T9	70A	30241	M7	70A	30326	700	70C	30427	L12	71A
30120	T9	71D	30242	M7	71A	30327	700	70C	30428	L12	71A
30121	T9	71A	30243	M7	71A	30328	M7	70C	30429	L12	70D
30122	T9	72C	30244	M7	70A	30330	H15	72B	30430	L12	70C
30123	M7	70A	30245	M7	72A	30331	H15	72B	30431	L12	70C
30124	M7	72A	30246	M7	70C	30332	H15	72B	30432	L12	70C
30125	M7	71A	30247	M7	72E	30333	H15	72B	30433	L12	70C
30127	M7	71A	30248	M7	70A	30334	H15	72B	30434	L12	70C
30128	M7	71A	30249	M7	70B	30335	H15	72B	30436	L11	70C
30129	M7	72C	30250	M7	72E	30336	T9	72C	30437	L11	71A
30130	M7	70A	30251	M7	71B	30337	T9	72C	30438	L11	70B
30131	M7	71B	30252	M7	72A	30338	T9	71C	30441	L11	71D
30132	M7	70A	30253	M7	72A	30339	700	70A	30442	L11	70C
30133	M7	72C	30254	M7	70B	30346	700	70B	30446	T14	70A
30134	L11	72C	30255	M7	72A	30349	G6	70A	30448*	N15	72B
30148	L11	71A	30256	M7	72A	30350	700	71A	30449*	N15	72B
30154	L11	71A	30258	G6	70C	30352	700	70B	30450*	N15	72B
30155	L11	71A	30260	G6	71B	30353	G6	70A	30451*	N15	72B
30156	L11	71A	30266	G6	70A	30355	700	70C	30452*	N15	72B
30157	L11	71A	30270	G6	70E	30356	M7	72D	30453*	N15	72B
30159	L11	71A	30274	G6	71H	30357	M7	71A	30454*	N15	72B
30160	G6	70A	30277	G6	70D	30367	T1	71A	30455*	N15	72B
30162	G6	71C	30280	T9	71D	30368	700	70D	30456*	N15	72B
30163	L11	70A	30281	T9	71A	30374	M7	72D	30457*	N15	72B
30164	L11	70B	30282	T9	71A	30375	M7	72D			
30165	L11	70A	30283	T9	71A	30376	M7	72A			
30170	L11	71D	30284	T9	71C	30377	M7	72A			
30171	L11	71A	30285	T9	71C	30378	M7	71A			

No.	Class	Shed	No.	Class	Shed	No.	Class	Shed	No.	Class	Shed
30458*	0458	70C	30520	H16	70B	30676	M7	70A	30748*	N15	71A
30461	T14	70A	30521	H15	70A	30687	700	70B	30749*	N15	71A
30463	D15	71A	30522	H15	70A	30688	700	70B	30750*	N15	71A
30464	D15	71A	30523	H15	70A	30689	700	70B	30751*	N15	71A
30465	D15	71A	30524	H15	70A	30690	700	70A	30752*	N15	71A
30466	D15	71A	30530	Q	71A	30691	700	72B	30753*	N15	71A
30467	D15	71A	30531	Q	71A	30692	700	70A	30754*	N15	71A
30468	D15	71A	30532	Q	71A	30693	700	70D	30755*	N15	71A
30469	D15	71A	30533	Q	75C	30694	700	70A	30756*	756	73A
30470	D15	71A	30534	Q	75C	30695	700	71B	30757*	757	72D
30471	D15	71A	30535	Q	71A	30696	700	70B	30758*	757	72D
30472	D15	71A	30536	Q	71A	30697	700	70B	30763*	N15	73A
30473	H15	71A	30537	Q	75C	30698	700	70B	30764*	N15	73A
30474	H15	71A	30538	Q	75C	30699	700	70A	30765*	N15	73A
30475	H15	71A	30539	Q	75C	30700	700	71A	30766*	N15	73A
30476	H15	71A	30540	Q	75E	30701	700	70A	30767*	N15	74C
30477	H15	71A	30541	Q	75E	30702	T9	72A	30768*	N15	74C
30478	H15	71A	30542	Q	71A	30703	T9	72A	30769*	N15	74C
30479	M7	70A	30543	Q	71A	30704	T9	72A	30770*	N15	74C
30480	M7	71D	30544	Q	71A	30705	T9	72A	30771*	N15	74C
30481	M7	70C	30545	Q	75D	30706	T9	72A	30772*	N15	74C
30482	H15	70A	30546	Q	75D	30707	T9	72A	30773*	N15	74C
30483	H15	70A	30547	Q	75C	30708	T9	72A	30774*	N15	74C
30484	H15	70A	30548	Q	71B	30709	T9	72B	30775*	N15	74C
30485	H15	70A	30549	Q	71B	30710	T9	72B	30776*	N15	74C
30486	H15	70A	30564	0395	72A	30711	T9	72A	30777*	N15	70A
30487	H15	70A	30565	0395	71A	30712	T9	72A	30778*	N15	70A
30488	H15	70A	30567	0395	70B	30713	T9	71A	30779*	N15	70A
30489	H15	70A	30568	0395	70C	30714	T9	72A	30780*	N15	71A
30490	H15	70A	30569	0395	70B	30715	T9	72A	30781*	N15	71A
30491	H15	70A	30570	0395	70B	30716	T9	72A	30782*	N15	71A
30492	G16	70B	30571	0395	71A	30717	T9	72A	30783*	N15	71A
30493	G16	70B	30572	0395	70B	30718	T9	70A	30784*	N15	71A
30494	G16	70B	30573	0395	70B	30719	T9	72B	30785*	N15	71A
30495	G16	70B	30574	0395	70C	30721	T9	70A	30786*	N15	71A
30496	S15	70B	30575	0395	70C	30722	T9	71A	30787*	N15	71A
30497	S15	70B	30576	0395	70C	30723	T9	72A	30788*	N15	71A
30498	S15	70B	30577	0395	70C	30724	T9	72B	30789*	N15	71A
30499	S15	70B	30578	0395	70B	30725	T9	72B	30790*	N15	70A
30500	S15	70B	30579	0395	70B	30726	T9	72B	30791*	N15	70A
30501	S15	70B	30580	0395	72A	30727	T9	72B	30792*	N15	71A
30502	S15	70B	30581	0395	72A	30728	T9	71B	30793*	N15	73A
30503	S15	70B	30582	0415	72A	30729	T9	71A	30794*	N15	73A
30504	S15	70B	30583	0415	72A	30730	T9	71B	30795*	N15	73A
30505	S15	70B	30584	0415	72A	30731	T9	71D	30796*	N15	73A
30506	S15	70B	30585	0298	72F	30732	T9	70B	30797*	N15	73B
30507	S15	70B	30586	0298	72F	30733	T9	70A	30798*	N15	73B
30508	S15	70B	30587	0298	72F	30736*	N15	71B	30799*	N15	73B
30509	S15	70B	30588	C14	71A	30737*	N15	71B	30800*	N15	74A
30510	S15	70B	30589	C14	71A	30738*	N15	71B	30801*	N15	74A
30511	S15	70B	30667	M7	71A	30739*	N15	71B	30802*	N15	74A
30512	S15	70B	30668	M7	72A	30740*	N15	71B	30803*	N15	74A
30513	S15	70B	30669	M7	72A	30741*	N15	71B	30804*	N15	74A
30514	S15	70B	30670	M7	72E	30742*	N15	71B	30805*	N15	74A
30515	S15	70B	30671	H16	72A	30743*	N15	71B	30806*	N15	73C
30516	H16	70B	30673	M7	71A	30744*	N15	70D	30823	S15	72A
30517	H16	70B	30674	M7	71A	30745*	N15	70D	30824	S15	72A
30518	H16	70B	30675	M7	72B	30746*	N15	71A	30825	S15	72A
30519	H16	70B				30747*	N15	71A	30826	S15	72B

No.	Class	Shed	No.	Class	Shed	No.	Class	Shed	No.	Class	Shed
30827	S15	72B	30922*	V	74C	31092	D	73D	31263	H	73A
30828	S15	72B	30923*	V	74C	31093	O1	74B	31265	H	74D
30829	S15	72B	30924*	V	74C	31102	C	73B	31266	H	73A
30830	S15	72B	30925*	V	74C	31107	R1	74C	31267	C	73D
30831	S15	72B	30926*	V	74C		(F)		31268	C	73E
30832	S15	72B	30927*	V	74C	31108	O1	74C	31269	H	74A
30833	S15	70B	30928*	V	73B	31112	C	73D	31270	C	73C
30834	S15	70B	30929*	V	73B	31113	C	74C	31271	C	74A
30835	S15	70B	30930*	V	73B	31128	R1	74C	31272	C	74D
30836	S15	70B	30931*	V	73B		(F)		31273	E	73B
30837	S15	70B	30932*	V	73B	31145	D1	74C	31274	H	74A
30838	S15	70B	30933*	V	73B	31147	R1	74C	31275	E	73B
30839	S15	70B	30934*	V	73B		(F)		31276	H	74C
30840	S15	70B	30935*	V	74E	31150	C.	73C	31277	C	74D
30841	S15	72A	30936*	V	73B	31154	R1	74C	31278	H	73B
30842	S15	72A	30937*	V	73B		(F)		31279	H	74E
30843	S15	72A	30938*	V	73B	31157	E	73E	31280	C	73B
30844	S15	72A	30939*	V	73B	31158	H	74A	31287	C	73D
30845	S15	72A	30950	Z	71A	31159	E	73C	31291	C	74C
30846	S15	72A	30951	Z	73D	31161	H	74A	31293	C	73B
30847	S15	72A	30952	Z	71A	31162	H	73B	31294	C	73B
30850*	LN	71A	30953	Z	74A	31164	H	74E	31295	H	73A
30851*	LN	71A	30954	Z	72A	31165	E1	73B	31297	C	73B
30852*	LN	71A	30955	Z	70A	31166	E	73B	31298	C	74B
30853*	LN	71A	30956	Z	71A	31174	R1	74E	31305	H	74A
30854*	LN	71A	30957	Z	72B	31175	E	73B	31306	H	74C
30855*	LN	71A	31004	C	74B	31176	E	73B	31307	H	73A
30856*	LN	71A	31005	H	73A	31177	H	73A	31308	H	73D
30857*	LN	71A	31010	R1	74A	31178	P	74C	31309	H	75B
30858*	LN	70A	31016	H	75F	31182	H	75F	31310	H	75B
30859*	LN	70A	31018	C	73C	31184	H	73A	31311	H	73A
30860*	LN	70A	31019	E1	73A	31191	C	74C	31315	E	73B
30861*	LN	71B	31027	P	74C	31193	H	74D	31317	C	73D
30862*	LN	71B	31033	C	73B	31218	C	74A	31319	H	73A
30863*	LN	71B	31036	E	73B	31219	C	74D	31320	H	74D
30864*	LN	71B	31037	C	74E	31221	C	73D	31321	H	73A
30865*	LN	71B	31038	C	74E	31223	C	73D	31322	H	74A
30900*	V	74E	31041	O1	74A	31225	C	73D	31323	P	74C
30901*	V	74E	31044	O1	73B	31227	C	73B	31324	H	73B
30902*	V	74E	31047	R1	74C	31229	C	73E	31325	P	75A
30903*	V	74E		(F)		31234	C	73A	31326	H	73B
30904*	V	74E	31048	O	74A	31239	H	74A	31327	H	74D
30905*	V	74E	31054	C	73C	31242	C	73E	31328	H	74E
30906*	V	74E	31057	D	70E	31243	C	74C	31329	H	73A
30907*	V	74E	31059	C	73C	31244	C	74D	31335	R1	74E
30908*	V	74E	31061	C	73C	31245	C	73C	31337	R1	74C
30909*	V	74E	31063	C	74C	31246	D1	74C		(F)	
30910*	V	74E	31064	O1	73B	31247	D1	74C	31339	R1	74A
30911*	V	74B		(NC)		31248	O1	73C	31340	R1	74C
30912*	V	74B	31065	O1	74B	31252	C	74B		(F)	
30913*	V	74B	31066	O1	73B	31253	C	73B	31369	O1	73E
30914*	V	74B		(NC)		31255	C	73D	31370	O1	74A
30915*	V	74B	31067	E1	73A	31256	C	73D	31373	O1	74C
30916*	V	74B	31068	C	73B	31258	O1	73C	31379	O1	74A
30917*	V	74B	31069	R1	74A	31259	H	73E	31381	O1	74C
30918*	V	74B	31071	C	73B	31260	C	74A	31383	O1	74C
30919*	V	73B	31075	D	70E	31261	H	73A	31390	O1	74B
30920*	V	73B	31086	C	73D				31391	O1	73C
30921*	V	73B	31090	C	73D						

No.	Class	Shed	No.	Class	Shed	No.	Class	Shed	No.	Class	Shed
31395	O1	73B (NC)	31519	H	74B	31615	U	70E	31700	R1	74D
31400	N	74A	31520	H	74A	31616	U	73C	31703	R1	74D
31401	N	74A	31521	H	74B	31617	U	73C	31704	R1	74D
31402	N	74A	31522	H	74B	31618	U	72B	31705	R1	73E
31403	N	74A	31523	H	74D	31619	U	70A	31706	R1	74D
31404	N	74A	31530	H	74C	31620	U	70C	31708	R1	74C
31405	N	74A	31531	H	74C	31621	U	70C	31710	R1	74A
31406	N	74A	31532	H	73E	31622	U	71B	31711	C	74A
31407	N	74A	31533	H	73B	31623	U	70A	31712	C	73D
31408	N	74A	31540	H	74C	31624	U	70C	31713	C	73D
31409	N	73A	31541	H	73B	31625	U	70A	31714	C	73A
31410	N	73A	31542	H	73B	31626	U	72B	31715	C	73E
31411	N	73A	31543	H	73B	31627	U	70C	31716	C	73A
31412	N	73A	31544	H	73B	31628	U	70C	31717	C	73A
31413	N	73A	31545	D1	74D	31629	U	70C	31718	C	73A
31414	N	73A	31548	H	74D	31630	U	70C	31719	C	73A
31425	O1	74C	31549	D	74D	31631	U	73E	31720	C	73C
31430	O1	74C	31550	H	74D	31632	U	71C	31721	C	74A
31432	O1	73C	31551	H	70A	31633	U	70D	31722	C	73A
31434	O1	74C	31552	H	70A	31634	U	72A	31723	C	73B
31443	B1	70E	31553	H	70A	31635	U	72A	31724	C	73D
31461	C	74D	31554	H	70A	31636	U	72A	31725	C	73B
31470	D1	74C	31555	P	74C	31637	U	70A	31727	D1	73E
31480	C	73C	31556	P	75A	31638	U	73E	31728	D	74D
31481	C	73E	31557	P	74C	31639	U	73C	31729	D	74D
31486	C	73C	31558	P	73A	31658	R	73D	31730	D	74D
31487	D1	73E	31572	C	74A	31659	R	73D	31731	D	74D
31488	D	73B	31573	C	73D	31660	R	73A	31732	D	74D
31489	D1	73E	31574	D	74A	31661	R	73E	31733	D	74D
31490	D	73B	31575	C	73A	31662	R	73D	31734	D	73E
31491	E	73B	31576	C	73A	31663	R	73D	31735	D1	73D
31492	D1	73B	31577	D	74A	31665	R	73D	31737	D	73E
31493	D	74E	31578	C	73A	31666	R	73D	31739	D1	73E
31494	D1	73E	31579	C	73D	31667	R	74D	31740	D	70E
31495	C	73E	31580	C	74D	31670	R	74D	31741	D1	73E
31496	D	74E	31581	C	73C	31671	R	74D	31743	D1	73A
31497	E1	73B	31582	C	73A	31673	R	74C	31744	D	70E
31498	C	73D	31583	C	73D	31674	R	73E	31745	D1	73A
31500	H	73B.	31584	C	73B	31675	R	74D	31746	D	74D
31501	D	73D	31585	C	73D	31681	C	73A	31748	D	73E
31502	D1	73E	31586	D	73E	31682	C	73D	31749	D1	73A
31503	H	74C	31587	E	74E	31683	C	73A	31750	D	70E
31504	E1	73A	31588	C	73D	31684	C	74D	31753	L1	74C
31505	D1	73E	31589	C	74A	31685	S	74A	31754	L1	74C
31506	E1	73A	31590	C	74D	31686	C	74D	31755	L1	74C
31507	E1	73B	31591	D	74A	31687	C	73B	31756	L1	74C
31508	C	73B	31592	C	74B	31688	C	73D	31757	L1	74C
31509	D1	74D	31593	C	74D	31689	C	73C	31758	L1	73B
31510	C	73D	31595	J	74A	31690	C	74B	31759	L1	73B
31512	H	74C	31596	J	74A	31691	C	73E	31760	L	74D
31513	C	74A	31602	T	70E	31692	C	73E	31761	L	74D
31514	E	74A	31610	U	70E	31693	C	73D	31762	L	74D
31515	E	70E	31611	U	70E	31694	C	73C	31763	L	74D
31516	E	74A	31612	U	70E	31695	C	73C	31764	L	74D
31517	H	74D	31613	U	70E	31696	R1	73E	31765	L	74D
31518	H	74C	31614	U	70E	31697	R1	73D	31766	L	74E
						31698	R1	73E	31767	L	74E

No.	Class	Shed	No.	Class	Shed	No.	Class	Shed	No.	Class	Shed
31768	L	74E	31827	N	73B	31894	U1	75A	32067	B4X	70D
31769	L	74E	31828	N	72A	31895	U1	75B	32068	B4	75G
31770	L	74A	31829	N	72A	31896	U1	75B	32070	B4X	73B
31771	L	74A	31830	N	72A	31897	U1	75B	32071	B4X	75G
31772	L	74A	31831	N	72A	31898	U1	75B	32072	B4X	75G
31773	L	74A	31832	N	72A	31899	U1	75A	32073	B4X	75G
31774	L	74A	31833	N	72A	31900	U1	75A	32075	13	73B
31775	L	74A	31834	N	72A	31901	U1	73B	32077	13	75G
31776	L	74A	31835	N	72A	31902	U1	73B	32081	13	75E
31777	L	74A	31836	N	72A	31903	U1	73B	32082	13	75E
31778	L	74B	31837	N	72A	31904	U1	73B	32083	13	75G
31779	L	74B	31838	N	72A	31905	U1	73A	32084	13	75E
31780	L	74B	31839	N	72A	31906	U1	73A	32086	13	75A
31781	L	74B	31840	N	72A	31907	U1	73A	32089	13	75G
31782	L1	73B	31841	N	72A	31908	U1	73A	32091	13	75E
31783	L1	73B	31842	N	72E	31909	U1	73A	32094	E1/R	72D
31784	L1	73B	31843	N	72A	31910	U1	73A	32095	E1/R	72E
31785	L1	73B	31844	N	72A	31911	W	73C	32096	E1/R	72E
31786	L1	73B	31845	N	72A	31912	W	73A	32100	E2	73A
31787	L1	73B	31846	N	72A	31913	W	73C	32101	E2	73A
31788	L1	74B	31847	N	72A	31914	W	73A	32102	E2	73A
31789	L1	74B	31848	N	75B	31915	W	73A	32103	E2	73A
31790	U	72C	31849	N	75B	31916	W	75C	32104	E2	73A
31791	U	72C	31850	N	73E	31917	W	75C	32105	E2	73A
31792	U	72C	31851	N	75B	31918	W	75C	32106	E2	73A
31793	U	72C	31852	N	72A	31919	W	75C	32107	E2	73A
31794	U	72C	31853	N	73E	31920	W	75C	32108	E2	74C
31795	U	70E	31854	N	73E	31921	W	73C	32109	E2	74C
31796	U	70E	31855	N	72A	31922	W	73C	32113	E1	73B
31797	U	70E	31856	N	75B	31923	W	73C	32124	E1/R	72A
31798	U	70C	31857	N	75B	31924	W	73C	32128	E1	73A
31799	U	70E	31858	N	75B	31925	W	73C	32129	E1	71D
31800	U	70C	31859	N	74C	32002	11X	75A	32133	E1	71A
31801	U	70C	31860	N	75B	32005	11X	75A	32135	E1/R	72A
31802	U	70C	31861	N	75B	32008	11X	73B	32138	E1	70A
31803	U	70C	31862	N	75B	32009	11X	75G (NC)	32139	E1	71D
31804	U	70C	31863	N	75B	32021	13	75F	32145	E1	75A
31805	U	71D	31864	N	75B	32022	13	75F	32147	E1	75A
31806	U	73E	31865	N	75B	32023	13	75F	32151	E1	71A
31807	U	71D	31866	N	72A	32026	13	75F	32156	E1	71I
31808	U	73E	31867	N	72A	32028	13	75F	32160	E1	70D
31809	U	71D	31868	N	73E	32029	13	75F	32165	E3	73B
31810	N	73A	31869	N	72A	32030	13	75G	32166	E3	73B
31811	N	73A	31870	N	71D	32037*	H1	75A	32167	E3	74D
31812	N	73A	31871	N	71D	32038*	H1	75A	32168	E3	73B
31813	N	73A	31872	N	72B	32039*	H1	73B	32169	E3	74D
31814	N	73A	31873	N	72B	32043	B4X	75A	32170	E3	73B
31815	N	73A	31874	N	72B	32045	B4X	70D	32300	C3	71D
31816	N	73A	31875	N	72B	32050	B4X	73B	32301	C3	71D
31817	N	73A	31876	N1	73C	32052	B4X	70D	32302	C3	71D
31818	N	73A	31877	N1	73C	32054	B4	75G	32303	C3	71D
31819	N	74C	31878	N1	73C	32055	B4X	75A	32306	C3	71D
31820	N	74C	31879	N1	73C	32056	B4X	73B	32325	J1	75A
31821	N	74C	31880	N1	73C	32060	B4X	75G			
31822	N1	73C	31890	U1	75A	32062	B4	75G			
31823	N	74C	31891	U1	75A	32063	B4	75G			
31824	N	73B	31892	U1	75A						
31825	N	73B	31893	U1	75A						
31826	N	73B									

No.	Class	Shed	No.	Class	Shed	No.	Class	Shed	No.	Class	Shed
32326	J2	75A	32417	E6	75C	32486	E4	75A	32544	C2X	75D
32327*	N15X	70D	32418	E6	75C	32487	E4	70C	32545	C2X	75E
32328*	N15X	70D	32421*	H2	75A	32488	E4	74D	32546	C2X	75C
32329*	N15X	70D			(N)	32489	E4X	75C	32547	C2X	75C
32330*	N15X	70D	32422*	H2	75A	32490	E4	70C	32548	C2X	75D
32331*	N15X	70D			(N)	32491	E4	71A	32549	C2X	73B
32332*	N15X	70D	32424*	H2	75A	32492	E4	71A	32550	C2X	75B
32333*	N15X	70D			(N)	32493	E4	70A	32551	C2X	73B
32337*	K	75A	32425*	H2	75A	32494	E4	75A	32552	C2X	75E
32338	K	75A	32426*	H2	75A			(N)	32553	C2X	75E
32339	K	75A	32434	C2X	75A	32495	E4	75C	32554	C2X	73B
32340	K	75A	32437	C2X	75A	32496	E4	75A	32556	E4	75D
32341	K	75A			(N)			(N)	32557	E4	71A
32342	K	75A	32438	C2X	75A	32497	E4	75E	32558	E4	71A
32343	K	75A	32440	C2X	75A	32498	E4	70A	32559	E4	71A
32344	K	75A	32441	C2X	75E	32499	E4	70A	32560	E4	75B
32345	K	75A	32442	C2X	73B	32500	E4	70A	32561	E4	75B
32346	K	75E	32443	C2X	75A	32501	E4	70A	32562	E4	71A
32347	K	75A	32444	C2X	75C	32502	E4	70A	32563	E4	71A
32348	K	75A	32445	C2X	75E	32503	E4	74D	32564	E4	73B
32349	K	75E	32446	C2X	73B	32504	E4	75A	32565	E4	73B
32350	K	75E	32447	C2X	75C			(N)	32566	E4	75A
32351	K	75E	32448	C2X	73B	32505	E4	75A	32568	E5	71D
32352	K	75E	32449	C2X	75B	32506	E4	75C	32570	E5X	75D
32353	K	75E	32450	C2X	75B	32507	E4	75B	32571	E5	75G
32359	D1/M	74C	32451	C2X	75E	32508	E4	75A	32573	E5	75A
32364	D3	75D	32453	E3	75A			(N)	32574	E5	75G
32365	D3	75D	32454	E3	74D	32509	E4	75A	32575	E5	75A
32368	D3	75A	32455	E3	75A	32510	E4	71A	32576	E5X	75A
32372	D3	75A	32456	E3	74D	32511	E4	75D	32577	E4	75A
32376	D3	75A	32458	E3	73B	32512	E4	75B	32578	E4	75C
32378	D3	74E	32459	E3	73B	32513	E4	75A	32579	E4	71A
32379	D3	75D	32460	E3	73B	32514	E4	75A	32580	E4	74D
32380	D3	75D	32461	E3	73B	32515	E4	75D	32581	E4	74D
32384	D3	75D	32462	E3	73B	32516	E4	75E	32582	E4	75E
32385	D3	75G	32463	E4	75C	32517	E4	75B	32583	E5	75A
32386	D3	75A	32464	E4	75D	32518	E4	75G	32585	E5	73B
32388	D3	74E	32465	E4	75E	32519	E4	75E	32586	E5X	75D
32390	D3	74E	32466	E4X	75A	32520	E4	75E	32587	E5	73B
32391	D3	74E	32467	E4	73B	32521	C2X	75D	32588	E5	75G
32393	D3	75A	32468	E4	70A	32522	C2X	75E	32590	E5	73B
32394	D3	75G	32469	E4	73B	32523	C2X	75A(N)	32591	E5	75E
32399	E5	75D	32470	E4	73B	32524	C2X	73B	32592	E5	73B
32400	E5	75A	32471	E4	75A	32525	C2X	73B	32593	E5	75G
32401	E5X	75D	32472	E4	73B	32526	C2X	75C	32594	E5	73B
32402	E5	75G	32473	E4	73B	32527	C2X	75E	32595	E5	75A
32404	E5	75G	32474	E4	73B	32528	C2X	75A	32596	11X	73B
32405	E5	75G	32475	E4	75A	32529	C2X	75E	32602	11X	73B
32406	E5	75C			(N)	32532	C2X	75E	32603	11X	75G
32407	E6X	75C	32476	E4	75C	32534	C2X	75A	32606	E1	71I
32408	E6	73B	32477	E4X	75C	32535	C2X	75C	32608	E1/R	72E
32409	E6	71A	32478	E4X	75C	32536	C2X	75C	32610	E1/R	72E
32410	E6	73B	32479	E4	75C	32537	C2X	75A	32636	A1X	75A
32411	E6X	75C	32480	E4	75E			(N)			(N)
32412	E6	71A	32481	E4	73B	32538	C2X	75A	32640	A1X	74A
32413	E6	73B	32482	E4	75D	32539	C2X	75D	32644	A1X	74A
32414	E6	75C	32484	E4	75E	32540	C2X	75B	32646	A1X	71D
32415	E6	73B	32485	E4	75G	32541	C2X	75B			
32416	E6	71A				32543	C2X	75A			

No.	Class	Shed	No.	Class	Shed	No.	Class	Shed	No.	Class	Shed
32647	AIX	75A	33036	Q1	74D	34046*	WC	72A	34096*	WC	74B
	(N)		33037	Q1	74D	34047*	WC	72A	34097*	WC	74B
32655	AIX	71D	33038	Q1	74D	34048*	WC	72B	34098*	WC	74B
32659	AIX	74A	33039	Q1	74E	34049*	BB	70A	34099*	WC	74B
32661	AIX	71D	33040	Q1	74E	34050*	BB	70A	34100*	WC	74B
32662	AIX	71D	34001*	WC	72A	34051*	BB	70A	34101*	WC	73A
32670	AIX	74A	34002*	WC	72A	34052*	BB	70A	34102*	WC	73A
32677	AIX	71D	34003*	WC	72A	34053*	BB	70A	34103*	WC	73A
32678	AIX	74A	34004*	WC	72A	34054*	BB	70A	34104*	WC	73A
32689	E1	75A	34005*	WC	72A	34055*	BB	70A	34105*	WC	71B
32691	E1	71D	34006*	WC	72A	34056*	BB	70A	34106*	WC	71B
32694	E1	71D	34007*	WC	72A	34057*	BB	70A	34107*	WC	71B
32695	E1/R	72A	34008*	WC	72A	34058*	BB	70A	34108*	WC	71B
32696	E1/R	72E	34009*	WC	72A	34059*	BB	70A	34109*	BB	71B
32697	E1/R	72A	34010*	WC	72A	34060*	BB	70A	34110*	BB	
33001	Q1	70C	34011*	WC	72D	34061*	BB	70A	35001*	MN	72A
33002	Q1	70C	34012*	WC	72B	34062*	BB	70A	35002*	MN	72A
33003	Q1	70C	34013*	WC	72A	34063*	BB	70A	35003*	MN	72A
33004	Q1	70C	34014*	WC	72B	34064*	BB	70A	35004*	MN	72A
33005	Q1	70C	34015*	WC	72A	34065*	BB	70A	35005*	MN	70A
33006	Q1	70B	34016*	WC	72A	34066*	BB	73A	35006*	MN	72B
33007	Q1	70B	34017*	WC	72A	34067*	BB	73A	35007*	MN	72B
33008	Q1	70B	34018*	WC	72A	34068*	BB	73A	35008*	MN	72B
33009	Q1	70B	34019*	WC	72A	34069*	BB	73A	35009*	MN	72B
33010	Q1	70B	34020*	WC	72A	34070*	BB	73A	35010*	MN	70A
33011	Q1	70B	34021*	WC	72A	34071*	BB	73A	35011*	MN	70A
33012	Q1	70B	34022*	WC	72B	34072*	BB	74C	35012*	MN	70A
33013	Q1	70B	34023*	WC	72B	34073*	BB	74C	35013*	MN	70A
33014	Q1	70C	34024*	WC	72A	34074*	BB	74C	35014*	MN	70A
33015	Q1	70C	34025*	WC	72A	34075*	BB	74C	35015*	MN	70A
33016	Q1	70C	34026*	WC	72A	34076*	BB	73A	35016*	MN	70A
33017	Q1	71A	34027*	WC	72A	34077*	BB	72A	35017*	MN	70A
33018	Q1	71A	34028*	WC	72B	34078*	BB	72B	35018*	MN	70A
33019	Q1	71A	34029*	WC	72A	34079*	BB	74B	35019*	MN	70A
33020	Q1	71A	34030*	WC	72A	34080*	BB	74B	35020*	MN	70A
33021	Q1	71A	34031*	WC	70A	34081*	BB	74B	35021*	MN	72A
33022	Q1	71A	34032*	WC	72B	34082*	BB	73A	35022*	MN	72A
33023	Q1	71A	34033*	WC	73A	34083*	BB	73A	35023*	MN	72A
33024	Q1	71A	34034*	WC	72D	34084*	BB	73A	35024*	MN	72A
33025	Q1	71A	34035*	WC	72D	34085*	BB	73A	35025*	MN	73A
33026	Q1	73D	34036*	WC	72D	34086*	BB	74B	35026*	MN	73A
33027	Q1	74D	34037*	WC	75A	34087*	BB	74B	35027*	MN	73A
33028	Q1	74D	34038*	WC	75A	34088*	BB	74B	35028*	MN	73A
33029	Q1	74D	34039*	WC	75A	34089*	BB	74B	35029*	MN	74C
33030	Q1	74D	34040*	WC	75A	34090*	BB	74B	35030*	MN	74C
33031	Q1	74D	34041*	WC	75A	34091*	WC	73A	36001	Lead	
33032	Q1	74D	34042*	WC	72B	34092*	WC	73A	36002	Lead	
33033	Q1	74D	34043*	WC	72B	34093*	WC	71B	36003	Lead	
33034	Q1	74D	34044*	WC	72A	34094*	WC	71B	36004	Lead	
33035	Q1	74D	34045*	WC	72A	34095*	WC	71B	36005	Lead	

Isle of Wight Locomotives

No.	Class	Shed	No.	Class	Shed	No.	Class	Shed
W1*	E1	71E	W15*	O2	71F	W30*	O2	71E
W2*	E1	71E	W16*	O2	71F	W31*	O2	71E
W3*	E1	71E	W17*	O2	71F	W32*	O2	71E
W4*	E1	71E	W18*	O2	71F	W33*	O2	71E
W14*	O2	71F	W19*	O2	71F	W34*	O2	71E
			W20*	O2	71F	W35*	O2	71E
			W21*	O2	71F	W36*	O2	71E
			W22*	O2	71F			
			W23*	O2	71F			
			W24*	O2	71F			
			W25*	O2	71F			
			W26*	O2	71E			
			W27*	O2	71E			
			W28*	O2	71E			
			W29*	O2	71E			

BRITISH RAILWAYS' LOCOMOTIVES

Nos. 30007-36003

NAMED ENGINES

CLASS B4 0–4–0T

30086	Havre		30096	Normandy
30089	Trouville		30102	Granville
30093	St. Malo			

CLASS N15 " KING ARTHUR " 4–6–0

30448	Sir Tristram		30453	King Arthur
30449	Sir Torre		30454	Queen Guinevere
30450	Sir Kay		30455	Sir Launcelot
30451	Sir Lamorak		30456	Sir Galahad
30452	Sir Meliagrance		30457	Sir Bedivere

CLASS 0458 0–4–0ST

30458	Ironside

CLASS N15 " KING ARTHUR " 4–6–0

30736	Excalibur		30746	Pendragon
30737	King Uther		30747	Elaine
30738	King Pellinore		30748	Vivien
30739	King Leodegrance		30749	Iseult
30740	Merlin		30750	Morgan le Fay
30741	Joyous Gard		30751	Etarre
30742	Camelot		30752	Linette
30743	Lyonnesse		30753	Melisande
30744	Maid of Astolat		30754	The Green Knight
30745	Tintagel		30755	The Red Knight

CLASS 756 0–6–0T

30756	A. S. Harris

CLASS 757 0-6-2T

30757	Earl of Mount Edgcumbe		30758	Lord St. Levan

NAMED LOCOMOTIVES
CLASS N15 "KING ARTHUR" 4–6–0

30763	Sir Bors de Ganis	30785	Sir Mador de la Porte
30764	Sir Gawain	30786	Sir Lionel
30765	Sir Gareth	30787	Sir Menadeuke
30766	Sir Geraint	30788	Sir Urre of the Mount
30767	Sir Valence	30789	Sir Guy
30768	Sir Balin	30790	Sir Villiars
30769	Sir Balan	30791	Sir Uwaine
30770	Sir Prianius	30792	Sir Hervis de Revel
30771	Sir Sagramore	30793	Sir Ontzlake
30772	Sir Percivale	30794	Sir Ector de Maris
30773	Sir Lavaine	30795	Sir Dinadan
30774	Sir Gaheris	30796	Sir Dodinas le Savage
30775	Sir Agravaine	30797	Sir Blamor de Ganis
30776	Sir Galagars	30798	Sir Hectimere
30777	Sir Lamiel	30799	Sir Ironside
30778	Sir Pelleas	30800	Sir Meleaus de Lile
30779	Sir Colgrevance	30801	Sir Meliot de Logres
30780	Sir Persant	30802	Sir Durnore
30781	Sir Aglovale	30803	Sir Harry le Fise Lake
30782	Sir Brian	30804	Sir Cador of Cornwall
30783	Sir Gillemere	30805	Sir Constantine
30784	Sir Nerovens	30806	Sir Galleron

CLASS LN "LORD NELSON" 4–6–0

30850	Lord Nelson	30858	Lord Duncan
30851	Sir Francis Drake	30859	Lord Hood
30852	Sir Walter Raleigh	30860	Lord Hawke
30853	Sir Richard Grenville	30861	Lord Anson
30854	Howard of Effingham	30862	Lord Collingwood
30855	Robert Blake	30863	Lord Rodney
30856	Lord St. Vincent	30864	Sir Martin Frobisher
30857	Lord Howe	30865	Sir John Hawkins

CLASS V "SCHOOLS" 4–4–0

30900	Eton	30903	Charterhouse
30901	Winchester	30904	Lancing
30902	Wellington	30905	Tonbridge

NAMED LOCOMOTIVES

30906	Sherborne		30923	Bradfield
30907	Dulwich		30924	Haileybury
30908	Westminster		30925	Cheltenham
30909	St. Paul's		30926	Repton
30910	Merchant Taylors		30927	Clifton
30911	Dover		30928	Stowe
30912	Downside		30929	Malvern
30913	Christ's Hospital		30930	Radley
30914	Eastbourne		30931	King's Wimbledon
30915	Brighton		30932	Blundells
30916	Whitgift		30933	King's Canterbury
30917	Ardingly		30934	St. Lawrence
30918	Hurstpierpoint		30935	Sevenoaks
30919	Harrow		30936	Cranleigh
30920	Rugby		30937	Epsom
30921	Shrewsbury		30938	St. Olave's
30922	Marlborough		30938	Leatherhead

CLASS H1 4-4-2

32037	Selsey Bill		32039	Hartland Point
32038	Portland Bill			

CLASS N15X " REMEMBRANCE " 4-6-0

32327	Trevithick		32331	Beattie
32328	Hackworth		32332	Stroudley
32329	Stephenson		32333	Remembrance
32330	Cudworth			

CLASS H2 4-4-2

32421	South Foreland		32425	Trevose Head
32422	North Foreland		32426	St. Alban's Head
32424	Beachy Head			

CLASSES WC & BB 4-6-2
" WEST COUNTRY " and " BATTLE OF BRITAIN "

34001	Exeter		34005	Barnstaple
34002	Salisbury		34006	Bude
34003	Plymouth		34007	Wadebridge
34004	Yeovil		34008	Padstow

Do you know a Real Spotter?

WHEN YOU SEE ONE

All genuine spotters wear this badge—to show they are members of the *Ian Allan* **LOCOSPOTTERS' CLUB**

THIS famous club aims to unite young people interested in railways through local and national activities. Full details of how to take part in these are given in a leaflet which is sent to you on joining, and you also receive a membership card bearing your number and a badge in any of six colours according to the British Railways regions. Many spotters like to have the badges of several regions, and you can have as many as you like by sending the extra remittance of sixpence per badge with your application. **SEND IN TO JOIN NOW** enclosing a 1/- membership fee, which entitles you to one badge. Write to:—

Ian Allan LOCOSPOTTERS' CLUB,
282, Vauxhall Bridge Road,
London, S.W.I.

Enclose a postal order and note that YOU MUST SEND A STAMPED ADDRESSED ENVELOPE for a reply. Note also that the declaration accepting the Club rule must be signed, otherwise you will not be accepted as a member.

Application Form to join
LOCOSPOTTERS' CLUB

(See previous page for details)

RULE : Members of the Locospotters' Club will not in any way interfere with railway working or material, nor be a nuisance or hindrance to railway staff nor, above all, trespass on railway property. No one will be admitted a member of the Club unless he solemnly agrees to keep this rule.

I, the undersigned, do hereby make application to join the Ian Allan Locospotters' Club, and undertake on my honour, if this application is accepted, to keep the rule of the Club ; I understand that if I break it in any way I cease to be a member and forfeit the right to wear the badge and take part in the Club's activities.

Date................................195.... Signed................................

These details to be completed in BLOCK LETTERS :

SURNAME................................ DATE OF BIRTH............19....

CHRISTIAN NAMES ....

ADDRESS................................

....

....

require the Badge(s) of : (Put cross (X) against badge(s) required):

WESTERN REGION	...	BROWN	
SOUTHERN REGION... ...	...	GREEN	
LONDON MIDLAND REGION	...	RED	
EASTERN REGION	...	DARK BLUE	
NORTH-EASTERN REGION	...	TANGERINE	
SCOTTISH REGION	...	LIGHT BLUE	

POSTAL ORDER enclosed for........................s.........................d.

MEMBERSHIP costs 1/-, and entitles you to 1 badge ; EACH EXTRA BADGE, 6d.

DON'T FORGET THE S.A.E.

34009	Lyme Regis	34054	Lord Beaverbrook
34010	Sidmouth	34055	Fighter Pilot
34011	Tavistock	34056	Croydon
34012	Launceston	34057	Biggin Hill
34013	Okehampton	34058	Sir Frederick Pile
34014	Budleigh Salterton	34059	Sir Archibald Sinclair
34015	Exmouth	34060	25 Squadron
34016	Bodmin	34061	73 Squadron
34017	Ilfracombe	34062	17 Squadron
34018	Axminster	34063	229 Squadron
34019	Bideford	34064	Fighter Command
34020	Seaton	34065	Hurricane
34021	Dartmoor	34066	Spitfire
34022	Exmoor	34067	Tangmere
34023	Blackmore Vale	34068	Kenley
34024	Tamar Valley	34069	Hawkinge
34025	Whimple	34070	Manston
34026	Yes Tor	34071	601 Squadron
34027	Taw Valley	34072	257 Squadron
34028	Eddystone	34073	249 Squadron
34029	Lundy	34074	46 Squadron
34030	Watersmeet	34075	264 Squadron
34031	Torrington	34076	41 Squadron
34032	Camelford	34077	603 Squadron
34033	Chard	34078	222 Squadron
34034	Honiton	34079	141 Squadron
34035	Shaftesbury	34080	74 Squadron
34036	Westward Ho	34081	92 Squadron
34037	Clovelly	34082	615 Squadron
34038	Lynton	34083	605 Squadron
34039	Boscastle	34084	253 Squadron
34040	Crewkerne	34085	501 Squadron
34041	Wilton	34086	219 Squadron
34042	Dorchester	34087	145 Squadron
34043	Combe Martin	34088	213 Squadron
34044	Woolacombe	34089	602 Squadron
34045	Ottery St. Mary	34090	Sir Eustace Missenden, Southern Railway
34046	Braunton		
34047	Callington	34091	Weymouth
34048	Crediton	34092	City of Wells
34049	Anti-Aircraft Command	34093	Saunton
34050	Royal Observer Corps	34094	Mortehoe
34051	Winston Churchill	34095	Brentor
34052	Lord Dowding	34096	Trevone
34053	Sir Keith Park	34097	Holsworthy

NAMED LOCOMOTIVES

34099	Templecombe	34105	Swanage
34099	Lynmouth	34106	Lydford
34100	Appledore	34107	Blandford
34101	Hartland	34108	Wincanton
34102	Lapford	34109	Sir Trafford
34103	Calstock		**Leigh-Mallory**
34104	Bere Alston	34110	66 Squadron

CLASS MN " MERCHANT NAVY " 4-6-2

35001	Channel Packet	35015	Rotterdam Lloyd
35002	Union Castle	35016	Elders Fyffes
35003	Royal Mail	35017	Belgian Marine
35004	Cunard White Star	35018	British India Line
35005	Canadian Pacific	35019	French Line CGT
35006	Peninsular & Oriental S.N. Co.	35020	Bibby Line
		35021	New Zealand Line
35007	Aberdeen	35022	Holland-America Line
	Commonwealth	35023	Holland-Afrika Line
35008	Orient Line	35024	East Asiatic Company
35009	Shaw Savill	35025	Brocklebank Line
35010	Blue Star	35026	Lamport & Holt Line
35011	General Steam Navigation	35027	Port Line
35012	United States Line	35028	Clan Line
35013	Blue Funnel	35029	Ellerman Lines
35014	Nederland Line	35030	Elder Dempster Lines

CLASS E1 0-6-0T

W 1	Medina	W 3	Ryde
W 2	Yarmouth	W 4	Wroxall

CLASS O2 0-4-4T

W14	Fishbourne	W22	Brading	W30	Shorwell
W15	Cowes	W23	Totland	W31	Chale
W16	Ventnor	W24	Calbourne	W32	Bonchurch
W17	Seaview	W25	Godshill	W33	Bembridge
W18	Ningwood	W26	Whitwell	W34	Newport
W19	Osborne	W27	Merstone	W35	Freshwater
W20	Shanklin	W28	Ashey	W36	Carisbrooke
W21	Sandown	W29	Alverstone		

(Facing Page). *Top to bottom:* Class N15 4-6-0 No. 30751 *Etarre;* Class N15X 4-6-0 No. 32329 *Stephenson;* Class V 4-4-0 No. 30935 *Sevenoaks.*
[*W. Gilburt, S. C. Townroe, P. Ransome-Wallis*

Above : Class 700 0-6-0 No. 30700.   *Below :* Class C2X 0-6-0 No. 32532.
[W. Gilburt.

Above : Class W 2-6-4T No. 31918.   *[A. F. Cook.*

Facing Page. *Top to Bottom :* Class K 2-6-0 No. 62350 ; Class Q1 0-6-0 No. 33019;
Class Q 0-6-0 No. 30544 ; Class 0395 0-6-0 No. 30578. .
[W. Gilburt (2), H. C. Casserley (2)

Top to bottom : E4
0-6-2T No. 32464 ;
E1/R 0-6-2T No.
32124; E1 0-6-0T No.
32606; A1X 0-6-0T
No. 32662.
Facing Page : *Top to
bottom :* R1 0-6-0Ts
Nos. 31154 & 31339 ;
G6 0-6-0T No.
DS3152 ; D3 0-4-4T
No. 32365 ; O2
0-4-4T No. W16.
[W. Gllburt, H. Cass-
erley, P. R.-Wallis,
C. Herbert. G. Sey-
mour, E. Smith, R.
Tunstall, R. Bowler.

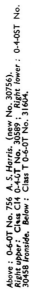

Above : 0-6-0T No. 756 A. S. Harris. (new No. 30756).
Right upper: Class C14 0-4-0T No. 30589 ; Right lower : 0-4-0ST No.
30458 Ironside. Below : Class T 0-6-0T No. 31604.

[P. Ransome-Wallis, P. J. Truscott, C. C. Herbert (2).

SUMMARY OF BRITISH RAILWAYS
NON-STEAM LOCOMOTIVE CLASSES
WITH HISTORICAL NOTES AND DIMENSIONS
INTERNAL COMBUSTION LOCOMOTIVES

Co+Co Diesel Electric
LONDON MIDLAND REGION

Introduced 1947 : English Electric Co. and H. A. Ivatt, main line passenger design for L.M.S.R.
Weight : 121 tons 10 cwt.
Driving Wheels : 3' 6".
T.E. : 41,400 lb.
Engine : English Electric Co. 16 cyls. 1,600 h.p.
Motors : Six nose-suspended motors, single reduction gear drive.

10000/1   Total 2

4-8-4 Diesel Mechanical

Under construction : H. G. Ivatt and Fell design for L.M.S.R.
Engines : Four 500 h.p.
Transmission : Fell patent differential drive and fluid couplings.

10100

1-Co+Co-1 Diesel Electric

English Electric Co. and Bulleid main line passenger design for S.R.
Engine : English Co. 16 cyls. 1,600 h.p.

10201/2

Bo+Bo Diesel Electric

Introduced 1950 : N.B. Loco. Co., B.T.H. Co. and H. A. Ivatt, branch line design for L.M.S.R.
Weight : 69 tons 16 cwt.
Driving Wheels : 3' 6".
T.E. : 34,500 lb.
Engine : Davey Paxman 16 cyls. 827 h.p.
Motors : Four nose-suspended motors, single reduction gear drive.

10800   Total 1

0-6-0 Diesel Mechanical

Introduced 1950 : Bulleid S.R. design for shunting and transfer work.
Weight : 49 tons 9 cwt.
Driving Wheels : 4' 6".
T.E. : 33,500 lb. (max. in low gear).
Engine : Davey Paxman 12 cyls. 500 h.p.
Transmission : S.S.S. Powerflow three-speed gearbox and fluid coupling.

11001
                                 Total 1

0-6-0 Diesel Electric
LONDON MIDLAND REGION

Introduced 1936 : English Electric–Hawthorn Leslie design for L.M.S.R.
Weight : {51 tons.*
         {47 tons.†
Driving Wheels : 4' 0½".
T.E. : 30,000 lb.
Engine : English Electric 6 cyl. 350 h.p.
Motors : Two nose-suspended motors, single reduction gear drive.

12000*/1*   12002†
                                 Total 3

0-6-0 Diesel Electric
LONDON MIDLAND REGION

Introduced 1939 : English Electric and Stanier design for L.M.S.R., development of previous design with jackshaft drive.
Weight : 54 tons 16 cwt.
Driving Wheels : 4' 3".
T.E. : 33,000 lb.
Engine : English Electric, 6 cyls. 350 h.p.
Motors : Single motor ; jackshaft drive

12003–32

                                 Total 30

0-6-0   Diesel Electric
LONDON MIDLAND REGION

Introduced 1945 : English Electric and Fairburn design for L.M.S.R., development of previous design with double reduction gear drive.

Weight : 50 tons.
Driving Wheels : 4′ 0½″.
T.E. : 33,000 lb.
Engine : English Electric, 6 cyls. 350 h.p.
Engine : Two nose-suspended motors, double reduction gear drive.

12033–82

N.B.—Locos of this class are still being delivered.

0-6-0 Diesel Electric DES 1
EASTERN REGION

Introduced 1944 : English Electric and Thompson design for L.N.E.R., (L.N.E.R. version of L.M.S. 12033 series).

Weight : 51 tons.
Driving Wheels : 4′ 0″.
T.E. : 32,000 lb.
Engine : English Electric, 6 cyl. 350 h.p.
Motors : Two nose-suspended motors, double reduction gear.

15000–3

                 Total 4

0-6-0 Diesel Electric DES 2
EASTERN REGION

Introduced 1949 : Brush design for E.R.

Weight : 51 tons.
Driving Wheels : 4′ 0″.
T.E. : 32,000 lb.
Engine : Petter 4 cyl. 360 h.p.

15004   **Total 1**

0-4-0   Petrol (Class Y11)
EASTERN REGION

Introduced 1921 : Motor, Rail and Tram Car Co., design (purchased by N.B.R. and L.N.E.R.).
Weight : 8 tons.
Driving Wheels : 3′ 1″.
Engine : 4 cyl. 40 h.p. petrol.
Drive : Chains and two speed gear box.

15097–9

                 Total 3

0-6-0   Diesel Electric
WESTERN REGION

Introduced 1936: Hawthorn Leslie and English Electric design for G.W.R. (G.W.R. version of L.M.S.R. Nos. 12000/1).
Weight : 51 tons 10 cwt.
Driving Wheels: 4′ 1″.
T.E. : 30,000 lb.
Engine: English Electric 6 cyl. 350 h.p.
Motors: Two nose-suspended motors, single reduction gear drive.

15100   **Total 1**

0-6-0   Diesel Electric
WESTERN REGION

Introduced 1948 : English Electric and Hawksworth design for Western Region (W.R. version of L.M.S. 12033 series).
Weight : 46 tons 9 cwt.
Driving Wheels : 4′ 0½″.
T. E.: 33,500 lb.
Engine: English Electric 6 cyl. 350 h.p.
Motors: Two nose-suspended motors, single reduction gear drive.

15101–6

                 Total 6

0-6-0   Diesel Electric
Introduced 1949 : Brush design for W.R.
15107   **Total 1**

0-6-0　　Diesel Electric
SOUTHERN REGION

Introduced 1937 : English Electric and Bulleid design for S.R.
Weight : 55 tons 5 cwt.
Driving Wheels : 4' 6".
T.E. : 30,000 lb.
Engine : English Electric 6 cyl. 350 h.p.
Motors : Two nose-suspended motors, single reduction gear drive.

15201–3

Total 3

0-6-0　　Diesel Electric
SOUTHERN REGION

Introduced 1949 : English Electric and Bulleid design for S.R. (S.R. version of L.M.S.R. 12033 series, but designed for higher speeds).
Weight : 49 tons.
Driving Wheels : 4' 6".
T.E. : 24,000 lb.
Engine : English Electric 6 cyl. 350 h.p.
Motors : Two nose-suspended motors, double reduction gear drive.

15211–25

Total 16

A-I-A+A-I-A
Gas Turbine

Introduced 1949 : Brown Boveri (Switzerland) design for W.R.
Weight : 115 tons.
Driving Wheels : 4' 0½".
T.E. : 31,500 lb. to 21 m.p.h.
Engine : 2,500 h.p. gas turbine.
Motors : Four independently mounted motors with spring drive.

18000

Total I

Co+Co　　Gas Turbine

Under construction : Metropolitan-Vickers and Hawksworth design for G.W.R.
Weight : 120 tons.
Driving Wheels : 3' 8".
T.E. : 60,000 lb.
Motors : Six nose-suspended motors with single reduction gear drive.

18001

> NOTE—There are a number of Diesel locomotives in the Service or Departmental stock of the Regions, but these have not been included in this section.

ELECTRIC LOCOMOTIVES

Co + Co　　Class CC
SOUTHERN REGION

*Introduced 1941 : Raworth & Bulleid design for S.R.
†Introduced 1948 : Later design with detail differences.
Weight : { 99 tons 14 cwt.*
　　　　　{ 104 tons 14 cwt.†
Driving Wheels : 3' 7".
T.E. : { 40,000 lb.*
　　　　{ 45,000 lb.†
Voltage : 660 D.C.
Current Collection : Overhead and third rail, with flywheel-driven generator for gaps in third rail.

20001/2*

20003†

Total 3

Bo + Bo　　Class EMI
EASTERN REGION

*Introduced 1941 : Metropolitan-Vickers and Gresley design for L.N.E.R.

Remainder. Introduced 1950. Production design with detail alterations.

Weight : 87 tons 18 cwt.
Driving Wheels : 4' 2".
T.E. : 45,000 lb.
Voltage : 1,500 D.C.
Current Collection : overhead.

26000*
26001–57

NOTE: Locomotives of this class are still being delivered.

Bo + Bo **Class EB1**

EASTERN REGION

EB1 Introduced 1946 : L.N.E.R. rebuild of N.E.R. Raven freight design (Introduced 1914) for banking work on Manchester-Wath line.
Weight : 74 tons 8 cwt.
Driving Wheels : 4′ 0″.
T.E. : 37,600 lb.
Voltage : 1,500 D.C.
Current collection : overhead.

26510   **Total 1**

Bo + Bo **Class ES1**

NORTH-EASTERN REGION

Built 1902 : Brush & Thomson-Houston shunting design for N.E.R.

Weight : 46 tons.
Voltage : 600 D.C.
T.E. : 25,000 lb.
26500/1   **Total 2**

Co + Co

EASTERN REGION

Under construction : Metropolitan Vickers and L.N.E.R. design, development of E.M.I. with six axles and higher speed range.
Weight: 102 tons.
Driving Wheels: 4′ 2″
T.E.: 45,000 lb.
Voltage: 1,500 D.C.
Current Collection: Overhead.
27 locomotives. Numbers not yet allocated.

SOUTHERN REGION SERVICE LOCOMOTIVES.

No.	Old No.	Class	Station
†49 S	—	Shunter	{ Broad Clyst Sleep. Depot
*74 S	—	Bo-Bo	{ Durnsford R Power Stn.
*75 S	—	Bo	{ Waterloo & City Rly.
77 S	0745	C14	{ Redbridge Sleep. Depot
†343 S	—	Shunter	{ Eastleigh Carr. Works
†346 S	—	Inspection Car	Engin'r's Dept.
‡377 S	2635	AIX	Brighton Wks.
§400 S	—	0-4-0	S'hamptonDks.
515 S	{ L.B.S.C. 650 I.W. 9 }	AIX	{ Lancing Carr. Wks.
600 S		0-4-0 diesel	
680 S	{ L.B.S.C. 654 SEC. 751. }	A 1	,,
701 S	2284	D 1	Fratton**
DS 1169	—	0–4–0 Diesel	Engineer's Dt.
DS 1173	2217	0–4–0 Diesel	Engineer's Dt.
DS 3152	30272	G 6	Meldon Quarry

* Electric   ‡ Repainted 1947 in Stroudley livery   † Petrol
** Ex-oil Pumping Engine   § Fowler Diesel

SUMMARY OF SOUTHERN REGION STEAM LOCOMOTIVE CLASSES

IN ALPHABETICAL ORDER
WITH HISTORICAL NOTES AND DIMENSIONS

0-6-0T OP Class A1 & A1X

*A1 Introduced 1872 : Stroudley L.B.S.C. " Terrier," later fitted with Marsh boiler, retaining original type smokebox (survivor built 1875).

†A1X Introduced 1911 : Rebuild of A1 with Marsh boiler and extended smokebox.

‡A1X Loco. with increased cylinder diameter.

N.B. Western Region No. 5 is also of this class.

Weight : $\begin{cases} 27 \text{ tons 10 cwt.*} \\ 28 \text{ tons 5 cwt.†‡} \end{cases}$

Pressure : 150 lb. Cyls. $\begin{cases} 12'' \times 20''† \\ 14\frac{3}{16}'' \times 20''‡ \end{cases}$

Driving Wheels : 4' 0".

T.E. : $\begin{cases} 7,650 \text{ lb.*†} \\ 10,695 \text{ lb.‡} \end{cases}$

*680S

†377S, 515S, 32640/4/6/7/55/9/61/2/70/7/8.

‡32636

	Totals : A1	1
	A1X	14

4-4-0 1P Class B1

Introduced 1910 : Wainwright rebuild with domed boiler and extended smokebox of Stirling S.E.R. domeless Class B (originally introduced 1898).

Weight : Loco. 45 tons 2 cwt.

Pressure : 170 lb.   Cyls. : 18" × 26"

Driving Wheels : 7' 0".

T.E. : 14,490 lb.

31443.

Total 1

0-4-0T OF Class B4

*Introduced 1891 : Adams L.S.W. design for dock shunting.

†Introduced 1908 : Drummond K14 locos., with smaller boiler and detail alterations.

‡Adams locos. fitted with Drummond boiler.

§Drummond loco. fitted with Adams boiler.

Weight : $\begin{cases} 33 \text{ tons 9 cwt.*‡} \\ 32 \text{ tons 18 cwt.†§} \end{cases}$

Pressure : 140 lb. Cyls (O) : 16" × 22"

Driving Wheels : 3' 9¾".

T.E. : 14,650 lb.

*30086/7/9/93/4/6, 30102.

†30082/3   ‡30088   §30084

Total 11

4-4-0 $\begin{cases} 1P & B4 \\ 3P & B4X \end{cases}$ Classes B4 & B4X

*B4 Introduced 1899 : R. J. Billinton L.B.S.C. design.

†B4X Introduced 1922 : L. B. Billinton design, incorporating parts from B4

Weights : Loco. $\begin{cases} 51 \text{ tons 10 cwt.*} \\ 58 \text{ tons 1 cwt.†} \end{cases}$

Pressure : $\begin{cases} 180 \text{ lb.*} \\ 180 \text{ lb. Su.†} \end{cases}$

Cyls. : $\begin{cases} 19'' \times 26''.* \\ 20'' \times 26''.† \end{cases}$

Driving Wheels : 6' 9".

T.E. : $\begin{cases} 17,730 \text{ lb.*} \\ 19,645 \text{ lb.†} \end{cases}$

P.V. (B4X).

*32054/62/3/8.

†32043/5/50/2/5/6/60/7/70–3.

	Totals : Class B4	4
	Class B4X	12

Classes BB–D1/M

4-6-2 6MT Class BB

(see Class WC & BB)

0-6-0 3F Class C

Introduced 1900 : Wainwright S.E.C.
design.
Weight : Loco. 43 tons 16 cwt.
Pressure : 160 lb. Cyls. : $18\frac{1}{2}'' \times 26''$
Driving Wheels : 5' 2".
T.E. : 19,520 lb.

31004/18/33/7/8/54/9/61/3/8/71/
86/90, 31102/12/3/50/91, 31218
/9/21/3/5/7/9/34/42–5/52/3/5/6
/60/7/8/70–2/7/80/7/91/3/4/7/8,
31317, 31461/80/1/6/95/8,
31508/10/3/72/3/5/6/8–85/8–90
/2/3, 31681–4/6–95, 31711–25.

Total 104

0-6-0 3F Class C2X

C2X Introduced 1908 : Marsh rebuild
of R. J. Billinton L.B.S.C. C2 with
larger C3-type boiler, extended
smokebox, etc.
Weights : Loco. 45 tons 5 cwt.
Pressure : 170 lb.†
Cyls. : $17\frac{1}{2}'' \times 26''$.
Driving Wheels : 5' 0".
T.E. 19,175 lb.†

32434/7/8/40–51, 32521–9/32/4–
41/3–54.

Total 45

0-6-0 3F Class C3

Introduced 1906 : Marsh L.B.S.C.
design.
Weight : Loco. 47 tons 10 cwt.
Pressure : 170 lb. Cyls. : $17\frac{1}{2}'' \times 26''$
Driving Wheels : 5' 0".
T.E. : 19,175 lb.

32300–3/6. **Total 5**

0-4-0T OF Class C14

Introduced 1913 : Urie rebuild as
shunting locos. of Drummond L.S.W.
motor-train 2–2–0T (originally introduced 1906).

Weight : 25 tons 15 cwt.
Pressure : 150 lb.
Cyls. (O) : $14'' \times 14''$.
Driving Wheels : 3' 0".
T.E. : 9,720 lb.
Walschaerts gear.

77S, 30588/9. **Total 3**

4-4-0 {1P D / 2P D1 Classes D & D1

*D Introduced 1901 : Wainwright
S.E.C. design,with round-top fire-box,
some later fitted with extended
smokebox.
†D1 Introduced 1921 : Maunsell rebuild
of Class D, with superheated Belpaire
boiler, and long-travel piston valves.
Weights : { 50 tons*
{ 52 tons 4 cwt.†
Pressure : { 175 lb.*
{ 180 lb. Su.†
Cyls. : $19'' \times 26''$.
Driving Wheels : 6' 8".
T.E. : { 17,450 lb.*
{ 17,950 lb.†

*31057/75/92, 31477/88/90/3/6,
31501/49/74/7/86/91, 31728–34
/7/40/4/6/8/50.
†31145, 31246/7, 31470/87/9/92/
4, 31502/5/9/45, 31727/35/6/9/
41/3/5/9.

Total : Class D 27
Class D1 20

0-4-2T 1P Classes D1 & D1/M

*D1/M Introduced 1909 : Stroudley
L.B.S.C. D1 fitted for push-and-pull
working (reclassified D1/M by S.R.)
†D1 Introduced 1947 . D1 fitted for oil
pumping.
Weight : 43 tons 10 cwt.
Pressure : 170 lb. Cyls. : $17'' \times 24''$
Driving Wheels : 5' 6".
T.E. : 15,185 lb.

*32359
†701S.

Total : D1 1   D1/M 1

0-4-4T 1P Class D3

Introduced 1892 : R. J. Billinton L.B.S.C. design, later reboilered by Marsh and fitted from 1934 for push-and-pull working.

Weight : 52 tons.
Pressure : 170 lb. Cyls. : $17\frac{1}{2}'' \times 26''$
Driving Wheels : 5' 6".
T.E. : 17,435 lb.

32364/5/8/72/6/8–80/4–6/8/90/1/3/4. **Total 16**

4-4-0 3P Class D15

Introduced 1912 : Drummond L.S.W. design, superheated by Urie from 1915.
Weight Loco. 61 tons 11 cwt.
Pressure : 180 lb. Su.
Cyls. : 20" × 26".
Driving Wheels : 6' 7".
T.E. : 20,140 lb.
Walschaerts gear, P.V.

30463–72. **Total 10**

4-4-0 {1P E / 2P E1} Classes E & E1

*E Introduced 1905 : Wainwright S.E.C. design with Belpaire boiler.
†E Introduced 1912 : Rebuilt with superheater in original boiler.
‡E1 Introduced 1919 : Maunsell rebuild of E, with larger superheated Belpaire boiler and long-travel piston valves.

Weight : Loco. { 52 tons 5 cwt.* / 53 tons 10 cwt.† / 53 tons 9 cwt.‡
Pressure : { 180 lb.* / 160 lb Su.† / 180 lb. Su.‡
Cyls. : { 19" × 26".* / $20\frac{1}{2}'' \times 26''$.† / 19" × 26".‡
T.E. : { 18,410 lb.* / 19,050 lb.† / 18,410 lb.‡
Driving Wheels : 6' 6".
*31157/9/66/75/6, 31273, 31315, 31491, 31514–6/47/87.

†31036, 31275.
‡31019/67, 31160/5/79, 31497, 31504/6/7/11.

Total : Class E 15
Class E1 10

0-6-0T 2F Class E1

Introduced 1874 : Stroudley L.B.S.C. design, reboilered by Marsh.
Weight : 44 tons 3 cwt.
Pressure : 170 lb. Cyls. : 17" × 24"
Driving Wheels : 4' 6".
T.E. : 18,560 lb.
32113/28/9/33/8/9/45/7/51/6/60, 32606/89/91/4,
(W) 1–4.

Total 19

0-6-2T 2MT Class E1/R

Introduced 1927 : Maunsell rebuild of Stroudley E1, with radial trailing axle and larger bunker for passenger service in West of England.
Weight : 50 tons 5 cwt.
Pressure : 170 lb. Cyls. : 17" × 24"
Driving Wheels : 4' 6".
T.E. : 18,560 lb.
32094–6, 32124/35, 32608/10/95–7.

Total 10

0-6-0T 3F Class E2

*Introduced 1913 : L. B. Billinton L.B.S.C. design.
†Introduced 1915 : Later locos. with tanks extended further forward.
Weight : { 52 tons 15 cwt.* / 53 tons 10 cwt.†
Pressure : 170 lb. Cyls. : $17\frac{1}{2}'' \times 26''$
Driving Wheels : 4' 6".
T.E. : 21,305 lb.
*32100–4.
†32105–9.

Total 10

Classes E3–G6

0-6-2T   3F   Class E3

Introduced 1894 : R. J. Billinton
L.B.S.C. design, development of
Stroudley " West Brighton " (introduced 1891), reboilered and fitted
with extended smokebox, 1918 onwards ; cylinder diameter reduced
from 18″ by S.R.

Weight : 56 tons 10 cwt.

Pressure : $\begin{cases} 160 \text{ lb.} \\ 170 \text{ lb.*} \end{cases}$

Cyls. : 17½″ × 26″

Driving Wheels : 4′ 6″

T.E. : $\begin{cases} 20,055 \text{ lb.} \\ 21,305 \text{ lb.*} \end{cases}$

*32165–70.
32453–6/8–61/2.

Total 15

0-6-2T   2 MT   Classes E4 & E4X

*E4 Introduced 1910   R. J. Billinton
L.B.S.C. design, development of E3
with larger wheels, reboilered with
Marsh boiler and extended smokebox,
cylinder diameter reduced from 18″
by S.R.

†E4X Introduced 1909 : E4 reboilered
with larger I2 4–4–2T type boiler.

Weights : $\begin{cases} 57 \text{ tons 10 cwt.*} \\ 59 \text{ tons 5 cwt.†} \end{cases}$

Pressure : 170 lb.   Cyls. : 17½″ × 26″

Driving Wheels : 5′ 0″

T.E. : 19,175 lb.

*32463–5/7–76/9–82/4–8/90–9,
32500–20/56–66/77–82.
†32466/77/8/89.

Totals E4 70
E4X 4

0-6-2T   2 MT   Classes E5 & E5X

*‡E5 Introduced 1902 : R. J. Billinton
L.B.S.C. design, development of E4
with larger wheels and firebox,
cylinder diameter reduced from 18″
by S.R.

†E5X Introduced 1911 : E5 reboilered
with larger C3-type boiler.

Weights : $\begin{cases} 60 \text{ tons.*} \\ 64 \text{ tons 5 cwt.†} \end{cases}$

Pressure : $\begin{cases} 160 \text{ lb.*} \\ 175 \text{ lb.‡} \\ 170 \text{ lb.†} \end{cases}$

Cyls. : 17½″ × 26″

Driving Wheels : 5′ 6″

T.E. : $\begin{cases} 16,410 \text{ lb.} \\ 17,945 \text{ lb.‡} \\ 17,435 \text{ lb.†} \end{cases}$

*‡32399, 32400/2/4–6, 32568/
71/3–5/83–5/7/8/90–4.
†32401, 32570/6/86.

Totals : E5 21   E5X 4

0-6-2T   4F   Classes E6 & E6X

*‡E6 Introduced 1904 : R. J. Billinton
L.B.S.C. design, development of E5
with smaller wheels.

†E6X Introduced 1911 : E6 reboilered
with larger C3-type boiler.

Weights : $\begin{cases} 61 \text{ tons.*} \\ 63 \text{ tons.†} \end{cases}$

Pressure : $\begin{cases} 160 \text{ lb.*} \\ 175 \text{ lb.‡} \\ 170 \text{ lb.†} \end{cases}$

Cyls. : 18″ × 26″

Driving Wheels : 4′ 6″

T.E. : $\begin{cases} 21,215 \text{ lb.} \\ 23,205 \text{ lb.‡} \\ 22,540 \text{ lb.†} \end{cases}$

*‡32408–10/2–8.
†32407/11.

Totals : E6 10   E6X 2

0-6-0T   2F   Class G6

*Introduced 1894 : Adams L.S.W.
design, later additions by Drummond,
but with Adams type boiler.

†Introduced 1925 : Fitted with Drummond type boiler.

Weight : 47 tons 13 cwt.
Pressure : 160 lb.   Cyls. : 17½″ × 24″
Driving Wheels : 4′ 10″
T.E. : 17,235 lb.

*30162, 30238/58/60/6/8/70/7,
30349/53, D.S. 1152
†30160, 30259/74.

Total 14

4-8-0T   7F   Class G16

Introduced 1921 : Urie L.S.W. "Hump"
loco.
Weight : 95 tons 2 cwt.
Pressure : 180 lb. Su.
Cyls. (O) : 22″ × 28″
Driving Wheels : 5′ 1″
T.E. : 33,990 lb.
Walschaerts gear, P.V.

30492–5   **Total 4**

0-4-4T   1P   Class H

Introduced 1904. Wainwright S.E.C.
design.
*Introduced 1949. Fitted for push-and-
pull working.
Weight : 54 tons 8 cwt.
Pressure : 160 lb.   Cyls. : 18″ × 26″
Driving Wheels : 5′ 6″
T.E. : 17,360 lb.

31005,   31162/77/84/93,
31239/59/61/3/5/6/9/74/6/8/9/
95, 31305–11/20/1/4/6–9,
31500/3/12/8/9/21/2/30–3/40–
4/6/50–4.
*31016, 31158/61/4/82, 31319/22,
31517/20/3/48

Total 64

4-4-2   3P   Class H1

*Introduced 1905 : Marsh L.B.S.C.
design, later superheated and re-
cylindered.
†Introduced 1947 : Rebuilt experimen-
tally with sleeve valves.
Weight : Loco. 68 tons 5 cwt.
Pressure : 200 lb. Su.
Cyls. : (O) 19″ × 26″.*
Driving Wheels : 6′ 7½″
T.E. : 20,070 lb.*

*32037/8   †32039

Total 3

4-4-2   4P   Class H2

Introduced 1911 : Marsh L.B.S.C.
design, superheated development of
H1 with large cylinders.
Weight : Loco. 68 tons 5 cwt.
Pressure : 200 lb. Su.
Cyls. : (O) 21″ × 26″
Driving Wheels : 6′ 7½″
T.E. : 24,520 lb.
P.V.

32421/2/4–6.

Total 5

4-6-0   4 MT   Class H15

*Introduced 1914 : Urie L.S.W. design,
fitted with "Maunsell" superheater
from 1927, replacing earlier types
(30490 built saturated).
†Introduced 1915 : Urie rebuild with
two outside cylinders of Drummond
E14, 4 cyl.4-6-0 introduced 1907, retaining original boiler retubed and
fitted with superheater.
‡Introduced 1924 : Maunsell locos.
with N15 type boiler and smaller
tenders.
§Introduced 1924 : Maunsell rebuild of
Drummond F13 4-cyl. 4-6-0 introduced 1905, with detail differences
from rebuild of E14.
¶Introduced 1927 : Urie loco. (built
1914 saturated) rebuilt with later
N15 class boiler, with smaller
firebox.

Weight : Loco. { 81 tons 5 cwt.*
{ 82 tons 1 cwt.†
{ 79 tons 19 cwt.‡¶
{ 80 tons 11 cwt.§
Pressure : { 180 lb. Su.*‡¶
{ 175 lb. Su.†§
Cyls. : 21″ × 28″
Driving Wheels : 6′ 0″
T.E. : { 26,240 lb *‡¶
{ 25,510 lb.†§
Walschaerts gear, P.V.

*30482–90
†30335
‡30473–8, 30521–4
§30330–4
¶30491

Total 26

4-6-2T 5F Class H16

Introduced 1921 : Urie L.S.W. design for heavy freight traffic.
Weight : 96 tons 8 cwt.
Pressure : 180 lb. Su.
Cyls. : (O) 21″ × 28″
Driving Wheels : 5′ 7″
T.E. : 28,200 lb.
Walschaerts valve gear, P.V.

30516–20   **Total 5**

4-4-2T 2P Class I IX

*Introduced 1925 : Maunsell rebuild with 13 class non-superheater boiler of Marsh L.B.S.C. II class (introduced 1906).
†Introduced 1929 : Maunsell rebuild of later II locos., with shorter coupled wheelbase (introduced 1907).
Weight : 71 tons 18 cwt.
Pressure : 180 lb. Cyls. : 17½″ × 26″
Driving Wheels : 5′ 6″
T.E. : 18,450 lb.

*32595/6, 32602/3
†32002/5/8/9

Total 8

4-4-2T 3P Class I3

*Introduced 1907 : Marsh L.B.S.C. design with slide valves, rebuilt 1919 with superheater and extended smokebox.
†Introduced 1908 : Marsh L.B.S.C. design with piston valves and smaller wheels, 32026-30/75/6 originally saturated, remainder built superheated.
‡Introduced 1912 : L. B. Billinton modification of 1908 design, built superheated with larger cylinders.
Weight : $\begin{cases} 75 \text{ tons } 10 \text{ cwt.}^* \\ 76 \text{ tons}†‡ \end{cases}$
Pressure : 180 lb. Su.
Cyls. : $\begin{cases} 19″ × 26″^* \\ 20″ × 26″† \\ 21″ × 26″‡ \end{cases}$
Driving Wheels : $\begin{cases} 6′ 9″^* \\ 6′ 7½″†‡ \end{cases}$
T.E. : $\begin{cases} 17,730 \text{ lb.}^* \\ 20,015 \text{ lb.}† \\ 22,065 \text{ lb.}‡ \end{cases}$

*32021
†32022/3/6–30/75–9/81.
‡32082–4/6/9–91

Total 21

0-6-4T 3 MT Class J

Introduced 1913 : Wainwright S.E.C. design.
Weight : 70 tons 4 cwt.
Pressure : 160 lb. Su.
Cyls. : 19½″ × 26″
Driving Wheels : 5′ 6″
T.E. : 20,370 lb.
P.V.

31595/6/8   **Total 3**

4-6-2T 4P

Classes J1 & J2

*J1 Introduced 1910 : Marsh L.B.S.C. design.
†J2 Introduced 1912 : L. B. Billinton development of J1 with Walschaerts valve gear and detail differences.
Weight : 89 tons.
Pressure : 170 lb. Su.
Cyls. : (O) 21″ × 26″
Driving Wheels : 6′ 7″
T.E. : 20,840 lb.
P.V. :

*32325   †32326

Total : Class J1 1
Class J2 1

2-6-0 4 MT Class K

Introduced 1913 : L. B. Billinton L.B.S.C. design.
Weight : Loco. 63 tons 15 cwt.
Pressure : 180 lb. Su.
Cyls. . (O) 21″ × 26″
Driving Wheels : 5′ 6″
T.E. : 26,580 lb.
P.V. :

32337–53   **Total 17**

4-4-0 1 MT Class K10

Introduced 1901. Drummond L.S.W. design, development of C8 express 4-4-0 for mixed traffic work.
Weight : Loco. 46 tons 14 cwt.
Pressure : 175 lb. Cyls. : 18½″ × 26″
Driving Wheels : 5′ 7″
T.E. : 19,755 lb.

30384/90   **Total 2**

4-4-0   2P   Class L

Introduced 1914 : Wainwright S.E.C.
design, with detail alterations by
Maunsell.
Weight : Loco. 57 tons 9 cwt.
Pressure : 160 lb. Su.
Cyls. : 20½" × 26"
Driving Wheels : 6' 8"
T.E. : 18,575 lb.
P.V.

31760–81   **Total 22**

4-4-0   2P   Class LI

Introduced 1926 : Post-grouping devel-
opment of L, with long-travel valves,
side window cab and detail alterations
Weight : Loco. 57 tons 16 cwt.
Pressure : 180 lb. Su.
Cyls. : 19½" × 26"
Driving Wheels : 6' 8"
T.E. : 18,910 lb.
P.V.

31753–9/82–9   **Total 15**

4-4-0   1 MT   Class LII

Introduced 1903. Drummond L.S.W.
design, development of K10 with T9-
type boiler, with larger firebox.
Weight : Loco. 50 tons 11 cwt.
Pressure : 175 lb.   Cyls. : 18½" × 26"
Driving Wheels : 5' 7"
T.E. : 19,755 lb.

30134/48/54–9/63–5/1/70–5,
   30405/6/8/9/11–4/36–8/41/2.
                           Total 30

4-4-0   2P   Class LI2

Introduced 1904 : Drummond L.S.W.
design, development of T9 with larger
boiler barrel, superheated from 1915.
Weight : Loco. 55 tons 5 cwt.
Pressure : 175 lb. Su.
Cyls. : 19" × 26"
Driving Wheels : 6' 7"
T.E. : 17,675 lb.

30415–34   **Total 20**

0-6-6-0T Uncl.
"Leader" Class

Introduced 1949 : Bulleid double-
bogie design, with chain-coupled
wheels.
Weight: 130 tons. (approx.)
Pressure : 280 lb. Su.
Cyls. : (6) 12½" × 15"
Driving Wheels : 5' 1"
T.E. : 26,350 lb.
Sleeve valves with modified Bulleid
valve gear.

36001

Nos. 36002–5 of this class are stored
in varying stages of construction.

4-6-0   6P   Class LN

*Introduced 1926 : Maunsell design.
cylinders and tender modified by
Bulleid from 1938, and fitted with
multiple-jet blast pipe and large
chimney.
†Introduced 1929 : Loco. fitted experi-
mentally with smaller driving wheels.
‡Introduced 1929 : Loco. fitted experi-
mentally with longer boiler barrel.
Weights : Loco. { 83 tons 10 cwt.*†
                  84 tons 16 cwt.‡
Pressure : 220 lb. Su.
Cyls. : (4) 16½" × 26"
Driving Wheels : { 6' 7"*‡
                   6' 3"†
T.E. { 33,510 lb.*‡
      35,300 lb.†
Walschaerts gear, P.V.
*30850–8/61–5.
†30859   ‡30860
                           Total 16

0-4-4T   2P   Class M7

*Introduced 1897 : Drummond L.S.W.
M7 design.
†Introduced 1903 : Drummond X14
design, with increased front over-
hang, steam reverser and detail
alterations, now classified M7 (30254
originally M7).
‡Introduced 1925 : X14 design fitted
for push-and-pull working.
Weights:{ 60 tons 4 cwt.*
          60 tons 3 cwt.†
          62 tons 0 cwt.‡
Pressure : 175 lb.   Cyls. : 18½" × 26"
Driving Wheels : 5' 7"
T.E. : 19,755 lb.

Classes MN–O1

*30022–6/31–44, 30112, 30241–
53/5/6, 30318–24/56/7, 30667–
71/3–6.

†30029/30, 30123/4/7/30/2/3,
30254, 30374–8, 30479.

‡30021/7/8/45–60, 30104–11/25/
8/9/31, 30328/79, 30480/1.

Total 103

4-6-2 7P Class MN

*Introduced 1941 : Bulleid design.
†Introduced 1948 : Loco. rebuilt with
mechanical stoker.
Weight : Loco. 94 tons 15 cwt.
Pressure : 280 lb. Su.
Cyls. : (3) 18″ × 24″
Driving Wheels : 6′ 2″
T.E. : 37,515 lb.
Bulleid valve gear, P.V.
*35001–4/6–30
†35005

Total 30

2-6-0 4 MT Classes N & N1

*N Introduced 1917 : Maunsell S.E.C.
mixed traffic design.
†N1 Introduced 1922 : 3-cylinder
development of N.
Weight : Loco. { 61 tons 4 cwt.*
{ 64 tons 5 cwt.†
Pressure : 200 lb. Su.
Cyls. : { (O) 19″ × 28″*
{ (3) 16″ × 28″†
Driving Wheels : 5′ 6″
T.E. : { 26,035 lb.*
{ 27,695 lb.†
Walschaerts gear, P.V.
*31400–14, 31810–21/3–75
†31822/76–80

**Totals : Class N 80
Class N1 6**

4-6-0 5P Class N15

*Introduced 1918 : Urie L.S.W. design.
†Introduced 1928 : Urie Locos modified
with cylinders of reduced diameter.
‡Introduced 1925 : Maunsell locos. with
long-travel valves, increased boiler
pressure, smaller fireboxes, and tenders from Drummond G14 4-6-0's.
§Introduced 1925 : Later locos. with
detail alterations and increased
weight.

‖Introduced 1925 : Locos. with modified cabs to suit Eastern Section and
new bogie tenders.
¶Introduced 1926 : Locos. with detail
alterations and six-wheeled tenders
for Central Section.
Weight : Loco. { 80 tons 7 cwt.*†
{ 79 tons 18 cwt.‡
{ 80 tons 19 cwt.§‖
{ 81 tons 17 cwt.¶
Pressure : { 180 lb. Su.*†
{ 200 lb Su.‡§‖¶
Cyls. : { (O) 22″ × 28″*
{ (O) 21″ × 28″†
{ (O) 20½″ × 28″‡§‖¶
Driving Wheels : 6′ 7″
T.E. : { 26,245 lb.*
{ 23,915 lb.†
{ 25,320 lb. §‡‖¶
Walschaerts gear, P.V.

NOTE : Nos. 30736/7/41/52/5 are fitted
with multiple jet blastpipe and
large diameter chimney.

*30755   †30736–54
‡30453–7   §30448–52
‖30763–92   ¶30793–30806

Total 74

4-6-0 4P Class N15X

Introduced 1934 : Maunsell rebuild of
L. B. Billinton L.B.S.C. Class L 4-6-4T
(introduced 1914).
Weight : Loco 73 tons 2 cwt.
Pressure : 180 lb. Su.
Cyls. : (O) 21″ × 28″
Driving Wheels : 6′ 9″
T.E. : 23,325 lb.
Walschaerts gear, P.V.
32327–33

Total 7

0-6-0 1F Class O1

*Introduced 1903 : Wainwright rebuild
with domed boiler and new cab of
Stirling S.E.R. Class O 0-6-0 (introduced 1878, oldest survivor built
1882).

†Introduced 1903 : Locos. with smaller
driving wheels.
Weight : Loco. 41 tons 1 cwt.
Pressure : 150 lb.   Cyls. : 18″ × 26″
Driving Wheels : { 5′ 2″*
{ 5′ 1″†
T.E. : { 17,325 lb.*
{ 17,610 lb.†

*31044/64–6/93, 31108, 31248/58,
  31369/70/3/9/81/3/90/1/5,
  31425/30/2/4,
†31041/8,

Total 23

0-4-4T   1P   Class O2

*Introduced 1889 : Adams L.S.W.
  design.
†Introduced 1923 : Fitted with West-
  inghouse brake for I.O.W., bunkers
  enlarged from 1932.
‡Fitted with Drummond-type boiler.
§Fitted for push-and-pull working.
Weight : $\begin{cases} 46 \text{ tons } 18 \text{ cwt.*}‡ \\ 48 \text{ tons } 8 \text{ cwt.}† \end{cases}$
Pressure : 160 lb.   Cyls. : $17\frac{1}{2}'' \times 24''$
Driving Wheels : 4' 10"
T.E. : 17,235 lb.

*30177/9/92/3/7/9,   30200/12/6/
  24/9–32/6.
† (W)14–34   †§ (W)35/6.
‡30203/4/13/21/3/5/33.
‡§30182/3, 30207.

Total 48

0-6-0T   0F   Class P

Introduced 1909 : Wainwright S.E.C.
  design for push-and-pull work, now
  used for shunting.
Weight : 28 tons 10 cwt.
Pressure : 160 lb.   Cyls. : $12'' \times 18''$
Driving Wheels : 3' 9$\frac{1}{2}$"
T.E. : 7,810 lb.

31027, 31178, 31323/5, 31555–8.
Total 8

0-6-0   4F   Class Q

Introduced 1938 : Maunsell design, later
  fitted with multiple-jet blast pipe and
  large chimney.
Weight : Loco. 49 tons 10 cwt.
Pressure : 200 lb. Su.
Cyls. : $19'' \times 26''$
Driving Wheels : 5' 1"
T.E. : 26,160 lb.
P.V.
30530–49
Total 20

Classes O2–R1

0-6-0   5F   Class Q1

Introduced 1942 : Bulleid " Austerity "
  design.
Weight : Loco. 51 tons 5 cwt.
Pressure : 230 lb. Su.
Cyls. : $19'' \times 26''$
Driving Wheels : 5' 1"
T.E. : 30,080 lb.
P.V.
33001–40
Total 40

0-4-4T   1P   Classes R & R1

*R Introduced 1891 : Kirtley L.C.D.
  design, since rebuilt with H. class
  boiler.
†R1 Introduced 1900 : Locos. built for
  S.E.C. with enlarged bunkers, since
  rebuilt with H class boiler.
‡Fitted for push-and-pull working.
Weight : $\begin{cases} 48 \text{ tons } 15 \text{ cwt.*} \\ 52 \text{ tons } 3 \text{ cwt.}† \end{cases}$
Pressure : 160 lb.   Cyls. : $17\frac{1}{2}'' \times 24''$
Driving Wheels : 5' 6"
T.E. : 15,145 lb.

*31661/71/3/4.
†31696/8, 31705/8.
*‡31658–60/2/3/5–7/70/5.
†‡31697, 31700/3/4/6/10.

**Total : Class R   15
Class R1 10**

0-6-0T   2F   Class R1

*Introduced 1888 : Stirling S.E. design,
  later rebuilt with domed boiler.
†Introduced 1938 : Fitted with Urie
  type short chimney for Whitstable
  branch, and fitted with or retaining
  original Stirling-type cab.
Weight : $\begin{cases} 46 \text{ tons } 15 \text{ cwt.*} \\ 46 \text{ tons } 8 \text{ cwt.}† \end{cases}$
Pressure : 160 lb.   Cyls. : $18'' \times 26''$
Driving Wheels : $\begin{cases} 5' 2''* \\ 5' 1''† \end{cases}$
T.E. : $\begin{cases} 18,480 \text{ lb.*} \\ 18,780 \text{ lb.}† \end{cases}$
*31047, 31128/54/74, 31335/7/40
†31010/69, 31107/47, 31339.
Total 12

Classes S–T9

0-6-0ST   2F   **Class S**

Introduced 1917 : Maunsell rebuild of Wainwright S.E.C. C Class (built 1900) with saddle-tank.
Weight : 53 tons 10 cwt.
Pressure : 160 lb.   Cyls. : 18½″ × 26″
Driving Wheels : 5′ 2″
T.E. : 19,520 lb.

31685   **Total 1**

4-4-0   2P   **Class S11**

Introduced 1903 : Drummond L.S.W. design, development of T9 with larger boiler barrel and smaller wheels for West of England, superheated from 1920.
Weight : Loco. 53 tons, 15 cwt.
Pressure : 175 lb. Su.
Cyls : 19″ × 26″
Driving Wheels : 6′ 0″
T.E. : 19,390 lb.

30395–30404   **Total 10**

4-6-0   6F   **Class S15**

*Introduced 1920 : Urie L.S.W. design, development of N15 for mixed traffic work.
†Introduced 1927 : Post-grouping locos. with higher pressure, smaller grate, modified footplating and other detail differences. 30833-7 with 6-wheel tenders for Central Section.
‡Introduced 1936 : Later locos. with detail differences and reduced weight.
Weight : Loco. $\begin{cases} 79 \text{ tons } 16 \text{ cwt.*} \\ 80 \text{ tons } 14 \text{ cwt.†} \\ 79 \text{ tons } 5 \text{ cwt.‡} \end{cases}$
Pressure : $\begin{cases} 180 \text{ lb. Su.*} \\ 200 \text{ lb. Su.†‡} \end{cases}$
Cyls. : $\begin{cases} (O) 21″ × 28″* \\ (O) 20½″ × 28″†‡ \end{cases}$
Driving Wheels : 5′ 7″
T.E. : $\begin{cases} 28,200 \text{ lb.*} \\ 29,855 \text{ lb.†‡} \end{cases}$
Walschaerts gear, P.V.

*30496–30515   †30823–37
‡30838–47

                Total 45

0-6-0T   2F   **Class T**

Introduced 1879 : Kirtley L.C.D. design (oldest survivor built 1890).
Weight : 40 tons 15 cwt.
Pressure : 160 lb.   Cyls. : 17½″ × 24″
Driving Wheels : 4′ 6″
T.E. : 18,510 lb.

31602/4

           Total 2

0-4-4T   1P   **Class T1**

Introduced 1894 : Adams L.S.W. design, originally designated F6, but later assimilated into Class T1 (introduced 1888).

Weight : 57 tons 2 cwt.
Pressure : 160 lb.   Cyls. : 18″ × 26″
Driving Wheels : 5′ 7″
T.E. : 17,100 lb.

30007/20, 30367

           Total 3

4-4-0   2P   **Class T9**

*Introduced 1899 : Drummond L.S.W. design, fitted with superheater and larger cylinders by Urie from 1922.
†Introduced 1899 : Locos. with detail differences (originally fitted with fire-box watertubes).
‡Introduced 1900 : Locos. with wider cab and splashers, and without coupling rod splashers (originally fitted with firebox watertubes.)

Weight : Loco. $\begin{cases} 51 \text{ tons } 18 \text{ cwt.*} \\ 51 \text{ tons } 16 \text{ cwt.†} \\ 51 \text{ tons } 7 \text{ cwt.‡} \end{cases}$

Pressure : 175 lb. Su.
Cyls. : 19″ × 26″
Driving Wheels : 6′ 7″
T.E. : 17,675 lb.

*30113–22, 30280–9
†30702–19/21–33
‡30300–5/7/10–4/36–8   **Total 66**

4-6-0   4P   **Class T14**

Introduced 1911 : Drummond L.S.W. design, fitted with superheater by Urie from 1915, and with Maunsell superheater, raised footplating and detail alterations from 1930.
Weight : Loco. 76 tons 10 cwt.
Pressure : 175 lb. Su.
Cyls. : (4) 15" × 26"
Driving Wheels : 6' 7"
T.E. : 22,030 lb.
Walschaerts gear and rocking arms.

30446/61   **Total 2**

2-6-0   4 MT
Classes U & U1

*U Introduced 1928 : Rebuild of Maunsell S.E.C. Class K (" River ") 2-6-4T (introduced 1917).
†U Introduced 1928 : Locos. built as Class U, with smaller splashers and detail alterations.
‡U1 Introduced 1928 : 3-cylinder development of Class U (prototype, 31890, rebuilt from 2-6-4T, originally built 1925).

Weight : Loco. { 63 tons*
                 62 tons 6 cwt.†
                 65 tons 6 cwt.‡
Pressure : 200 lb. Su.
Cyls. : { (O) 19" × 28"*†
         (3) 16" × 28"‡
Driving Wheels : 6' 0"
T.E. : { 23,865 lb.*†
      25,385 lb.‡
Walschaerts gear, P.V.
*31790–31809   †31610–39
‡31890–31910

Total : Class U   **50**
           Class U1   **21**

0-6-0T   3F   **Class USA**

Introduced 1942 : U.S. Army Transportation Corps design, purchased by S.R. 1946, and fitted with modified cab and bunker and other detail alterations.
Weight : 46 tons 10 cwt.
Pressure : 210 lb.
Cyls. : (O) 16½" × 24"
Driving Wheels : 4' 6"
T.E. : 21,600 lb.
Walschaerts gear, P.V.

30061–74   **Total 14**

Classes T14–WC & BB

4-4-0   5P   **Class V**

*Introduced 1930 : Maunsell design.
†Introduced 1938 : Fitted with multiple jet blastpipe and larger chimney by Bulleid.
Weight : Loco. 67 tons 2 cwt.
Pressure : 220 lb. Su.
Cyls. : (3) 16½" × 26"
Driving Wheels : 6' 7"
T.E. : 25,135 lb.
Walschaerts gear, P.V.
*30902–6/8/10–2/6/22/3/5–8/32/5/6.
†30900/1/7/9/13–5/7–21/4/29–31/3/4/7–9.

                    Total 40

2-6-4T   5F   **Class W**

Introduced 1931 : Maunsell design, developed from Class N1 2-6-0.
Weight : 90 tons 14 cwt.
Pressure : 200 lb. Su.
Cyls. : (3) 16½" × 28"
Driving Wheels : 5' 6"
T.E. : 29,450 lb.
Walschaerts gear, P.V.

31911–25   **Total 15**

4-6-2   6 MT
Classes WC & BB

*Introduced 1945 : Bulleid " West Country " Class.
†Introduced 1946 : Bulleid " Battle of Britain " Class.
‡Introduced 1948 : Locos. with larger tenders.
Weight : Loco. 86 tons 0 cwt.
Pressure : 280 lb. Su.
Cyls. : (3) 16⅜" × 24"
Driving Wheels : 6' 2"
T.E. : 31,050 lb.
Bulleid valve gear, P.V.
   *34001–48   †34049–70
††34071–90, 34109/10
*‡34091–34108

N.B.—Locos. of this class are still being delivered.

Classes Z-0458

0-8-0T 7F Class Z

Introduced 1929 : Maunsell design for heavy shunting.
Weight : 71 tons 12 cwt.
Pressure : 180 lb. Cyls : (3) 16″ × 18″
Driving Wheels : 4′ 8″
T.E. : 29,375 lb.
Walschaerts gear, P.V.
30950-7   **Total 8**

0-6-0 4F Class 700

Introduced 1897 : Drummond L.S.W. design, superheated from 1921.
Weight : Loco. 46 tons 14 cwt.
Pressure : 180 lb. Su.
Cyls. : 19″ × 26″
Driving Wheels : 5′ 1″
T.E. : 23,540 lb.
30306/8/9/15-7/25-7/39/46/50/2/5/68, 30687-30701.   **Total 30**

0-6-0T 1F Class 756

Introduced 1907 : Hawthorn Leslie design for P.D.S.W.J.
Weight : 35 tons 15 cwt.
Pressure : 170 lb.
Cyls. : (O) 14″ × 22″
Driving Wheels : 3′ 10″
T.E. : 13,545 lb.
30756   **Total 1**

0-6-2T 1MT Class 757

Introduced 1907 : Hawthorn Leslie design for P.D.S.W.J.
Weight : 49 tons 19 cwt.
Pressure : 170 lb.
Cyls. : (O) 16″ × 24″
Driving Wheels : 4′ 0″
T.E. : 18,495 lb.
30757-8   **Total 2**

2-4-0WT 0F Class 0298

Introduced 1874 : Beattie L.S.W. design, rebuilt by Adams (1884-92), Urie (1921-2) and Maunsell (1931-5).
Weight : 37 tons 16 cwt.
Pressure : 160 lb.
Cyls. : (O) 16½″ × 20″
Driving Wheels : 5′ 7″
T.E. : 11,050 lb.
30585-7   **Total 3**

0-6-0 1F Class 0395

*Introduced 1881 : Adams L.S.W. design.
†Introduced 1885 : Adams " 496 " class, with longer front overhang.
‡Introduced 1928 : Reboilered with ex-S.E.C. Class M3 4-4-0 boiler.
§Fitted with Drummond type boiler.
Weight : Loco. { 37 tons 12 cwt.*
{ 38 tons 14 cwt.†
Pressure : { 140 lb.*
{ 150 lb.†
Driving Wheels : 5′ 1″
T.E. : { 15,535 lb.*
{ 16,645 lb.†

*30568-72/4-8
†30566/79/81
*‡30573
*§30567
†‡30565/80
†§30564

                                           Total 18

4-4-2T 1P Class 0415

Introduced 1882 : Adams L.S.W. design later reboilered (oldest survivor built 1883).
Weight : 55 tons 2 cwt.
Pressure : 160 lb.
Cyls. : (O) 17½″ × 24″
Driving Wheels : 5′ 7″
T.E. : 14,920 lb.
30582-4   **Total 3**

0-4-0ST 0F Class 0458

Introduced 1890 : Hawthorn Leslie design for Southampton Docks Co., absorbed by L.S.W., 1892.
Weight : 21 tons 2 cwt.
Pressure : 120 lb.
Cyls. : (O) 12″ × 20″
Driving Wheels : 3′ 2″
T.E. : 7,730 lb.
30458   **Total 1**

THE ABC OF
BRITISH RAILWAYS
LOCOMOTIVES

PART 3—Nos. 40000-59999

LONDON MIDLAND & SCOTTISH
REGION STEAM
LOCOMOTIVES

LONDON

Ian Allan Ltd

FOREWORD

THIS booklet lists all British Railways locomotives numbered between 40000 and 59999. This series of numbers includes all London Midland Region and Scottish (ex-L.M.S.) Region steam locos., i.e. steam locomotives of the former L.M.S.R. Under the general British Railways numbering scheme, the numbers of L.M.S.R. steam locomotives were increased by 40000, with certain exceptions which were to be completely renumbered.

Former L.M.S.R. diesel and diesel-electric locomotives were to be renumbered, in common with all British Railways locomotives of similar propulsion, between 10000 and 29999, and details of them will be found in the ABC OF BRITISH RAILWAYS LOCOMOTIVES, PART II, Nos. 10000-39999.

THE BOILERS OF STANIER LOCOMOTIVES

THE early taper boilers of Sir William Stanier's design were domeless, with a smokebox regulator and a top feed toward the rear of the barrel. The superheaters were small, and the proportions of the boilers followed G.W.R. practice.

In the light of experience with these locos., successive developments were made in the boilers built from 1935 onward. The superheaters (sometimes in several stages) and the fireboxes were enlarged, the latter by sloping the back plate and increasing the length of grate ; domes were fitted, incorporating the regulator valve. In recent boilers the top feed casing has been moved much further forward.

Earlier boilers have, in many cases, been fitted with domes and larger superheaters, and this, combined with the routine boiler changes which are made under the L.M.R. repair system, makes it impossible to tabulate the current condition of the locos. Furthermore, the variations of weight between different types of boiler fitted to each class produce variations in the loco. weights. The figures given in this book are therefore those applicable to recent locos. of the class.

The following gives an indication of the principal changes in certain classes :—

Class 3 2-6-2 T

Nos. 40071–40144 were built domeless, and 40145–40209 with domes and larger fireboxes. The firebox distinction seems to be maintained.

Class 4 2–6–4 T

Nos. 42500–36 were built domeless with 12-element superheaters, but many have now been fitted with domes. Nos. 42537–44 had larger barrels and fireboxes (but still with 25 sq. ft. grates) and 18 element superheaters. Nos. 42425–94 and 42545–42617 were built domed, with 18-element superheaters and 26.7 sq. ft. grates. From No. 42618 onward, and on all the Fairburn locos., the superheater was further increased to 21 elements.

Class 5 4–6–0

Nos. 45000–69 were built domeless with 14-element superheaters. These boilers have now been rebuilt with domes and 24-element superheaters. Nos. 45070–45224 were also domeless, but with 21-element superheaters. These boilers are in course of rebuilding. Boilers are interchanged freely between locos. 45000–45224. From No. 45225 onward domes were fitted, and the superheaters increased to 24 elements. The grate area was also increased from the previous figure of 27.8 sq. ft. to 28.65 sq. ft. On Nos. 45472–99 the superheater was further increased to 28 elements, and this applies to all locos. below No. 45000. The larger firebox boilers are freely interchanged between locos. from No. 45225 onward, and some of the locos. in the earlier series have also been modified to take these boilers. This process will be continued as the original boilers wear out.

Class 5X 4–6–0

Nos. 45552–45664 were built domeless, with 14-element superheaters and 29.5 sq. ft. of grate. From No. 45665 the superheater was increased to 21 elements, the grate to 31 sq. ft., and domes were fitted. Nos. 45702–42 had the superheater further increased to 24 elements. In this class there has been extensive rebuilding of boilers and interchange between locos. A number of the class still carry domeless boilers.

Class 8 2–8–0

Nos. 48000–11 were domeless with 27.8 sq. ft. of grate, but all other locos. were built with domes and 28.65 sq. ft. grates. The whole class has 21-element superheaters. No. 48003 was soon modified to take the larger firebox, and other locos. of this batch will eventually follow suit.

3

THE CLASS 8 2-8-0 LOCOMOTIVES

THE Stanier Class 7 2–8–0 was introduced in 1935 and reclassified 8F in 1936. In 1935–9 Nos. 48000–26/96–48110 were built by the L.M.S. and 48027–95 by the Vulcan Foundry. Early in the war the Ministry of Supply ordered 240 locos. of similar design for overseas service from private builders : these were delivered in 1940–2, the actual total being 208. Prior to shipment overseas in 1941 a number of these locos. worked on the L.M.S. and G.W.R., and 53 of them carried L.M.S. numbers temporarily, 8226–63 (North British Loco. Co.) and 8286–8300 (Beyer Peacock).

When the remainder were shipped, No. 8293 was under repair following an accident, and it was permanently transferred to L.M.S. stock in 1943. In addition, 22 of the later M.o.S. locos., which had never received L.M.S. numbers, remained in England and in 1943 became L.M.S. Nos. 8264–85.

When shipment of this class began in 1941 the need for locos. in the Middle East was so great that 51 of the original L.M.S. locos. were prepared for shipment ; 43 actually left the country, and the remainder (Nos. 8024/69/78–80/5/8/93) were later returned to the L.M.S.

With a view to standardising the production of heavy freight locos. for home use the M.o.S. ordered further Class 8 locos. from the other railway companies. These were built as follows in 1943–5 : Nos. 8400–79 by the G.W.R., Nos. 8500–59 by the L.N.E.R. and Nos. 8600–8704 by the S.R. The G.W. and L.N.E.-built locos. were loaned to the companies which built them until 1946–47, but were regarded as L.M.S. stock from the outset.

As the L.N.E.R. required further freight locos. for its own stock the S.R. delivered 25 Class 8 locos. in 1944, and the L.N.E.R. shops built a further 43 in 1944–6. These locos. eventually became L.N.E.R. Nos. 3500–67, and in 1947–8 were loaned to the L.M.S., becoming Nos. 8705–72.

In the meantime construction proceeded steadily in the L.M.S. shops, and between 1939 and 1945 Nos. 8111–75, 8301–99 and 8490–5 were built at Crewe and Horwich. In addition, concurrently with its M.o.S. deliveries, the N.B. Loco. Co. built 8176–8225.

In 1948, 39 of the W.D. locos. were returned from the Middle East and were added to L.M.S. stock after overhaul. Those which had been taken from the L.M.S., 8000–95, had their former numbers restored (plus 40,000). The remainder were allotted blank numbers in the 48200 series : 48246–63/86–92/4–7.

The present stock of 663 locos. can be summarized thus :—

Built by L.M.S. or by private builders for L.M.S.	...	288
Built by other railways on L.M.S. account	... ...	245
Built by other railways on L.N.E.R. account	... ...	68
Built by private builders on M.o.S. account	... ...	62

4

CHIEF MECHANICAL ENGINEERS

BRITISH RAILWAYS (L. M. Region)

H. G. Ivatt ... 1948—

L.M.S.

George Hughes ...	...	1923—1925	Sir William Stanier	...	1932—1944
Sir Henry Fowler	...	1925—1931	Charles E. Fairburn	...	1944—1945
E. H. J. Lemon	...	1931—1932	H. G. Ivatt	...	1945—1947
(Sir Ernest Lemon)				

LOCOMOTIVE SUPERINTENDENTS AND C.M.E.'S—L.M.S. CONSTITUENT COMPANIES†

CALEDONIAN RAILWAY

Robert Sinclair		
(First loco engineer)‡	1847—1856	
Benjamin Connor	...	1856—1876
George Brittain	...	1876—1882
Dugald Drummond	...	1882—1890
Hugh Smellie	...	1890
J. Lambie	...	1890—1895
J. F. McIntosh	...	1895—1914
William Pickersgill	...	1914—1923

FURNESS RAILWAY

R. Mason ...	...	1890—1897
W. F. Pettigrew	...	1897—1918
D. J. Rutherford ...	...	1918—1923

Previous to Mason, F.R. locomotives were designed by contract with " outside " builders.

GLASGOW AND SOUTH WESTERN RLY.

Patrick Stirling	...	1853—1866
James Stirling	...	1866—1877
Hugh Smellie	...	1877—1890
James Manson	...	1890—1912
Peter Drummond	...	1912—1918
R H. Whitelegg ...	...	1918—1923

HIGHLAND RAILWAY

William Stroudley		
(First loco engineer) ...	1866—1869	
David Jones ...	...	1869—1896
Peter Drummond	...	1896—1911
F. G. Smith	...	1912—1915
C. Cumming	...	1915—1923

L. & Y.R.

Sir John Hawkshaw (Consultant),*		
Hurst and Jenkins successively to 1868		
W. Hurst ...	...	1868—1876
W. Barton Wright	...	1876—1886
John A. F. Aspinall	...	1886—1899
H. A. Hoy...	...	1899—1904
George Hughes ...	...	1904—1922

L.N.W.R.

Francis Trevithick and J. E. McConnell, first loco engineers, 1846, with Alexander Allan largely responsible for design at Crewe.*

John Ramsbottom	...	1857—1871
Francis William Webb	...	1871—1903
George Whale ...	...	1903—1909
Charles John Bowen-Cooke ...	...	1909—1920
Capt. Hewitt Pearson Montague Beames ...	...	1920—1921
George Hughes ...	...	1922

The L. & Y. amalgamated with L.N.W.R. in 1921.

L.T. & S.R.

Thomas Whitelegg	...	1880—1910
Robert Harben Whitelegg	...	1910—1912

(LTSR absorbed by M.R., control of locos. transferred to Derby as from Aug., 1912.)

LOCOMOTIVE SUPERINTENDENTS
AND C.M.E.'S *(continued)*

MARYPORT & CARLISLE

Hugh Smellie	...	1870—1878
J. Campbell	...	1878—
William Coulthard	* —1904
J. B. Adamson		1904—1923

MIDLAND RAILWAY

Matthew Kirtley (First loco engineer)	...	1844—1873
Samuel Waite Johnson	...	1873—1903
Richard Mountford Deeley	1903—1909
Henry Fowler	...	1909—1923

SOMERSET AND DORSET JOINT RAILWAY

Until leased by Mid. and L. & S.W. (as from 1st Nov., 1875) locomotives were bought from outside builders, principally George England of Hatcham Iron Works, S.E. After the above date, Derby and its various Loco. Supts. and CMEs have acted for S. & D.J., aided by a resident Loco. Supt. stationed at Highbridge works.

NORTH STAFFORDSHIRE RAILWAY

L. Clare	...	1876—1882
L. Longbottom	...	1882—1902
J. H. Adams	...	1902—1915
J. A. Hookham	...	1915—1923

W. Angus was Loco. Supt. at Stoke prior to 1876. No earlier records can be traced.

WIRRAL

Eric G. Barker	...	1892—1902
T. B. Hunter	...	1903—1923

Barker of the Wirral Railway is noteworthy for originating the 4-4-4 tank type in this country (1896).

NORTH LONDON RAILWAY

(Worked by L. & N.W. by agreement dated Dec., 1908.)

William Adams	...	1853—1873
J. C. Park	...	1873—1893
Henry J. Pryce	...	1893—1908

* Date of actual entry into office not known.

MOTIVE POWER DEPOTS, AND CODES

LONDON MIDLAND REGION

Heavy type thus, **Rugby**, indicates a main district depot. Sub-depots, the engines attached to which bear the code of the main district depot, are those listed without codes.

1A	**Willesden**	9A	**Longsight**
1B	Camden	9B	Stockport
1C	Watford	9C	Macclesfield
1D	Devons Road	9D	Buxton
		9E	Trafford Park
2A	**Rugby**	9F	Heaton Mersey
	Market Harborough	9G	Northwich
	Seaton		
2B	Nuneaton	10A	**Springs Branch**
2C	Warwick	10B	Preston
2D	Coventry	10C	Patricroft
		10D	Plodder Lane
3A	**Bescot**	10E	Sutton Oak
3B	Bushbury	10F	Wigan (L.I.)
3C	Walsall		
3D	Aston	11A	**Carnforth**
3E	Monument Lane	11B	Barrow
			Coniston
4A	**Bletchley**	11C	Oxenholme
	Leighton Buzzard	11D	Tebay
	Oxford		
	Newport Pagnell	12A	**Carlisle** (Upperby)
	Aylesbury	12B	Carlisle (Canal)
4B	Northampton	12C	Penrith
		12D	Workington
5A	**Crewe North**	12E	Moor Row
	Whitchurch		
5B	Crewe South	14A	**Cricklewood**
5C	Stafford	14B	Kentish Town
5D	Stoke	14C	St. Albans
5E	Alsager		
5F	Uttoxeter	15A	**Wellingboro'**
		15B	Kettering
6A	**Chester**	15C	Leicester
6B	Mold Junction	15D	Bedford
6C	Birkenhead		
6D	Chester (Northgate)	16A	**Nottingham**
6E	Wrexham		Southwell
6F	Bidston		Lincoln (Midland)
		16C	Kirkby
7A	**Llandudno Junc.**	16D	Mansfield
7B	Bangor		
7C	Holyhead	17A	**Derby**
7D	Rhyl	17B	Burton
			Overseal
8A	**Edge Hill**	17C	Coalville
8B	Warrington	17D	Rowsley
8C	Speke Junction		Crompton
8D	Widnes		Middleton
8E	Brunswick		Sheep Pasture
	Warrington		

18A	**Toton**		23C	Lancaster
18B	Westhouses			
18C	Hasland		24A	**Accrington**
	Clay Cross		24B	Rose Grove
18D	Staveley		24C	Lostock Hall
	Sheepbridge		24D	Lower Darwen

19A	**Sheffield**		25A	**Wakefield**
	York (Queen's St.)		25B	Huddersfield
19B	Millhouses		25C	Goole
19C	Canklow		25D	Mirfield
			25E	Sowerby Bridge
20A	**Leeds**		25F	Low Moor
20B	Stourton		25G	Farnley Junction
20C	Royston			
20D	Normanton		26A	**Newton Heath**
20E	Manningham		26B	Agecroft
	Ilkley		26C	Bolton
			26D	Bury
21A	**Saltley**		26E	Bacup
21B	Bourneville		26F	Lees
	Redditch		26G	Belle Vue
21C	Bromsgrove			
21D	Stratford-on-Avon		27A	**Bank Hall**
			27B	Aintree
22A	**Bristol**		27C	Southport
22B	Gloucester		27D	Wigan (C)
	Tewkesbury		27E	Walton
	Dursley			Southport
23A	**Skipton**		28A	**Blackpool**
	Keighley			Blackpool N.
23B	Hellifield		28B	Fleetwood
	Ingleton			

Scottish Region

60A	**Inverness**		62B	Dundee
	Dingwall			Arbroath
	Fortrose			Dundee West
	Kyle of Lochalsh			Montrose
60B	Aviemore			St. Andrews
	Boat of Garten			Tayport
60C	Helmsdale		62C	Dunfermline
	Dornoch			Alloa
	Tain			Inverkeithing
60D	Wick			Kelty
	Thurso			Loch Leven
60E	Forres			
			63A	**Perth**
				Aberfeldy
				Blair Atholl
				Crieff
61A	**Kittybrewster**		63B	Stirling
	Ballater			Killin
	Fraserburgh			Stirling (Shore Rd.)
	Macduff		63C	Forfar
	Peterhead			Brechin
61B	Ferryhill		63D	Fort William
61C	Keith			Mallaig
	Banff		63E	Oban
	Elgin			Ballachulish
62A	**Thornton**		64A	**St. Margarets**
	Anstruther			Dunbar
	Burntisland			Galashiels
	Ladybank			

	Hardengreen	65G	Yoker
	Longniddry	65H	Helensburgh
	North Berwick		Arrochar
	Peebles	65I	Balloch
	Penicuik		
	Polton		
	Seafield	66A	**Polmadie**
64B	Haymarket		Paisley
64C	Dalry Road	66B	Motherwell
64D	Carstairs		Morningside
64E	Polmont	66C	Hamilton
	Kinniel	66D	Greenock (Ladyburn)
64F	Bathgate		Greenock (Princes Pier)
64G	Hawick		
	Kelso		
	Riccarton	67A	**Corkerhill**
		67B	Hurlford
			Beith
			Muirkirk
65A	**Eastfield**	67C	Ayr
	Aberfoyle	67D	Ardrossan
	Kilsyth		
	Lennoxtown		
65B	St. Rollox	68A	**Carlisle Kingmoor**
65C	Parkhead	68B	Dumfries
65D	Dawsholm		Kirkcudbright
	Dumbarton	68C	Stranraer
	Stobcross		Newton Stewart
65E	Kipps	68D	Beattock
65F	Grangemouth		Lockerbie

NOTES ON THE USE OF THIS BOOK

1. At the head of each class will be found a list of any important sub-divisions of the class, usually in order of introduction. Each sub-division is given a reference mark, by which its relevant dimensions (if differing from those of other sub-divisions) and the locomotives it comprises (if known) may be identified.

2. The lists of dimensions at the head of each class show locomotives fitted with two inside cylinders unless otherwise stated, e.g. (O)= two outside cylinders.

3. Superheated locos. are denoted by the letters " Su " after the boiler pressure. " SS " denotes that some are superheated.

4. The date on which the first locomotive of a class was built is denoted by " Introduced." If the oldest loco. still running was built at a later date, that also is indicated.

5. Where locomotives have been renumbered other than by the addition of 40000 to their former L.M.S. numbers, the details of former L.M.S. numbers are given.

6. Tender weights have not been included in the lists of dimensions, owing to the numerous variations in weight within individual classes.

7. The numbers of locomotives in service have been checked to February 24, 1951.

2-6-2T   3MT

Introduced 1930. Fowler L.M.S. design with parallel boiler.
*Introduced 1930. Condensing locos. for working to Moorgate, London.
Weight : {70 tons 10 cwt.
{71 tons 16 cwt.*
Pressure : 200 lb Su.
Cyls. : (O) 17½″ × 26″.
Dr. Wheels : 5′ 3″.   T.E. : 21,485 lb.
Walschaerts Valve Gear P.V.

40001	40019	40037*	40054
40002	40020	40038*	40055
40003	40021*	40039*	40056
40004	40022*	40040*	40057
40005	40023*	40041	40058
40006	40024*	40042	40059
40007	40025*	40043	40060
40008	40026*	40044	40061
40009	40027*	40045	40062
40010	40028*	40046	40063
40011	40029*	40047	40064
40012	40030*	40048	40065
40013	40031*	40049	40066
40014	40032*	40050	40067
40015	40033*	40051	40068
40016	40034*	40052	40069
40017	40035*	40053	40070
40018	40036*		Total 70

2-6-2T   3MT

Introduced 1935. Stanier L.M.S. taper boiler development of Fowler design (above).
*Introduced 1941. Rebuilt with larger boiler.
Weight : {71 tons 5 cwt.
{72 tons 10 cwt.*
Pressure : 200 lb Su.
Cyls. : (O) 17½″ × 26″.
Dr. Wheels : 5′ 3″.   T.E. : 21,485 lb.
Walschaerts Valve Gear P.V.

40071	40080	40089	40098
40072	40081	40090	40099
40073	40082	40091	40100
40074	40083	40092	40101
40075	40084	40093	40102
40076	40085	40094	40103
40077	40086	40095	40104
40078	40087	40096	40105
40079	40088	40097	40106

40107	40133	40159	40185
40108	40134	40160	40186
40109	40135	40161	40187
40110	40136	40162	40188
40111	40137	40163*	40189
40112	40138	40164	40190
40113	40139	40165	40191
40114	40140	40166	40192
40115	40141	40167	40193
40116	40142	40168	40194
40117	40143	40169*	40195
40118	40144	40170	40196
40119	40145	40171	40197
40120	40146	40172	40198
40121	40147	40173	40199
40122	40148*	40174	40200
40123	40149	40175	40201
40124	40150	40176	40202
40125	40151	40177	40203*
40126	40152	40178	40204
40127	40153	40179	40205
40128	40154	40180	40206
40129	40155	40181	40207
40130	40156	40182	40208
40131	40157	40183	40209
40132	40158	40184	Total 139

4-4-0   2P

*Introduced 1909. Fowler rebuild of Johnson Midland loco. (introduced 1882).
Introduced 1912. Fowler rebuild of Johnson locos. with superheater and piston valves.
†Introduced 1914. Locos. built new to superheated design for S. & D.J.R. (taken into L.M.S. stock, 1930).
Weight : Loco. 53 tons 7 cwt.
Pressure : 160 lb. SS.
Cyls : {18″ × 26″.*
{20¼″ × 26″. Su.
Dr. Wheels : {6′ 6½″.*
{7′ 0½″ Su.
T.E. : {15,960 lb.*
{17,585 lb. Su.

40322†	40332	40359	40395
40323†	40337	40362	40396
40324†	40351	40364	40397
40325†	40353	40377	40401
40326†	40356	40383*	40402

40404	40438	40493	40531	40571	40604	40636	40669
40405	40439	40495	40532	40572	40605	40637	40670
40406	40443	40497	40534	40573	40606	40638	40671
40407	40444	40499	40535	40574	40607	40640	40672
40409	40447	40501	40536	40575	40608	40641	40673
40410	40448	40502	40537	40576	40609	40642	40674
40411	40450	40503	40538	40577	40610	40643	40675
40412	40452	40504	40539	40578	40611	40644	40676
40413	40453	40505	40540	40579	40612	40645	40677
40414	40454	40507	40541	40580	40613	40646	40678
40415	40455	40508	40542	40581	40614	40647	40679
40416	40458	40509	40543	40582	40615	40648	40680
40417	40461	40511	40546	40583	40616	40649	40681
40418	40462	40513	40547	40584	40617	40650	40682
40419	40463	40514	40548	40585	40618	40651	40683
40420	40464	40518	40549	40586	40619	40652	40684
40421	40470	40519	40550	40587	40620	40653†	40685
40422	40471	40520	40551	40588	40621	40654	40686
40423	40472	40521	40552	40589	40622	40655	40687
40424	40480	40522	40553	40590	40623	40656	40688
40425	40482	40523	40556	40592	40624	40657	40689
40426	40484	40524	40557	40593	40625	40658	40690
40430	40485	40525	40558	40594	40626	40659	40691
40432	40486	40526	40559	40595	40627	40660	40692
40433	40487	40527	40560	40596	40628	40661	40693
40434	40489	40528	40562	40597	40629	40662	40694
40436	40491	40529		40598	40630	40663	40695
				40599	40631	40664	40696
				40600	40632	40665	40697
				40601	40633*†	40666	40698
				40602	40634*	40667	40699
				40603	40635*	40668	40700

Total 127

Total 136

4-4-0   2P

Introduced 1928. Post-Grouping development of Midland design, with modified dimensions and reduced boiler mountings.
*Introduced 1929. Locos. built for S. & D.J.R. (taken into L.M.S. stock, 1930).
†Fitted experimentally in 1933 with Dabeg feed-water heater.
Weight : Loco. 54 tons 1 cwt.
Pressure : 180 lb. Su.
Cyls. : 19″ × 26″.
Dr. Wheels : 6′ 9″.   T.E. : 17,730 lb. P.V.

40563	40565	40567	40569
40564	40566	40568	40570

4-4-0   3P

Introduced 1901. Johnson Midland design rebuilt by Fowler from 1916 with larger cyls., superheater, etc.
Weight : Loco. 55 tons 7 cwt.
Pressure : 175 lb. Su.
Cyls. : 20½″ × 26″.
Dr. Wheels : 6′ 9″.   T.E. : 20,065 lb. P.V.

40726	40729	40743	40758
40728	40741	40747	

Total 7

11

4-4-0 (3-Cyl. Compd.) 4P

*Introduced 1905. Development by Deeley of Johnson Midland compound, later superheated by Fowler.
†Introduced 1914. Fowler superheated rebuild of Johnson locos. (originally built 1902).
Remainder. Introduced 1924. Post-Grouping locos. with modified dimensions and (except 61045–64) reduced boiler mountings.
Weight : Loco. 61 tons 14 cwt.
Pressure : 200 lb Su.
Cyls. : L.P. (2) 21″ × 26″.
H.P. (1) 19″ × 26″.
Dr. Wheels : $\begin{cases} 7′\ 0″*†. \\ 6′\ 9″. \end{cases}$
T.E. (of L.P. cyls. at 80% boiler pressure) $\begin{cases} 21,840\ \text{lb.}*† \\ 22,650\ \text{lb.} \end{cases}$
P.V. (H.P. cyl. only)

40900	40929	41032†	41066
40901	40930	41035†	41067
40902	40931	41037†	41068
40903	40932	41038†	41069
40904	40933	41040†	41070
40905	40934	41041†	41071
40906	40935	41043†	41072
40907	40936	41044†	41073
40908	40937	41045	41074
40909	40938	41046	41075
40910	40939	41047	41076
40911	41000*	41048	41077
40912	41001*	41049	41078
40913	41003*	41050	41079
40914	41004*	41051	41080
40915	41005†	41052	41081
40916	41006†	41053	41082
40917	41007†	41054	41083
40918	41009†	41055	41084
40919	41014†	41056	41085
40920	41015†	41057	41086
40921	41016†	41058	41087
40922	41019†	41059	41088
40923	41020†	41060	41089
40924	41021†	41061	41090
40925	41023†	41062	41091
40926	41025†	41063	41092
40927	41028†	41064	41093
40928	41030†	41065	41094

41095	41122	41148	41174
41096	41123	41149	41175
41097	41124	41150	41176
41098	41125	41151	41177
41099	41126	41152	41178
41100	41127	41153	41179
41101	41128	41154	41180
41102	41129	41155	41181
41103	41130	41156	41182
41104	41131	41157	41183
41105	41132	41158	41184
41106	41133	41159	41185
41107	41134	41160	41186
41108	41135	41161	41187
41109	41136	41162	41188
41110	41137	41163	41189
41111	41138	41164	41190
41112	41139	41165	41191
41113	41140	41166	41192
41114	41141	41167	41193
41115	41142	41168	41194
41116	41143	41169	41195
41117	41144	41170	41196
41118	41145	41171	41197
41119	41146	41172	41198
41120	41147	41173	41199
41121			

Total 221

2-6-2T   2MT

Introduced 1946. Ivatt L.M.S taper boiler design.
Weight : 63 tons 5 cwt.
Pressure : 200 lb. Su.
Cyls. : (O) 16″ × 24″.
Dr. Wheels : 5′ 0″.   T.E. : 17,410 lb.
Walschaerts Valve Gear.   P.V.

41200	41210	41220	41230
41201	41211	41221	41231
41202	41212	41222	41232
41203	41213	41223	41233
41204	41214	41224	41234
41205	41215	41225	41235
41206	41216	41226	41236
41207	41217	41227	41237
41208	41218	41228	41238
41209	41219	41229	41239

41240	41263	41286	41309
41241	41264	41287	41310
41242	41265	41288	41311
41243	41266	41289	41312
41244	41267	41290	41313
41245	41268	41291	41314
41246	41269	41292	41315
41247	41270	41293	41316
41248	41271	41294	41317
41249	41272	41295	41318
41250	41273	41296	41319
41251	41274	41297	41320
41252	41275	41298	41321
41253	41276	41299	41322
41254	41277	41300	41323
41255	41278	41301	41324
41256	41279	41302	41325
41257	41280	41303	41326
41258	41281	41304	41327
41259	41282	41305	41328
41260	41283	41306	41329
41261	41284	41307	
41262	41285	41308	

(N.B. Locos of this class are still being delivered.)

0-4-0ST   0F

*Introduced 1883. Johnson Midland design.

†‡Introduced 1897. Larger Johnson Midland design.
Dr. Wheels : 3' 10".
Pressure : $\begin{cases} 140 \text{ lb.}*† \\ 150 \text{ lb.}‡ \end{cases}$

	Weight tons cwt.		Cyls. (O)	T.E.
41516*	23	3	13"×20"	8,745
41518†	32	3	15"×20"	11,640
41523‡	32	3	15"×20"	12,475
				Total 3

0-4-0T   0F

Introduced 1907. Deeley Midland design.
Weight : 32 tons 16 cwt.
Pressure : 160 lb.
Cyls. : (O) 15"×22".
Dr. Wheels : 3' 9¾".   T.E. : 14,635 lb.
Walschaerts Valve Gear.

41528	41531	41534	41536
41529	41532	41535	41537
41530	41533		
			Total 10

0-6-0T   1F

Introduced 1878. Johnson Midland design.
* Rebuilt with Belpaire boilers.
Weight : 39 tons 11 cwt.
Pressure : $\begin{cases} 150 \text{ lb.} \\ 140 \text{ lb.}* \end{cases}$
Cyls. : 17"×24".
Dr. Wheels : 4' 7".
T.E. : $\begin{cases} 16,080 \text{ lb.} \\ 15,005 \text{ lb.}* \end{cases}$

41660*	41725*	41781	41846*
41661*	41726	41793	41847*
41664*	41727*	41794*	41852*
41666	41734*	41795	41853
41671	41739*	41797*	41854*
41672*	41745*	41803*	41855*
41682*	41747*	41804*	41856*
41686	41748	41805	41857
41690*	41749*	41811*	41859*
41695*	41752*	41813*	41860*
41699*	41753*	41814*	41865
41702*	41754*	41820*	41869*
41706*	41763	41826*	41874*
41708*	41767	41829*	41875*
41710*	41769*	41833*	41878*
41711*	41770*	41835	41879*
41712*	41773*	41838*	41885
41713	41777	41839*	41889*
41720*	41779	41844*	41890*
41724*	41780*		
			Total 78

0-4-4T   2P

Introduced : 1932. Stanier L.M.S. design.
Weight : 58 tons 1 cwt.
Pressure : 160 lb.
Cyls. : 18"×26".
Dr. Wheels : 5' 7".   T.E. : 17,100 lb.

41900	41903	41906	41908
41901	41904	41907	41909
41902	41905		**Total 10**

13

4-4-2T   2P

Introduced : 1900. Whitelegg L.T. & S.
"51" Class.
Weight : 67 tons 15 cwt.
Pressure : 170 lb.
Cyls. : (O) 19″×26″:.
Dr. Wheels : 6′ 6″.   T.E. : 17,390 lb.

41911	41917	41921	41925
41915	41919	41922	41926
41916			**Total 9**

4-4-2T   3P

*Introduced 1905. Rebuild of White-
legg L.T. & S. "37" Class (originally
introduced 1897).
†Introduced 1909. L.T. & S. Whitelegg
"79" Class.
Remainder. Introduced 1923. Midland
and L.M.S. development of L.T. &
S. "79" Class.
Weight :⎰ 71 tons 10 cwt.†
⎱ 71 tons 10 cwt.
⎱ 70 tons 15 cwt.*
Pressure : 170 lb.
Cyls. : (O) 19″×26″.
Dr. Wheels : 6′ 6″.   T.E. : 17,390 lb

41928	41939	41950	41967†
41929	41940	41951	41969
41930	41941	41952	41970
41931	41942	41953*	41971
41932	41943	41954*	41972
41933	41944	41956*	41973
41934	41945	41957*	41974
41935	41946	41958*	41975
41936	41947	41959*	41976
41937	41948	41961*	41977
41938	41949	41966†	41978
			Total 44

0-6-2T   3F

Introduced 1903. Whitelegg L.T. & S.
"69" Class (Nos. 41990–3 built 1912.
taken directly into M.R. stock).
Weight : 64 tons 13 cwt.
Pressure : 170 lb.
Cyls. : 18″×26″.
Dr. Wheels : 5′ 3″.   T.E. : 19,320 lb

41980	41984	41988	41991
41981	41985	41989	41992
41982	41986	41990	41993
41983	41987		**Total 14**

2-6-4T   4MT

*Introduced 1927. Fowler L.M.S. parallel
boiler design.
†Introduced 1933. As earlier engines,
but with side-window cabs and doors.
‡Introduced 1934. Stanier taper-
boiler 3-cylinder design for L.T. & S.
section.
§Introduced 1935. Stanier taper
boiler 2-cylinder design.
¶Introduced 1945. Fairburn development of Stanier design with shorter
wheelbase and detail alterations.
Weights :⎰ 86 tons 5 cwt.*†
⎱ 92 tons 5 cwt.‡
⎱ 87 tons 17 cwt.§
⎱ 85 tons 5 cwt.¶
Pressure (all types) : 200 lb. Su.
Cyls. :⎰ (O) 19″×26″*†
⎱ (3) 16″×26″‡
⎱ (O) 19⅞″×26″§¶
Dr. Wheels (all types) : 5′ 9″.
T.E. :⎰ 23,125 lb.*†
⎱ 24,600 lb‡
⎱ 24,670 lb.§¶
Walschaerts valve gear.   P.V.

**¶Nos.   42050–42299   FAIRBURN
LOCOS.**

42050	42072	42094	42116
42051	42073	42095	42117
42052	42074	42096	42118
42053	42075	42097	42119
42054	42076	42098	42120
42055	42077	42099	42121
42056	42078	42100	42122
42057	42079	42101	42123
42058	42080	42102	42124
42059	42081	42103	42125
42060	42082	42104	42126
42061	42083	42105	42127
42062	42084	42106	42128
42063	42085	42107	42129
42064	42086	42108	42130
42065	42087	42109	42131
42066	42088	42110	42132
42067	42089	42111	42133
42068	42090	42112	42134
42069	42091	42113	42135
42070	42092	42114	42136
42071	42093	42115	42137

42138	42179	42220	42260
42139	42180	42221	42261
42140	42181	42222	42262
42141	42182	42223	42263
42142	42183	42224	42264
42143	42184	42225	42265
42144	42185	42226	42266
42145	42186	42227	42267
42146	42187	42228	42268
42147	42188	42229	42269
42148	42189	42230	42270
42149	42190	42231	42271
42150	42191	42232	42272
42151	42192	42233	42273
42152	42193	42234	42274
42153	42194	42235	42275
42154	42195	42236	42276
42155	42196	42237	42277
42156	42197	42238	42278
42157	42198	42239	42279
42158	42199	42240	42280
42159	42200	42241	42281
42160	42201	42242	42282
42161	42202	42243	42283
42162	42203	42244	42284
42163	42204	42245	42285
42164	42205	42246	42286
42165	42206	42247	42287
42166	42207	42248	42288
42167	42208	42249	42289
42168	42209	42250	42290
42169	42210	42251	42291
42170	42211	42252	42292
42171	42212	42253	42293
42172	42213	42254	42294
42173	42214	42255	42295
42174	42215	42256	42296
42175	42216	42257	42297
42176	42217	42258	42298
42177	42218	42259	42299
42178	42219		

*Nos. 42300–94 FOWLER LOCOS.

42300	42303	42306	42309
42301	42304	42307	42310
42302	42305	42308	42311

42312	42333	42354	42375
42313	42334	42355	42376
42314	42335	42356	42377
42315	42336	42357	42378
42316	42337	42358	42379
42317	42338	42359	42380
42318	42339	42360	42381
42319	42340	42361	42382
42320	42341	42362	42383
42321	42342	42363	42384
42322	42343	42364	42385
42323	42344	42365	42386
42324	42345	42366	42387
42325	42346	42367	42388
42326	42347	42368	42389
42327	42348	42369	42390
42328	42349	42370	42391
42329	42350	42371	42392
42330	42351	42372	42393
42331	42352	42373	42394
42332	42353	42374	

†Nos. 42395–42424 FOWLER LOCOS. WITH SIDE-WINDOW CAB.

42395	42403	42411	42418
42396	42404	42412	42419
42397	42405	42413	42420
42398	42406	42414	42421
42399	42407	42415	42422
42400	42408	42416	42423
42401	42409	42417	42424
42402	42410		

§Nos. 42425–94 STANIER 2-CYL LOCOS.

42425	42436	42447	42458
42426	42437	42448	42459
42427	42438	42449	42460
42428	42439	42450	42461
42429	42440	42451	42462
42430	42441	42452	42463
42431	42442	42453	42464
42432	42443	42454	42465
42433	42444	42455	42466
42434	42445	42456	42467
42435	42446	42457	42468

42469–42755

42469	42476	42483	42489
42470	42477	42484	42490
42471	42478	42485	42491
42472	42479	42486	42492
42473	42480	42487	42493
42474	42481	42488	42494
42475	42482		

‡Nos. 42500–36 STANIER 3·CYL. LOCOS.

42500	42510	42519	42528
42501	42511	42520	42529
42502	42512	42521	42530
42503	42513	42522	42531
42504	42514	42523	42532
42505	42515	42524	42533
42506	42516	42525	42534
42507	42517	42526	42535
42508	42518	42527	42536
42509			

§Nos. 42537–42672 STANIER 2·CYL. LOCOS.

42537	42560	42583	42606
42538	42561	42584	42607
42539	42562	42585	42608
42540	42563	42586	42609
42541	42564	42587	42610
42542	42565	42588	42611
42543	42566	42589	42612
42544	42567	42590	42613
42545	42568	42591	42614
42546	42569	42592	42615
42547	42570	42593	42616
42548	42571	42594	42617
42549	42572	42595	42618
42550	42573	42596	42619
42551	42574	42597	42620
42552	42575	42598	42621
42553	42576	42599	42622
42554	42577	42600	42623
42555	42578	42601	42624
42556	42579	42602	42625
42557	42580	42603	42626
42558	42581	42604	42627
42559	42582	42605	42628

42629	42640	42651	42662
42630	42641	42652	42663
42631	42642	42653	42664
42632	42643	42654	42665
42633	42644	42655	42666
42634	42645	42656	42667
42635	42646	42657	42668
42636	42647	42658	42669
42637	42648	42659	42670
42638	42649	42660	42671
42639	42650	42661	42672

¶Nos. 42673–99 FAIRBURN LOCOS.

42673	42680	42687	42694
42674	42681	42688	42695
42675	42682	42689	42696
42676	42683	42690	42697
42677	42684	42691	42698
42678	42685	42692	42699
42679	42686	42693	

Total **645**

2-6-0　　　　　　　**5MT**

Introduced 1926. Hughes L.M.S. design built under Fowler's direction. With Walschaerts Valve Gear and P.V.
*Introduced 1931. Locos. rebuilt experimentally with Lentz R.C. poppet valves.
Weight : Loco. 66 tons 0 cwt.
Pressure : 180 lb. Su.
Cyls. : (O) 21″ × 26″.
Dr. Wheels : 5′ 6″.　　T.E. : 26,580 lb.

42700	42714	42728	42742
42701	42715	42729	42743
42702	42716	42730	42744
42703	42717	42731	42745
42704	42718	42732	42746
42705	42719	42733	42747
42706	42720	42734	42748
42707	42721	42735	42749
42708	42722	42736	42750
42709	42723	42737	42751
42710	42724	42738	42752
42711	42725	42739	42753
42712	42726	42740	42754
42713	42727	42741	42755

Top to bottom : Class 3MT (Stanier) 2–6–2T No. 40204 ; Class 3MT (Fowler) 2–6–2T No. 40024 (Condensing) ; Class 3MT (Fowler) 2–6–2T No. 40021 (with outside steampipe) ; Class 2MT 2–6–2T No. 41262

This page—*Above* : Class 2P (M.R.) 4–4–0 No. 40562. *Below* : Class 2P (L.M.S.) 4–4–0 No. 40688. *Right upper* : Class 0F 0–4–0T No. 41536. *Right lower* : Class 2F 0–6–0T No. 47166.
[P. Ransome-Wallis, E. Treacy, H. C. Casserley, P. J. Truscott

Facing page—*Left* : Class 7F 2–8–0s No. 53808 (with large boiler) and 53804. *Right upper* : Class 4P 4–4–0 No. 41030. *Right lower* : Class 3P 4–4–0 No. 40741.
[H. C. Casserley (2), J. Davenport, L.G.R.P. 23297

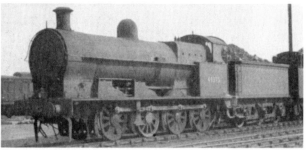

Top to bottom: 2–6–0
+ 0–6–2 No. 47979 ;
0–10–0 No. 58100 ;
Class 7F (G2a) 0–8–0
No. 49375 ; Class 7F
0–8–0 No. 49592

[R. E. Vincent (2),
H. C. Casserley,
B. W. Brooksbank

Class 5MT (Caprotti) 4–6–0 No. 44738   [*F. F. Moss*

Class 4F 0–6–0 No. 44442   [*P. Ransome-Wallis*

Class 4F (ex-S. & D.J.) 0–6–0 No. 44559   [*H. C. Casserley*

Top to bottom:

Class 7P 4–6–0 No. 461
Lancashire Fusilier; Cla
8P 4–6–2 No. 462
Princess Elizabeth ; Cla
8P 4–6–2 No. 46255 C
of Hereford

[W. J. Reynol
C. R. L. Coles, E. Tree

42756	42802	42848	42894	42940	42942	42943	42944
42757	42803	42849	42895	42941			Total 245

2-6-0   5MT

Introduced 1933. Stanier L.M.S. taper boiler design.
Weight : Loco. 69 tons 2 cwt.
Pressure : 225 lb. Su.
Cyls. : (O) 18″×28″.
Dr. Wheels : 5′ 6″.   T.E. : 26,290 lb.
Walschaerts Valve Gear P.V.

42758	42804	42850	42896				
42759	42805	42851	42897				
42760	42806	42852	42893	42945	42955	42965	42975
42761	42807	42853	42899	42946	42956	42966	42976
42762	42808	42854	42900	42947	42957	42967	42977
42763	42809	42855	42901	42948	42958	42968	42978
42764	42810	42856	42902	42949	42959	42969	42979
42765	42811	42357	42903	42950	42960	42970	42980
42766	42812	42858	42904	42951	42961	42971	42981
42767	42813	42859	42905	42952	42962	42972	42982
42768	42814	42860	42906	42953	42963	42973	42983
42769	42815	42861	42907	42954	42964	42974	42984

Total 40

42770	42816	42862	42908				
42771	42817	42863	42909				
42772	42818*	42864	42910				
42773	42819	42865	42911				

2-6-0   4MT

Introduced 1947. Ivatt L.M.S. taper boiler design.
*Introduced 1949, with single chimney.
Weight : Loco. 59 tons 2 cwt.
Pressure : 225 lb. Su.
Cyls. : (O) 17½″×26″.
Dr. Wheels : 5′ 3″.   T.E. : 24,170 lb.
Walschaerts Valve Gear P.V.

42774	42820	42866	42912	43000	43018	43036	43054*
42775	42821	42867	42913	43001	43019	43037	43055*
42776	42822*	42868	42914	43002	43020	43038	43056*
42777	42823	42869	42915	43003	43021	43039	43057*
42778	42824*	42870	42916	43004	43022	43040	43058*
42779	42825*	42871	42917	43005	43023	43041	43059*
42780	42826	42872	42918	43006	43024	43042	43060*
42781	42827	42873	42919	43007	43025	43043	43061*
42782	42828	42874	42920	43008	43026	43044	43062*
42783	42829*	42875	42921	43009	43027*	43045	43063*
42784	42830	42876	42922	43010	43028	43046	43064*
42785	42831	42877	42923	43011	43029	43047	43065*
42786	42832	42878	42924	43012	43030	43048	43066*
42787	42833	42879	42925	43013	43031	43049	43067*
42788	42834	42880	42926	43014	43032	43050*	43068*
42789	42835	42881	42927	43015	43033	43051*	43069*
42790	42836	42882	42928	43016	43034	43052*	43070*
42791	42837	42883	42929	43017	43035	43053*	43071*
42792	42838	42884	42930				
42793	42839	42835	42931				
42794	42840	42886	42932				
42795	42841	42887	42933				
42796	42842	42888	42934				
42797	42843	42889	42935				
42798	42844	42890	42936				
42799	42845	42891	42937				
42800	42846	42892	42938				
42801	42847	42893	42939				

43072*	43095*	43118*	43140*
43073*	43096*	43119*	43141*
43074*	43097*	43120*	43142*
43075*	43098*	43121*	43143*
43076*	43099*	43122*	43144*
43077*	43100*	43123*	43145*
43078*	43101*	43124*	43146*
43079*	43102*	43125*	43147*
43080*	43103*	43126*	43148*
43081*	43104*	43127*	43149*
43082*	43105*	43128*	43150*
43083*	43106*	43129*	43151*
43084*	43107*	43130*	43152*
43085*	43108*	43131*	43153*
43086*	43109*	43132*	43154*
43087*	43110*	43133*	43155*
43088*	43111*	43134*	43156*
43089*	43112*	43135*	43157*
43090*	43113*	43136*	43158*
43091*	43114*	43137*	43159*
43092*	43115*	43138*	43160*
43093*	43116*	43139*	43161*
43094*	43117*		

N.B.—Locos. of this class are still being delivered.

0-6-0 3F

Introduced 1885. Johnson Midland locos., rebuilt from 1920 by Fowler with Belpaire boilers.
Weight : Loco. 43 tons 17 cwt.
Pressure : 175 lb.
Cyls. : 18″ × 26″.
Dr. Wheels : 4′ 11″. T.E. : 21,240 lb.

43137	**43180**	43185	43188
43174	**43181**	43186	43189
43178	**43183**	43187	

Total 11

0-6-0 3F

Introduced 1885. Johnson Midland locos., rebuilt from 1916 by Fowler with Belpaire boilers.
*Introduced 1896. Locos. built for S. & D.J. (taken into L.M.S. stock 1930).
Weight : Loco. 43 tons 17 cwt.
Pressure : 175 lb.
Cyls. : 18″ × 26″.
Dr. Wheels : 5′ 3″. T.E. : 19,890 lb.

43191	43254	43324	43401
43192	43256	43325	43402
43193	43257	43326	43405
43194*	43258	43327	43406
43200	43259	43329	43410
43201*	43261	43330	43411
43203	43263	43331	43419
43204*	43266	43332	43427
43205	43267	43333	43428
43207	43268	43334	43429
43208	43271	43335	43431
43210	43273	43336	43433
43211*	43274	43337	43435
43212	43275	43339	43436
43213	43277	43340	43440
43214	43278	43341	43441
43216*	43281	43342	43443
43218*	43282	43344	43444
43219	43283	43351	43446
43222	43284	43355	43448
43223	43286	43356	43449
43224	43287	43357	43453
43225	43290	43359	43454
43226	43292	43361	43456
43228*	43293	43364	43457
43231	43294	43367	43459
43232	43295	43368	43462
43233	43296	43369	43463
43234	43298	43370	43464
43235	43299	43371	43468
43237	43300	43373	43469
43239	43301	43374	43474
43240	43305	43378	43475
43241	43306	43379	43482
43242	43307	43381	43484
43243	43308	43386	43490
43244	43309	43387	43491
43245	43310	43388	43494
43246	43312	43389	43496
43247	43313	43392	43497
43248*	43314	43394	43499
43249	43315	43395	43502
43250	43317	43396	43506
43251	43318	43398	43507
43252	43321	43399	43509
43253	43323	43400	43510

43514	43594	43653	43715
43515	43595	43656	43717
43520	43596	43657	43721
43521	43598	43658	43723
43522	43599	43660	43727
43523	43600	43661	43728
43524	43604	43662	43729
43529	43605	43664	43731
43531	43607	43665	43734
43538	43608	43667	43735
43540	43612	43668	43737
43544	43615	43669	43742
43546	43618	43673	43745
43548	43619	43674	43747
43550	43620	43675	43748
43553	43621	43676	43749
43558	43622	43678	43751
43562	43623	43679	43753
43565	43624	43680	43754
43568	43627	43681	43755
43570	43629	43682	43756
43572	43630	43683	43757
43574	43631	43684	43759
43575	43633	43686	43760
43578	43634	43687	43762
43579	43636	43690	43763
43580	43637	43693	43765
43581	43638	43698	43766
43582	43639	43705	43767
43583	43644	43709	43770
43584	43645	43710	43771
43585	43650	43711	43773
43586	43651	43712	
43587	43652	43714	
43593			

Total 320

0-6-0   3F

Introduced 1906. Deeley Midland design, rebuilt by Fowler with Belpaire boiler.
Weight : Loco. 46 tons 3 cwt.
Pressure : 175 lb.
Cyls. : $18\frac{1}{2}'' \times 26''$.
Dr. Wheels : 5' 3".   T.E. : 21,010 lb.

43775	43777	43779	43782
43776	43778	43781	43784

43785	43798	43810	43824
43786	43799	43812	43825
43787	43800	43814	43826
43789	43801	43815	43828
43790	43803	43817	43829
43791	43804	43819	43832
43792	43806	43820	43833
43793	43807	43821	
43795	43808	43822	
43797	43809	43823	

Total 45

0-6-0   4F

Introduced 1911. Fowler superheated Midland design.
Weight : 48 tons 15 cwt.
Pressure : 175 lb. Su.
Cyls. : $20'' \times 26''$.
Dr. Wheels : 5' 3".   T.E. : 24,555 lb.
P.V.

43835	43862	43889	43916
43836	43863	43890	43917
43837	43864	43891	43918
43838	43865	43892	43919
43839	43866	43893	43920
43840	43867	43894	43921
43841	43868	43895	43922
43842	43869	43896	43923
43843	43870	43897	43924
43844	43871	43898	43925
43845	43872	43899	43926
43846	43873	43900	43927
43847	43874	43901	43928
43848	43875	43902	43929
43849	43876	43903	43930
43850	43877	43904	43931
43851	43878	43905	43932
43852	43879	43906	43933
43853	43880	43907	43934
43854	43881	43908	43935
43855	43882	43909	43936
43856	43883	43910	43937
43857	43884	43911	43938
43858	43885	43912	43939
43859	43886	43913	43940
43860	43887	43914	43941
43861	43888	43915	43942

43943	43964	43985	44006	44075	44121	44167	44213
43944	43965	43986	44007	44076	44122	44168	44214
43945	43966	43987	44008	44077	44123	44169	44215
43946	43967	43988	44009	44078	44124	44170	44216
43947	43968	43989	44010	44079	44125	44171	44217
43948	43969	43990	44011	44080	44126	44172	44218
43949	43970	43991	44012	44081	44127	44173	44219
43950	43971	43992	44013	44082	44128	44174	44220
43951	43972	43993	44014	44083	44129	44175	44221
43952	43973	43994	44015	44084	44130	44176	44222
43953	43974	43995	44016	44085	44131	44177	44223
43954	43975	43996	44017	44086	44132	44178	44224
43955	43976	43997	44018	44087	44133	44179	44225
43956	43977	43998	44019	44088	44134	44180	44226
43957	43978	43999	44020	44089	44135	44181	44227
43958	43979	44000	44021	44090	44136	44182	44228
43959	43980	44001	44022	44091	44137	44183	44229
43960	43981	44002	44023	44092	44138	44184	44230
43961	43982	44003	44024	44093	44139	44185	44231
43962	43983	44004	44025	44094	44140	44186	44232
43963	43984	44005	44026	44095	44141	44187	44233

Total 192

0-6-0   4F

Introduced 1924. Post-grouping development of Midland design with reduced boiler mountings.
*Introduced 1922. Locos. built for S.D. & J.R. to M.R. design (taken into L.M.S. stock, 1930).
Weight : Loco. 48 tons 15 cwt.
Pressure : 175 lb. Su.
Cyls. : 20″×26″.
Dr. Wheels : 5′ 3″.   T.E. : 24,555 lb
P.V.

44027	44039	44051	44063	44096	44142	44188	44234
44028	44040	44052	44064	44097	44143	44189	44235
44029	44041	44053	44065	44098	44144	44190	44236
44030	44042	44054	44066	44099	44145	44191	44237
44031	44043	44055	44067	44100	44146	44192	44238
44032	44044	44056	44068	44101	44147	44193	44239
44033	44045	44057	44069	44102	44148	44194	44240
44034	44046	44058	44070	44103	44149	44195	44241
44035	44047	44059	44071	44104	44150	44196	44242
44036	44048	44060	44072	44105	44151	44197	44243
44037	44049	44061	44073	44106	44152	44198	44244
44038	44050	44062	44074	44107	44153	44199	44245
				44108	44154	44200	44246
				44109	44155	44201	44247
				44110	44156	44202	44248
				44111	44157	44203	44249
				44112	44158	44204	44250
				44113	44159	44205	44251
				44114	44160	44206	44252
				44115	44161	44207	44253
				44116	44162	44208	44254
				44117	44163	44209	44255
				44118	44164	44210	44256
				44119	44165	44211	44257
				44120	44166	44212	44258

44259	44305	44351	44397	44443	44484	44525	44566
44260	44306	44352	44398	44444	44485	44526	44567
44261	44307	44353	44399	44445	44486	44527	44568
44262	44308	44354	44400	44446	44487	44528	44569
44263	44309	44355	44401	44447	44488	44529	44570
44264	44310	44356	44402	44448	44489	44530	44571
44265	44311	44357	44403	44449	44490	44531	44572
44266	44312	44358	44404	44450	44491	44532	44573
44267	44313	44359	44405	44451	44492	44533	44574
44268	44314	44360	44406	44452	44493	44534	44575
44269	44315	44361	44407	44453	44494	44535	44576
44270	44316	44362	44408	44454	44495	44536	44577
44271	44317	44363	44409	44455	44496	44537	44578
44272	44318	44364	44410	44456	44497	44538	44579
44273	44319	44365	44411	44457	44498	44539	44580
44274	44320	44366	44412	44458	44499	44540	44581
44275	44321	44367	44413	44459	44500	44541	44582
44276	44322	44368	44414	44460	44501	44542	44583
44277	44323	44369	44415	44461	44502	44543	44584
44278	44324	44370	44416	44462	44503	44544	44585
44279	44325	44371	44417	44463	44504	44545	44586
44280	44326	44372	44418	44464	44505	44546	44587
44281	44327	44373	44419	44465	44506	44547	44588
44282	44328	44374	44420	44466	44507	44548	44589
44283	44329	44375	44421	44467	44508	44549	44590
44284	44330	44376	44422	44468	44509	44550	44591
44285	44331	44377	44423	44469	44510	44551	44592
44286	44332	44378	44424	44470	44511	44552	44593
44287	44333	44379	44425	44471	44512	44553	44594
44288	44334	44380	44426	44472	44513	44554	44595
44289	44335	44381	44427	44473	44514	44555	44596
44290	44336	44382	44428	44474	44515	44556	44597
44291	44337	44383	44429	44475	44516	44557*	44598
44292	44338	44384	44430	44476	44517	44558*	44599
44293	44339	44385	44431	44477	44518	44559*	44600
44294	44340	44386	44432	44478	44519	44560*	44601
44295	44341	44387	44433	44479	44520	44561*	44602
44296	44342	44388	44434	44480	44521	44562	44603
44297	44343	44389	44435	44481	44522	44563	44604
44298	44344	44390	44436	44482	44523	44564	44605
44299	44345	44391	44437	44483	44524	44565	44606
44300	44346	44392	44438				
44301	44347	44393	44439				Total 580
44302	44348	44394	44440				
44303	44349	44395	44441				
44304	44350	44396	44442				

4-6-0   5MT

Introduced 1934. Stanier L.M.S. taper
boiler design.

Experimental locomotives :—
1. Introduced 1947. Stephenson link
   motion (outside), Timken roller
   bearings, double chimney.
2. Introduced 1948. Caprotti Valve
   Gear.
3. Introduced 1948. Caprotti Valve
   Gear, Timken roller bearings.
4. Introduced 1948. Caprotti Valve
   Gear, Timken roller bearings,
   double chimney.
5. Introduced 1948. Timken roller
   bearings.
6. Introduced 1948. Timken roller
   bearings, double chimney.
7. Introduced 1949. Fitted with steel
   firebox.
8. Introduced 1950. Skefco roller
   bearings.
9. Introduced 1950. Timken roller
   bearing on driving coupled axle
   only.
10. Introduced 1950. Skefco roller
    bearings on driving coupled axle
    only.
11. Introduced 1951. Caprotti valve
    gear, Skefco roller bearings.

Weights : Loco. $\begin{cases} \text{72 tons 2 cwt.} \\ \text{75 tons 6 cwt.(1, 5, 6,} \\ \text{8, 9, 10).} \\ \text{74 tons 0 cwt.(2, 3, 4,} \\ \text{11).} \\ \text{72 tons 2 cwt. (7).} \end{cases}$

Pressure : 225 lb. Su.
Cyls. : (O) 18½″×28″.
Dr. Wheels : 6′ 0″.   T.E. : 25,455 lb.
Walschaerts Valve Gear, and P.V. except
where otherwise shown.

44658	44671[10]	44684[8]	44697[9]
44659	44672[10]	44685[8]	44698
44660	44673[10]	44686[11]	44699
44661	44674[10]	44687[11]	44700
44662	44675[10]	44688[9]	44701
44663	44676[10]	44689[9]	44702
44664	44677[10]	44690[9]	44703
44665	44678[8]	44691[9]	44704
44666	44679[8]	44692[9]	44705
44667	44680[8]	44693[9]	44706
44668[10]	44681[8]	44694[9]	44707
44669[10]	44682[8]	44695[9]	44708
44670[10]	44683[8]	44696[9]	44709

44710	44756[4]	44802	44848
44711	44757[4]	44803	44849
44712	44758[5]	44804	44850
44713	44759[5]	44805	44851
44714	44760[5]	44806	44852
44715	44761[5]	44807	44853
44716	44762[5]	44808	44854
44717	44763[5]	44809	44855
44718[7]	44764[5]	44810	44856
44719[7]	44765[6]	44811	44857
44720[7]	44766[6]	44812	44858
44721[7]	44767[1]	44813	44859
44722[7]	44768	44814	44860
44723[7]	44769	44815	44861
44724[7]	44770	44816	44862
44725[7]	44771	44817	44863
44726[7]	44772	44818	44864
44727[7]	44773	44819	44865
44728	44774	44820	44866
44729	44775	44821	44867
44730	44776	44822	44868
44731	44777	44823	44869
44732	44778	44824	44870
44733	44779	44825	44871
44734	44780	44826	44872
44735	44781	44827	44873
44736	44782	44828	44874
44737	44783	44829	44875
44738[2]	44784	44830	44876
44739[2]	44785	44831	44877
44740[2]	44786	44832	44878
44741[2]	44787	44833	44879
44742[2]	44788	44834	44880
44743[2]	44789	44835	44881
44744[2]	44790	44836	44882
44745[2]	44791	44837	44883
44746[2]	44792	44838	44884
44747[2]	44793	44839	44885
44748[3]	44794	44840	44886
44749[3]	44795	44841	44887
44750[3]	44796	44842	44888
44751[3]	44797	44843	44889
44752[3]	44798	44844	44890
44753[3]	44799	44845	44891
44754[3]	44800	44846	44892
44755[4]	44801	44847	44893

44894	44934	44974	45014	45054	45095	45136	45177
44895	44935	44975	45015	45055	45096	45137	45178
44896	44936	44976	45016	45056	45097	45138	45179
44897	44937	44977	45017	45057	45098	45139	45180
44898	44938	44978	45018	45058	45099	45140	45181
44899	44939	44979	45019	45059	45100	45141	45182
44900	44940	44980	45020	45060	45101	45142	45183
44901	44941	44981	45021	45061	45102	45143	45184
44902	44942	44982	45022	45062	45103	45144	45185
44903	44943	44983	45023	45063	45104	45145	45186
44904	44944	44984	45024	45064	45105	45146	45187
44905	44945	44985	45025	45065	45106	45147	45188
44906	44946	44986	45026	45066	45107	45148	45189
44907	44947	44987	45027	45067	45108	45149	45190
44908	44948	44988	45028	45068	45109	45150	45191
44909	44949	44989	45029	45069	45110	45151	45192
44910	44950	44990	45030	45070	45111	45152	45193
44911	44951	44991	45031	45071	45112	45153	45194
44912	44952	44992	45032	45072	45113	45154 [1]	45195
44913	44953	44993	45033	45073	45114	45155	45196
44914	44954	44994	45034	45074	45115	45156 [1]	45197
44915	44955	44995	45035	45075	45116	45157 [1]	45198
44916	44956	44996	45036	45076	45117	45158 [1]	45199
44917	44957	44997	45037	45077	45118	45159	45200
44918	44958	44998	45038	45078	45119	45160	45201
44919	44959	44999	45039	45079	45120	45161	45202
44920	44960	45000	45040	45080	45121	45162	45203
44921	44961	45001	45041	45081	45122	45163	45204
44922	44962	45002	45042	45082	45123	45164	45205
44923	44963	45003	45043	45083	45124	45165	45206
44924	44964	45004	45044	45084	45125	45166	45207
44925	44965	45005	45045	45085	45126	45167	45208
44926	44966	45006	45046	45086	45127	45168	45209
44927	44967	45007	45047	45087	45128	45169	45210
44928	44968	45008	45048	45088	45129	45170	45211
44929	44969	45009	45049	45089	45130	45171	45212
44930	44970	45010	45050	45090	45131	45172	45213
44931	44971	45011	45051	45091	45132	45173	45214
44932	44972	45012	45052	45092	45133	45174	45215
44933	44973	45013	45053	45093	45134	45175	45216
				45094	45135	45176	45217

NOTE

To understand the system of reference marks used in this book it is essential to read the notes on page 9.

[1] NAMES :

45154 Lanarkshire Yeomanry.
45156 Ayrshire Yeomanry.
45157 The Glasgow Highlander.
45158 Glasgow Yeomanry.

31

45218	45264	45310	45356	45402	45427	45452	45476
45219	45265	45311	45357	45403	45428	45453	45477
45220	45266	45312	45258	45404	45429	45454	45478
45221	45267	45313	45359	45405	45430	45455	45479
45222	45268	45314	45360	45406	45431	45456	45480
45223	45269	45315	45361	45407	45432	45457	45481
45224	45270	45316	45362	45408	45433	45458	45482
45225	45271	45317	45363	45409	45434	45459	45483
45226	45272	45318	45364	45410	45435	45460	45484
45227	45273	45319	45365	45411	45436	45461	45485
45228	45274	45320	45366	45412	45437	45462	45486
45229	45275	45321	45367	45413	45438	45463	45487
45230	45276	45322	45368	45414	45439	45464	45488
45231	45277	45323	45369	45415	45440	45465	45489
45232	45278	45324	45370	45416	45441	45466	45490
45233	45279	45325	45371	45417	45442	45467	45491
45234	45280	45326	45372	45418	45443	45468	45492
45235	45281	45327	45373	45419	45444	45469	45493
45236	45282	45328	45374	45420	45445	45470	45494
45237	45283	45329	45375	45421	45446	45471	45495
45238	45284	45330	45376	45422	45447	45472	45496
45239	45285	45331	45377	45423	45448	45473	45497
45240	45286	45332	45378	45424	45449	45474	45498
45241	45287	45333	45379	45425	45450	45475	45499
45242	45288	45334	45380	45426	45451		
45243	45289	45335	45381				
45244	45290	45336	45382				
45245	45291	45337	45383				
45246	45292	45338	45384				
45247	45293	45339	45385				
45248	45294	45340	45386				
45249	45295	45341	45387				
45250	45296	45342	45388				
45251	45297	45343	45389				
45252	45298	45344	45390				
45253	45299	45345	45391				
45254	45300	45346	45392				
45255	45301	45347	45393				
45256	45302	45348	45394				
45257	45303	45349	45395				
45258	45304	45350	45396				
45259	45305	45351	45397				
45260	45306	45352	45398				
45261	45307	45353	45399				
45262	45308	45354	45400				
45263	45309	45355	45401				

Total 842

4-6-0 " Patriot " 6P & 7P

*6P Introduced 1930. Fowler 3-cyl-rebuild of L.N.W. " Claughton " Class (introduced 1912), retaining original wheels and other details.

Remainder. Introduced 1933. New locos. to Fowler design (45502–41 were officially considered as rebuilds).

†7P Introduced 1946. Ivatt rebuild of Fowler locos. with large taper boiler, new cylinders and double chimney.

Weight : Loco. $\begin{cases} 80 & \text{tons} \quad 15 \quad \text{cwt.*} \\ 82 & \text{tons} \quad 0 \quad \text{cwt.†} \end{cases}$

Pressure : $\begin{cases} 200 \text{ lb. Su.*} \\ 250 \text{ lb. Su.†} \end{cases}$

Cyls. : $\begin{cases} (3) \ 18'' \times 26''* \\ (3) \ 17'' \times 26''† \end{cases}$
Dr. Wheels : 6′ 9″.

T.E. : $\begin{cases} 26,520 \text{ lb.*} \\ 29,570 \text{ lb.†} \end{cases}$
Walschaerts Valve Gear P.V.

45500*Patriot
45501*St. Dunstan's
45502 Royal Naval Division
45503 The Royal Leicestershire
      Regiment
45504 Royal Signals
45505 The Royal Army
      Ordnance Corps
45506 The Royal Pioneer Corps
45507 Royal Tank Corps
45508
45509
45510
45511 Isle of Man
45512†Bunsen
45513
45514†Holyhead
45515 Caernarvon
45516 The Bedfordshire and
      Hertfordshire Regiment.
45517
45518 Bradshaw
45519 Lady Godiva
45520 Llandudno
45521†Rhyl
45522†Prestatyn
45523†Bangor
45524 Blackpool
45525†Colwyn Bay
45526†Morecambe and Heysham
45527†Southport
45528†
45529†Stephenson
45530†Sir Frank Ree
45531†Sir Frederick Harrison
45532†Illustrious
45533 Lord Rathmore
45534†E. Tootal Broadhurst
45535†Sir Herbert Walker,
      K.C.B.
45536†Private W. Wood, V.C.
45537 Private E. Sykes, V.C.
45538 Giggleswick
45539 E. C. Trench
45540†Sir Robert Turnbull
45541 Duke of Sutherland

45542
45543 Home Guard
45544
45545†Planet
45546 Fleetwood
45547
45548 Lytham St. Annes
45549
45550
45551

Total 52

"Jubilee" Class

4-6-0   **6P & 7P**

6P Introduced 1934. Stanier L.M.S. taper boiler development of the "Patriot" class.

*Introduced 1936. Boiler fitted with double chimney. Double chimney fitted to 45742 in 1940.

†**7P** Introduced 1942. Rebuilt with larger boiler and double chimney.

Weight : Loco. : $\begin{cases} 79 \text{ tons } 11 \text{ cwt.} \\ 82 \text{ tons } 0 \text{ cwt.}† \end{cases}$

Pressure : $\begin{cases} 225 \text{ lb. Su.} \\ 250 \text{ lb. Su.}† \end{cases}$

Cyls. : 17"×26".
Dr. Wheels : 6' 9".

T.E. : $\begin{cases} 26,610 \text{ lb.} \\ 29,570 \text{ lb.}† \end{cases}$

Walschaerts Valve Gear. P.V.

45552 Silver Jubilee
45553 Canada
45554 Ontario
45555 Quebec
45556 Nova Scotia
45557 New Brunswick
45558 Manitoba
45559 British Columbia
45560 Prince Edward Island
45561 Saskatchewan
45562 Alberta
45563 Australia
45564 New South Wales
45565 Victoria

45566 Queensland	45612 Jamaica
45567 South Australia	45613 Kenya
45568 Western Australia	45614 Leeward Islands
45569 Tasmania	45615 Malay States
45570 New Zealand	45616 Malta G.C.
45571 South Africa	45617 Mauritius
45572 Eire	45618 New Hebrides
45573 Newfoundland	45619 Nigeria
45574 India	45620 North Borneo
45575 Madras	45621 Northern Rhodesia
45576 Bombay	45622 Nyasaland
45577 Bengal	45623 Palestine
45578 United Provinces	45624 St. Helena
45579 Punjab	45625 Sarawak
45580 Burma	45626 Seychelles
45581 Bihar and Orissa	45627 Sierra Leone
45582 Central Provinces	45628 Somaliland
45583 Assam	45629 Straits Settlements
45584 North West Frontier	45630 Swaziland
45585 Hyderabad	45631 Tanganyika
45586 Mysore	45632 Tonga
45587 Baroda	45633 Aden
45588 Kashmir	45634 Trinidad
45589 Gwalior	45635 Tobago
45590 Travancore	45636 Uganda
45591 Udaipur	45637 Windward Islands
45592 Indore	45638 Zanzibar
45593 Kolhapur	45639 Raleigh
45594 Bhopal	45640 Frobisher
45595 Southern Rhodesia	45641 Sandwich
45596 Bahamas	45642 Boscawen
45597 Barbados	45643 Rodney
45598 Basutoland	45644 Howe
45599 Bechuanaland	45645 Collingwood
45600 Bermuda	45646 Napier
45601 British Guiana	45647 Sturdee
45602 British Honduras	45648 Wemyss
45603 Solomon Islands	45649 Hawkins
45604 Ceylon	45650 Blake
45605 Cyprus	45651 Shovell
45606 Falkland Islands	45652 Hawke
45607 Fiji	45653 Barham
45608 Gibraltar	45654 Hood
45609 Gilbert and Ellice Islands	45655 Keith
45610 Gold Coast	45656 Cochrane
45611 Hong Kong	45657 Tyrwhitt

45658 Keyes
45659 Drake
45660 Rooke
45661 Vernon
45662 Kempenfelt
45663 Jervis
45664 Nelson
45665 Lord Rutherford of
45666 Cornwallis   [Nelson
45667 Jellicoe
45668 Madden
45669 Fisher
45670 Howard of Effingham
45671 Prince Rupert
45672 Anson
45673 Keppel
45674 Duncan
45675 Hardy
45676 Codrington
45677 Beatty
45678 De Robeck
45679 Armada
45680 Camperdown
45681 Aboukir
45682 Trafalgar
45683 Hogue
45684 Jutland
45685 Barfleur
45686 St. Vincent
45687 Neptune
45688 Polyphemus
45689 Ajax
45690 Leander
45691 Orion
45692 Cyclops
45693 Agamemnon
45694 Bellerophon
45695 Minotaur
45696 Arethusa
45697 Achilles
45698 Mars
45699 Galatea
45700
45701 Conqueror
45702 Colossus
45703 Thunderer

45704 Leviathan
45705 Seahorse
45706 Express
45707 Valiant
45708 Resolution
45709 Implacable
45710 Irresistible
45711 Courageous
45712 Victory
45713 Renown
45714 Revenge
45715 Invincible
45716 Swiftsure
45717 Dauntless
45718 Dreadnought
45719 Glorious
45720 Indomitable
45721 Impregnable
45722 Defence
45723 Fearless
45724 Warspite
45725 Repulse
45726 Vindictive
45727 Inflexible
45728 Defiance
45729 Furious
45730 Ocean
45731 Perseverance
45732 Sanspareil
45733 Novelty
45734 Meteor
45735†Comet
45736†Phoenix
45737 Atlas
45738 Samson
45739 Ulster
45740 Munster
45741 Leinster
45742*Connaught

Total 191

```
For full details of
BRITISH  RAILWAYS  CLASS
" WD " 2-8-0s
see the
A.B.C. OF BRITISH RAILWAYS
LOCOMOTIVES  PT. IV.
```

" Royal Scot " Class

4-6-0   7P

Introduced 1927. Fowler L.M.S. parallel boiler design.

*Introduced 1935. Stanier taper boiler rebuild with simple cyls. of experimental high pressure loco. No. 6399 *Fury*.

†Introduced 1943. Stanier rebuild of Fowler locos. with taper boiler, new cyls. and double chimney.

Weight : Loco.
$\begin{cases} 84 \text{ tons } 18 \text{ cwt.} \\ 84 \text{ tons } 1 \text{ cwt.*} \\ 83 \text{ tons†} \end{cases}$

Pressure : 250 lb. Su.

Cyls. : (3) $18'' \times 26''$.

Dr. Wheels : 6' 9".   T.E. : 33,150 lb.

Walschaerts Valve Gear. P.V.

46100†Royal Scot
46101†Royal Scots Grey
46102†Black Watch
46103†Royal Scots Fusilier
46104†Scottish Borderer
46105†Cameron Highlander
46106†Gordon Highlander
46107†Argyll and Sutherland Highlander
46108†Seaforth Highlander
46109†Royal Engineer
46110 Grenadier Guardsman
46111†Royal Fusilier
46112†Sherwood Forester
46113†Cameronian
46114†Coldstream Guardsman
46115†Scots Guardsman
46116†Irish Guardsman
46117†Welsh Guardsman
46118†Royal Welch Fusilier
46119†Lancashire Fusilier
46120†Royal Inniskilling Fusilier
46121†Highland Light Infantry, City of Glasgow Regiment
46122†Royal Ulster Rifleman
46123†Royal Irish Fusilier
46124†London Scottish
46125†3rd Carabinier
46126†Royal Army Service Corps
46127†Old Contemptibles
46128†The Lovat Scouts
46129†The Scottish Horse
46130 The West Yorkshire Regiment
46131†The Royal Warwickshire Regiment
46132†The King's Regiment Liverpool
46133†The Green Howards
46134 The Cheshire Regiment
46135†The East Lancashire Regiment
46136†The Border Regiment
46137 The Prince of Wales's Volunteers (South Lancashire)
46138†The London Irish Rifleman
46139†The Welch Regiment
46140 The King's Royal Rifle Corps
46141†The North Staffordshire Regiment
46142 The York & Lancaster Regiment
46143†The South Staffordshire Regiment
46144†Honourable Artillery Company
46145†The Duke of Wellington's Regt. (West Riding)
46146†The Rifle Brigade
46147†The Northamptonshire Regiment
46148 The Manchester Regiment
46149†The Middlesex Regiment
46150†The Life Guardsman
46151 The Royal Horse Guardsman
46152†The King's Dragoon Guardsman

46153†The Royal Dragoon
46154†The Hussar
46155†The Lancer
46156 The South Wales Borderer
46157†The Royal Artilleryman
46158†The Loyal Regiment
46159†The Royal Air Force
46160†Queen Victoria's Rifleman
46161†King's Own
46162†Queen's Westminster Rifleman
46163 Civil Service Rifleman
46164 The Artists' Rifleman
46165 The Ranger (12tn London Regt.)
46166†London Rifle Brigade
46167†The Hertfordshire Regiment
46168†The Girl Guide
46169†The Boy Scout
46170*British Legion   Total 71

46200*The Princess Royal
46201*Princess Elizabeth
46202†
46203 Princess Margaret Rose
46204 Princess Louise
46205 Princess Victoria
46206 Princess Marie Louise
46207 Princess Arthur of Connaught
46208 Princess Helena Victoria
46209 Princess Beatrice
46210 Lady Patricia
46211 Queen Maud
46212 Duchess of Kent   Total 13

"Princess Coronation" Class
4-6-2   8P

Introduced 1938. Stanier L.M.S. enlargement of "Princess Royal" class. All except Nos. 46230–4/49–55 originally streamlined (introduced 1937. Streamlining removed from 1946).
*Introduced 1947. Ivatt development with roller bearings and detail alterations.

Weight : { 105 tons 5 cwt.
106 tons 8 cwt.*

Pressure : 250 lb. Su.

Cyls. : (4) 16¼″ × 28″.

Dr. Wheels : 6′ 9″.   T.E. : 40,000 lb.
Walschaerts Valve Gear and rocking shafts, P.V.

46220 Coronation
46221 Queen Elizabeth
46222 Queen Mary
46223 Princess Alice
46224 Princess Alexandra
46225 Duchess of Gloucester
46226 Duchess of Norfolk
46227 Duchess of Devonshire
46228 Duchess of Rutland
46229 Duchess of Hamilton
46230 Duchess of Buccleuch

"Princess Royal" Class
4-6-2   8P

*Introduced 1933. Stanier L.M.S. taper boiler design.

†Introduced 1935. Experimental turbine-driven locomotive ("Turbomotive"). (NOTE : Cyl. and T.E. figures given below do not apply to this locomotive.)

Remainder. Introduced 1935. Development of original design with alterations to valve gear, boiler and other details.

Weight : Loco. { 110 tons 11 cwt.†
104 tons 10 cwt. (remainder).

Pressure : 250 lb. Su.
Cyls. : (4) 16¼″ × 28″.
Dr. Wheels : 6′ 6″.   T.E. : 40,285 lb.
Walschaerts Valve Gear and rocking shafts, P.V.

46231 Duchess of Atholl			
46232 Duchess of Montrose			
46233 Duchess of Sutherland			
46234 Duchess of Abercorn			
46235 City of Birmingham			
46236 City of Bradford			
46237 City of Bristol			
46238 City of Carlisle			
46239 City of Chester			
46240 City of Coventry			
46241 City of Edinburgh			
46242 City of Glasgow			
46243 City of Lancaster			
46244 King George VI			
46245 City of London			
46246 City of Manchester			
46247 City of Liverpool			
46248 City of Leeds			
46249 City of Sheffield			
46250 City of Lichfield			
46251 City of Nottingham			
46252 City of Leicester			
46253 City of St. Albans			
46254 City of Stoke-on-Trent			
46255 City of Hereford			
46256*Sir William A. Stanier, F.R.S.			
46257*City of Salford			

Total 38

46432	46456	46480	46504
46433	46457	46481	46505
46434	46458	46482	46506
46435	46459	46483	46507
46436	46460	46484	46508
46437	46461	46485	46509
46438	46462	46486	46510
46439	46463	46487	46511
46440	46464	46488	46512
46441	46465	46489	46513
46442	46466	46490	46514
46443	46467	46491	46515
46444	46468	46492	46516
46445	46469	46493	46517
46446	46470	46494	46518
46447	46471	46495	46519
46448	46472	46496	46520
46449	46473	46497	46521
46450	46474	46498	46522
46451	46475	46499	46523
46452	46476	46500	46524
46453	46477	46501	46525
46454	46478	46502	46526
46455	46479	46503	46527

N.B. Locos. of this class are still being delivered.

2-6-0   2MT

Introduced 1946. Ivatt L.M.S. taper boiler design.
Weight : Loco. 47 tons 2 cwt.
Pressure : 200 lb. Su.
Cyls. : (O) 16″ × 24″.
Dr. Wheels : 5′ 0″.   T.E. : 17,410 lb.
Walschaerts Valve Gear, P.V.

46400	46408	46416	46424
46401	46409	46417	46425
46402	46410	46418	46426
46403	46411	46419	46427
46404	46412	46420	46428
46405	46413	46421	46429
46406	46414	46422	46430
46407	46415	46423	46431

2-4-2T　　　　1P

Introduced 1890. Webb L.N.W. design.
Weight : 50 tons 10 cwt.
Pressure : 150 lb.
Cyls. : 17″×24″.
Dr. Wheels : 5′ 8½″. T.E. : 12,910 lb.

Allan straight link gear.

46601	46628	46680	46712
46603	46643	46683	46727
46604	46654	46688	46749
46616	46656	46701	46757
46620	46666		

Total 18

2-4-2T　　　　2P

Introduced 1889. Aspinall L. & Y. design, sold to Wirral Rly., 1921 (loco. built 1890), and numbered by the L.M.S.R. in the ex-L.N.W.R. Series with other Wirral locos. The number 50638 in the present L. & Y. class was allotted to this engine.
Weight : 55 tons 19 cwt.
Pressure : 180 lb.
Cyls. : 17½″×26″.
Dr. Wheels : 5′ 8″. T.E. : 18,360 lb.
Joy valve gear

46762　　　　**Total 1**

0-6-2T　　　　2MT

Introduced 1898. Webb L.N.W. " 18″ Passenger tank."
Weight : 52 tons 6 cwt.
Pressure : 150 lb.
Cyls. : 18″×24″.
Dr. Wheels : 5′ 2½″. T.E. : 15,865 lb.
Joy valve gear.

46899	46906	46912	46922
46900			

Total 5

0-4-0ST　　　　0F

Introduced 1932. Kitson design prepared to Stanier's requirements for L.M.S.
Weight : 33 tons 0 cwt.
Pressure : 160 lb.
Cyls. : (O) 15½″×30″.
Dr. Wheels : 3′ 10″. T.E. : 14.205 lb.

47000	47003	47006	47008
47001	47004	47007	47009
47002	47005		

N.B. Locos. of this class are still being delivered.

0-6-0T　　　　2F

Introduced 1928. Fowler L.M.S. short-wheel-base dock tanks.
Weight : 43 tons 12 cwt.
Pressure : 160 lb.
Cyls. : (O) 17″×22″.
Dr. Wheels : 3′ 11″. T.E. : 18,400 lb.
Walschaerts Valve Gear.

47160	47163	47166	47168
47161	47164	47167	47169
47162	47165		

Total 10

0-4-0T　　　　Sentinel

Geared Sentinel locos.
*Introduced 1929. Single-speed locos. for S.D. & J. (taken into L.M.S. stock 1930).
†Introduced 1930. Two-speed locos. for L.M.S.
‡Introduced 1932. Single-speed loco. for L.M.S.
Weight : { 27 tons 15 cwt.* / 20 tons 17 cwt.† / 18 tons 18 cwt.‡
Pressure : 275 lb. Su.
Cyls. : { (4)6¾″×9″.* / 6¾″×9†‡.
Dr. Wheels : { 3′ 1½″* / 2′ 6″†‡
T.E. : { 15,500 lb.* / 11,800 lb.†‡
Poppet Valves

47180†	47182†	47184‡	47191*
47181†	47183†	47190*	

Total 7

0-6-0T   3F

'ntroduced 1899. Johnson large Midland design, rebuilt with Belpaire boiler from 1919 ; fitted with condensers for London area.

*Introduced 1899. Non-condensing 'ocos

Weight : 48 tons 15 cwt.
Pressure : 160 lb.
Cyls. : 18″×26″.
Dr. Wheels : 4′ 7″.   T.E. : 20,835 lb

47200	47215	47230*	47245
47201	47216	47231*	47246*
47202	47217	47232*	47247
47203	47218	47233*	47248*
47204	47219	47234*	47249
47205	47220	47235*	47250*
47206	47221	47236*	47251
47207	47222	47237*	47252*
47208	47223	47238*	47253*
47209	47224	47239*	47254*
47210	47225	47240	47255*
47211	47226	47241	47256*
47212	47227	47242	47257*
47213	47228	47243	47258*
47214	47229	47244	47259*

Total 60

0-6-0T   3F

Introduced 1924. Post-grouping development of Midland design with detail alterations.

*Introduced 1929. Locos. built for S. & D.J. (taken into L.M.S. stock 1930).

Weight : 49 tons 10 cwt.
Pressure : 160 lb.
Cyls. : 18″×26″.
Dr. Wheels : 4′ 7″.   T.E. : 20,835 lb.

47260	47270	47280	47290
47261	47271	47281	47291
47262	47272	47282	47292
47263	47273	47283	47293
47264	47274	47284	47294
47265	47275	47285	47295
47266	47276	47286	47296
47267	47277	47287	47297
47268	47278	47288	47298
47269	47279	47289	47299

47300	47346	47392	47438
47301	47347	47393	47439
47302	47348	47394	47440
47303	47349	47395	47441
47304	47350	47396	47442
47305	47351	47397	47443
47306	47352	47398	47444
47307	47353	47399	47445
47308	47354	47400	47446
47309	47355	47401	47447
47310*	47356	47402	47448
47311*	47357	47403	47449
47312*	47358	47404	47450
47313*	47359	47405	47451
47314*	47360	47406	47452
47315*	47361	47407	47453
47316*	47362	47408	47454
47317	47363	47409	47455
47318	47364	47410	47457
47319	47365	47411	47458
47320	47366	47412	47459
47321	47367	47413	47460
47322	47368	47414	47461
47323	47369	47415	47462
47324	47370	47416	47463
47325	47371	47417	47464
47326	47372	47418	47465
47327	47373	47419	47466
47328	47374	47420	47467
47329	47375	47421	47468
47330	47376	47422	47469
47331	47377	47423	47470
47332	47378	47424	47471
47333	47379	47425	47472
47334	47380	47426	47473
47335	47381	47427	47474
47336	47382	47428	47475
47337	47383	47429	47476
47338	47384	47430	47477
47339	47385	47431	47478
47340	47386	47432	47479
47341	47387	47433	47480
47342	47383	47434	47481
47343	47389	47435	47482
47344	47390	47436	47483
47345	47391	47437	47484

Top to bottom:
Class 7P 4-6-0 No.
46163 *Civil Service
Rifleman*; Class 6P
4-6-0 No. 45520
Llandudno; Class 6P
4-6-0 No. 45742
Connaught (with
double chimney)

[J. Davenport,
F. F. Moss,
P. Ransome-Wallis]

Left upper : Class 2P 2–4–2T No. 50648. Left lower : Class 2P 2–4–2T No. 50655 (with Belpaire boiler and extended smokebox). Above : Class 3F (ex-Furness) 0–6–0 No. 52510. Below : Class 7F 0–8–0 No. 52870

[H. C. Casserley (3), J. Davenport

Top to bottom: Class
2F 0–6–0 No. 52016 ;
Class 3F 0–6–0 No.
52517 ; Class 3F
(Superheated) 0–6–0
No. 52549 ; Class 3F
0–6–0 No. 52132
(unsuperheated but
with Belpaire boiler
and extended smoke-
box)

[H. C. Casserley (2)
C. C. B. Herbert,
J. Davenport

This page. Top to bottom: Class 2F 0–6–0 No. 57336 ; Class 3F (McIntosh) 0–6–0 No. 57579; Class 3F (Pickersgill) 0–6–0 No. 57689 ; Class 2P 0–4–4T No. 55222

[H. C. Casserley (2).
J. Davenport,
P. L. Melvill

Facing page. Top to bottom: Class 4MT 4–6–0 No. 54638 ; Class 3P (McIntosh) 4–4–0 No. 54443 ; Class 3P (Pickersgill) 4–4–0 No. 54493 ; Class 4P 4–6–2T No. 55353

[H. N. A. Shelton,
D. S. Currie,
H. C. Casserley,
A. Ashley

Left upper : Class 2F 0-6-0 No. 58400. Above : Class 2F (4' 11")
0-6-0 No. 58115. Left lower : Class 2F (5' 3") 0-6-0 No. 58265.
Below : Class 3F 0-6-0 No. 43459

[E. Oldham, A. Rowse, H. C. Casserley (2)]

Above : Class 1P 2-4-2T No. 46654. *Right upper* : Class 6F
0-8-2T No. 47884. *Right lower* : Class 2F 0-6-2T No. 58837.
Below : Class 2MT 0-6-2T No. 46912.
[J. Davenport, B. Canning, H. C. Casserley (2)

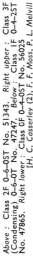

Above: Class 2F 0-6-0ST No. 51343.   Right upper: Class 3F
(Condensing) 0-6-0T No. 47247.   Below: Class 1F 0-4-2ST
No. 47865.   Right lower: Class 0F 0-4-0ST No. 56025
[H. C. Casserley (2), F. F. Moss, P. L. Melvill]

47485	47531	47578	47626
47486	47532	47579	47627
47487	47533	47580	47628
47488	47534	47581	47629
47489	47535	47582	47630
47490	47536	47583	47631
47491	47537	47584	47632
47492	47538	47585	47633
47493	47539	47586	47634
47494	47540	47587	47635
47495	47541	47588	47636
47496	47542	47589	47637
47497	47543	47590	47638
47498	47544	47591	47639
47499	47545	47592	47640
47500	47546	47593	47641
47501	47547	47594	47642
47502	47548	47595	47643
47503	47549	47596	47644
47504	47550	47597	47645
47505	47551	47598	47646
47506	47552	47599	47647
47507	47554	47600	47648
47508	47555	47601	47649
47509	47556	47602	47650
47510	47557	47603	47651
47511	47558	47604	47652
47512	47559	47605	47653
47513	47560	47606	47654
47514	47561	47607	47655
47515	47562	47608	47656
47516	47563	47609	47657
47517	47564	47610	47658
47518	47565	47611	47659
47519	47566	47612	47660
47520	47567	47614	47661
47521	47568	47615	47662
47522	47569	47616	47664
47523	47570	47618	47665
47524	47571	47619	47666
47525	47572	47620	47667
47526	47573	47621	47668
47527	47574	47622	47669
47528	47575	47623	47670
47529	47576	47624	47671
47530	47577	47625	47672

47673	47676	47678	47680
47674	47677	47679	47681
47675			

Total 417

0-4-2ST **1F**

Introduced 1896. Webb L.N.W. Bissel truck design (oldest survivor built 1901).
Weight : 34 tons 17 cwt.
Pressure : 150 lb.
Cyls. : 17″×24″.
Dr. Wheels : 4′ 5½″. T.E. : 16,530 lb.

47862 47865 **Total 2**

0-8-2T **6F**

Introduced 1911. Bowen Cooke L.N.W. design (tank version of " G " 0-8-0).
Weight : 72 tons 10 cwt.
Pressure : 170 lb.
Cyls. : 20½″×24″.
Dr. Wheels : 4′ 5½″. T.E. : 27,240 lb.
Joy valve gear.

47877 | 47881 | 47884

Total 3

0-8-4T **7F**

Introduced 1923. Beames L.N.W. design, built after grouping (tank version of G2 0-8-0).
Weight : 88 tons 0 cwt.
Pressure : 185 lb. Su.
Cyls. : 20½″×24″.
Dr. Wheels : 4′ 5½″. T.E. : 29,815 lb.
Joy valve gear, P.V.

47931 **Total 1**

2-6-6-2T Beyer-Garratt

*Introduced 1927. Fowler & Beyer-Peacock, L.M.S. design with fixed coal bunker.

Remainder. Introduced 1930. Development with detail alterations, later fitted with revolving coal bunkers.

No. 47997 built 1927 to original design.

Weight : { 148 tons 15 cwt*
155 tons 10 cwt. }
Pressure ; 190 lb. Su.
Cyls. (4) 18½″×26″.
Dr. Wheels : 5′ 3″. T.E. : 45,620 lb.
Walschaerts Valve Gear, P.V.

47967	47976	47984	47992
47968	47977	47985	47993
47969	47978	47986	47994
47970	47979	47987	47995
47971	47980	47988	47996
47972	47981	47989	47997
47973	47982	47990	47998*
47974	47983	47991	47999*
47975			

Total 33

2-8-0   8F

Introduced 1935. Stanier L.M.S. taper
  boiler design.
Weight : Loco. 72 tons 2 cwt.
Pressure : 225 lb. Su.
Cyls. : (O) $18\frac{1}{2}''\times28''$.
Dr. Wheels : 4' $8\frac{1}{2}''$.   T.E. : 32,440 lb.
Walschaerts Valve Gear, P.V.

48000	48046	48084	48114	48141	48187	48253	48302
48001	48050	48085	48115	48142	48188	48254	48303
48002	48053	48088	48116	48143	48189	48255	48304
48003	48054	48089	48117	48144	48190	48256	48305
48004	48055	48090	48118	48145	48191	48257	48306
48005	48056	48092	48119	48146	48192	48258	48307
48006	48057	48093	48120	48147	48193	48259	48308
48007	48060	48094	48121	48148	48194	48260	48309
48008	48061	48095	48122	48149	48195	48261	48310
48009	48062	48096	48123	48150	48196	48262	48311
48010	48063	48097	48124	48151	48197	48263	48312
48011	48064	48098	48125	48152	48198	48264	48313
48012	48065	48099	48126	48153	48199	48265	48314
48016	48067	48100	48127	48154	48200	48266	48315
48017	48069	48101	48128	48155	48201	48267	48316
48018	48070	48102	48129	48156	48202	48268	48317
48020	48073	48103	48130	48157	48203	48269	48318
48024	48074	48104	48131	48158	48204	48270	48319
48026	48075	48105	48132	48159	48205	48271	48320
48027	48076	48106	48133	48160	48206	48272	48321
48029	48077	48107	48134	48161	48207	48273	48322
48033	48078	48108	48135	48162	48208	48274	48323
48035	48079	48109	48136	48163	48209	48275	48324
48036	48080	48110	48137	48164	48210	48276	48325
48037	48081	48111	48138	48165	48211	48277	48326
48039	48082	48112	48139	48166	48212	48278	48327
48045	48083	48113	48140	48167	48213	48279	48328
				48168	48214	48280	48329
				48169	48215	48281	48330
				48170	48216	48282	48331
				48171	48217	48283	48332
				48172	48218	48284	48333
				48173	48219	48285	48334
				48174	48220	48286	48335
				48175	48221	48287	48336
				48176	48222	48288	48337
				48177	48223	48289	48338
				48178	48224	48290	48339
				48179	48225	48291	48340
				48180	48246	48292	48341
				48181	48247	48293	48342
				48182	48248	48294	48343
				48183	48249	48295	48344
				48184	48250	48296	48345
				48185	48251	48297	48346
				48186	48252	48301	48347

48348	48394	48440	48500	48546	48632	48678	48724
48349	48395	48441	4t501	48547	48633	48679	48725
48350	48396	48442	48502	48548	48634	48680	48726
48351	48397	48443	48503	48549	48635	48681	48727
48352	48398	48444	48504	48550	48636	48682	48728
48353	48399	48445	48505	48551	48637	48683	48729
48354	48400	48446	48506	48552	48638	48684	48730
48355	48401	48447	48507	48553	48639	48685	48731
48356	48402	48448	48508	48554	48640	48686	48732
48357	48403	48449	48509	48555	48641	48687	48733
48358	48404	48450	48510	48556	48642	48688	48734
48359	48405	48451	48511	48557	48643	48689	48735
48360	48406	48452	48512	48558	48644	48690	48736
48361	48407	48453	48513	48559	48645	48691	48737
48362	48408	48454	48514	48600	48646	48692	48738
48363	48409	48455	48515	48601	48647	48693	48739
48364	48410	48456	48516	48602	48648	48694	48740
48365	48411	48457	48517	48603	48649	48695	48741
48366	48412	48458	48518	48604	48650	48696	48742
48367	48413	48459	48519	48605	48651	48697	48743
48368	48414	48460	48520	48606	48652	48698	48744
48369	48415	48461	48521	48607	48653	48699	48745
48370	48416	48462	48522	48608	48654	48700	48746
48371	48417	48463	48523	48609	48655	48701	48747
48372	48418	48464	48524	48610	48656	48702	48748
48373	48419	48465	48525	48611	48657	48703	48749
48374	48420	48466	48526	48612	48658	48704	48750
48375	48421	48467	48527	48613	48659	48705	48751
48376	48422	48468	48528	48614	48660	48706	48752
48377	48423	48469	48529	48615	48661	48707	48753
48378	48424	48470	48530	48616	48662	48708	48754
48379	48425	48471	48531	48617	48663	48709	48755
48380	48426	48472	48532	48618	48664	48710	48756
48381	48427	48473	48533	48619	48665	48711	48757
48382	48428	48474	48534	48620	48666	48712	48758
48383	48429	48475	48535	48621	48667	48713	48759
48384	48430	48476	48536	48622	48668	48714	48760
48385	48431	48477	48537	48623	48669	48715	48761
48386	48432	48478	48538	48624	48670	48716	48762
48387	48433	48479	48539	48625	48671	48717	48763
48388	48434	48490	48540	48626	48672	48718	48764
48389	48435	48491	48541	48627	48673	48719	48765
48390	48436	48492	48542	48628	48674	48720	48766
48391	48437	48493	48543	48629	48675	48721	48767
48392	48438	48494	48544	48630	48676	48722	48768
48393	48439	48495	48545	48631	48677	48723	48769

51

48770   48771   48772

Total 663

0-8-0   6F & 7F

G1 Class 6F
*Introduced 1912. Bowen Cooke
L.N.W. superheated design, developed from earlier saturated design
(many rebuilt from earlier Webb,
Whale and Bowen Cooke compound
and simple designs introduced 1892
onwards). Many later rebuilt with
Belpaire boilers.

G2 Class 7F
†Introduced 1921. Development of
G1 with higher pressure boiler.
Many later rebuilt with Belpaire
boilers.

G2a Class 7F
Remainder. Introduced 1936. G1 locos.
rebuilt with G2 Belpaire boilers.

Weights : Loco.$\begin{cases} 60 \text{ tons 15 cwt. (G1)} \\ 62 \text{ tons 0 cwt. (G2, G2a).} \end{cases}$

Pressure :$\begin{cases} 160 \text{ lb. Su. (G1).} \\ 175 \text{ lb. Su. (G2, G2a).} \end{cases}$
Cyls. : $20\frac{1}{2}'' \times 24''$.
Dr. Wheels : 4' 5½".
T.E. :$\begin{cases} 25,640 \text{ lb. (G1).} \\ 28,045 \text{ lb. (G2, G2a).} \end{cases}$

Joy valve gear, P.V.

**Nos. 48893–49394 CLASSES G1*
AND G2a.**

48893	48930	49007	49031
48895	48932	49008	49033
48898	48936	49009	49034
48899	48940	49010	49035
48901	48942	49014	49037
48902*	48943	49017*	49044
48905	48944	49018	49045
48907	48945	49020	49046
48914	48950	49021	49047
48915	48951	49022	49048
48917	48952	49023	49049
48920	48953	49024	49051
48921	48964	49025	49057
48922	49002	49027	49061
48926	49005	49028	49062
48927	49006	49030*	49063

49064	49143	49214	49302
49066	49144	49216	49304
49068	49145	49218	49306
49070	49146	49222*	49308
49073	49147	49223	49310
49077	49148	49224	49311
49078	49149	49226	49312
49079	49150	49228	49313
49081	49151*	49229	49314
49082	49153	49230	49315
49087	49154	49234	49316
49088	49155	49239	49318
49089*	49157	49240	49321
49092*	49158	49241*	49322
49093	49160	49243	49323
49094	49161	49244	49326*
49096	49162*	49245	49327
49098*	49163	49246	49328
49099	49164	49247	49330
49104	49167	49249	49335
49105	49168	49252	49339
49106	49171*	49253	49340
49108	49172	49254	49341
49109	49173	49258	49342
49112	49174	49260	49343
49113	49177	49261*	49344
49114	49178	49262	49345
49115	49180	49265	49346*
49116	49181	49266	49348
49117	49186	49267	49350
49119	49187*	49268	49352
49120	49189	49270	49354
49121	49191	49271	49355
49122	49193*	49275	49357
49125	49196	49276	49358
49126	49198	49277	49359*
49129	49199	49278	49361
49130	49200	49281	49366
49132	49202	49287	49367
49134	49203	49288	49368
49137	49204*	49289	49370*
49138	49205	49292	49371*
49139	49209	49293	49373
49140*	49210	49296	49375
49141	49212	49300	49376
49142	49213*	49301	49377

49378	49386	49390	49394
49381	49387	49391	
49382	49388	49392	
49385	49389	49393	

Nos. 49395–49454† CLASS G2.

49395	49410	49425	49440
49396	49411	49426	49441
49397	49412	49427	49442
49398	49413	49428	49443
49399	49414	49429	49444
49400	49415	49430	49445
49401	49416	49431	49446
49402	49417	49432	49447
49403	49418	49433	49448
49404	49419	49434	49449
49405	49420	49435	49450
49406	49421	49436	49451
49407	49422	49437	49452
49408	49423	49438	49453
49409	49424	49439	49454

Totals G2 60 G1 22 G2a 239

0-8-0   7F

Introduced 1929. Fowler L.M.S. design, developed from L.N.W. G2.
Weight : Loco. 60 tons 15 cwt.
Pressure : 200 lb. Su.
Cyls. : $19\frac{1}{2}'' \times 26''$.
Dr. Wheels : 4' 8½".   T.E. : 29,745 lb.
Walschaerts Valve Gear. P.V.

49502	49540	49568	49594
49503	49544	49570	49595
49505	49545	49571	49598
49506	49547	49578	49600
49508	49548	49580	49602
49509	49552	49582	49603
49510	49554	49586	49608
49511	49555	49587	49610
49515	49557	49589	49612
49524	49558	49590	49617
49532	49560	49591	49618
49536	49563	49592	49620
49538	49566	49593	49624

49627	49648	49661	49667
49631	49650	49662	49668
49637	49657	49663	49671
49638	49659	49664	49672
49640	49660	49666	49674

Total 72

4-6-0   5P

Introduced 1924. Development of Hughes superheated L. & Y. Class 8 with longer wheelbase, larger firebox and parts originally made for 4-6-4T.
Weight : Loco. 77 tons 18 cwt.
Pressure ; 180 lb. Su.
Cyls. : (4) $16\frac{1}{2}'' \times 26''$
Dr. Wheels : 6' 3".
T.E. : 28,880 lb.
Walschaerts Valve Gear and rocking shafts, P.V.

50455   **Total 1**

2-4-2T   2P & 3P

2P Introduced 1889. Aspinall L. & Y. Class 5 with 2 tons coal capacity.
*Introduced 1892. Locos. built or re-built with smaller cylinders.
†Introduced 1898. Locos. with longer tanks and 4 tons coal capacity.
‡Introduced 1905. Hughes locos. built with Belpaire boiler and extended smokebox.
φIntroduced 1910. Loco. rebuilt with Belpaire boiler.
Weight :$\begin{cases} 55 \text{ tons } 19 \text{ cwt.} \\ 55 \text{ tons } 19 \text{ cwt.*} \\ 59 \text{ tons } 3 \text{ cwt.}†‡ø \end{cases}$
Pressure : 180 lb.
Cyls. :$\begin{cases} 17\frac{1}{2}'' \times 26''* \\ 18'' \times 26'' \text{ (remainder)} \end{cases}$
Dr. Wheels : 5' 8".
T.E. :$\begin{cases} 18,360 \text{ lb.*} \\ 18,955 \text{ lb.} † \text{ (remainder)} \end{cases}$
Joy valve gear.

50621–52043

3P §Introduced 1911. Hughes L. & Y.
Class 6 (superheated development of
Class 5).
¶ Loco. as § but with reduced cylinder
diameters.
Weight : 66 tons 9 cwt.
Pressure : ¹80 lb. Su.
Cyls. : $\begin{cases} 19\frac{1}{2}'' \times 26''\P. \\ 20\frac{1}{4}'' \times 26'' \S \end{cases}$
T.E. : $\begin{cases} 22,445 \text{ lb.}\P \\ 24,585 \text{ lb.}\S \end{cases}$
Dr. Wheels : 5' 8".
Joy valve gear, P.V.

50621	50656*	50735	50818
50622	50660	50736φ	50829†φ
50623	50671	50746	50831†
50625	50676	50749	50840†
50633	50678*	50752*	50842†
50634*	50681	50757	50850†
50636	50686	50762	50852†
50639	50687	50764	50855*†
50640	50689	50765	50859†
50642	50695	50766*	50865*†
50643*	50697	50777	50869†
50644	50703	50778	50872‡
50646	50705	50781	50873‡
50647	50712	50788	50886‡
50648	50714*	50795*	50887‡
50650φ	50715*	50799*	50892‡
50651φ	50720	50802	50897‡
50652*φ	50721	50806	50898‡
50653*	50725	50807*	50909§
50654	50731	50812	50925¶
50655φ			

Totals 2P 79
3P 2

0-4-0ST **0F**
Introduced 1891. Aspinall L. & Y.
Class 21.
Weight : 21 tons 5 cwt.
Pressure : 160 lb.
Cyls. : (O) 13" × 18".
Dr. Wheels : 3' 0¾". T.E. : 11,335 lb.

51202	51217	51230	51240
51204	51218	51231	51241
51206	51221	51232	51244
51207	51222	51234	51246
51212	51227	51235	51253
51216	51229	51237	

Total 23

0-6-0ST **2F**
Introduced 1891. Aspinall rebuild of
L. & Y. Barton Wright Class 23 0-6-0.
Originally introduced 1876.
Weight : 43 tons 17 cwt.
Pressure : 140 lb. Cyls. : 17½" × 26".
Dr. Wheels : 4' 6". T.E. : 17,545 lb.

51307	51396	51447	51496
51313	51397	51453	51497
51316	51404	51457	51498
51319	51408	51458	51499
51321	51410	51460	51500
51323	51412	51462	51503
51336	51413	51464	51504
51338	51415	51470	51506
51343	51419	51471	51510
51345	51423	51472	51511
51348	51424	51474	51512
51353	51425	51477	51513
51358	51429	51479	51514
51361	51432	51481	51516
51371	51436	51484	51519
51375	51439	51486	51521
51376	51441	51488	51524
51379	51444	51489	51526
51381	51445	51490	51530
51390	51446	51491	

Total 79

0-6-0T **1F**
Introduced 1897. Aspinall L. & Y.
Class 24 dock tanks.
Weight : 50 tons 0 cwt.
Pressure : 140 lb.
Cyls. : (O) 17" × 24".
Dr. Wheels : 4' 0". T.E. : 15,285 lb.
Allan straight link gear.

51535	51537	51544	51546
51536			

Total 5

0-6-0 **2F**
Introduced 1887. Barton Wright L.
& Y. Class 25.
Weight : Loco. 39 tons 1 cwt.
Pressure : 140 lb.
Cyls. : 17½" × 26".
Dr. Wheels : 4' 6". T.E. : 17,545 lb.

52016	52024	52031	52037
52021	52030	52034	52043

52044	52051	52056	52059
52045	52053		

Total 14

0-6-0   3F

Introduced 1889. Aspinall L. & Y. Class 27.

*Introduced 1911. Rebuilt with Belpaire boiler and extended smokebox.

†Introduced 1913. Pettigrew Furness Rly. design.

Weight : Loco. $\begin{cases} 42 \text{ tons } 3 \text{ cwt.} \\ 42 \text{ tons } 13 \text{ cwt.}† \\ 43 \text{ tons } 11 \text{ cwt.}* \end{cases}$

Pressure : $\begin{cases} 180 \text{ lb.} \\ 170 \text{ lb.}† \end{cases}$

Cyls. : $18'' \times 26''$.

Dr. Wheels : $\begin{cases} 5' \ 1''. \\ 4' \ 7\frac{1}{2}''.† \end{cases}$

T.E. : $\begin{cases} 21,130 \text{ lb.} \\ 21,935 \text{ lb.}† \end{cases}$

Joy valve gear.

52088*	52135	52177	52237
52089	52136	52179	52238
52091*	52137	52182	52239
52093	52138	52183	52240
52094	52139	52186	52243
52095	52140*	52189	52244
52098	52141	52191	52245
52099	52143	52194	52246
52100	52150	52196	52248
52102	52154*	52197	52250*
52104	52156	52201*	52252
52105	52157	52203	52255
52107	52159	52207	52258
52108	52160	52212	52260
52111	52161*	52215	52262
52112	52162	52216	52266*
52118	52163	52217	52268
52119	52164	52218	52269
52120	52165	52219	52270
52121	52166	52220	52271
52123	52167	52225	52272
52124	52169	52230	52273*
52125	52171	52231	52275
52126	52172	52232	52278
52129	52174	52233	52279
52132*	52175	52235	52280
52133	52176	52236	52284

52285	52350	52405	52450
52288	52351	52408	52452
52289	52353	52410	52453
52290	52355	52411	52455
52293	52356	52412	52456
52296	52357	52413	52458
52299	52358	52414	52459
52300	52360	52415	52460
52304	52362	52416	52461
52305	52363	52418	52464
52309	52365	52427	52465
52311	52366	52428*	52466
52312*	52368	52429	52494†
52317	52369	52430	52499†
52319*	52376	52431*	52501†
52321	52378	52432	52509†
52322	52379*	52433	52510†
52328	52381	52435	52515
52330*	52382	52437	52517
52331	52386	52438*	52518
52333	52387	52440	52521
52334	52388	52441	52522
52336	52389	52443	52523
52338	52390	52444*	52524
52341	52393	52445	52525
52343	52397	52446	52526
52345	52399	52447	52527
52348	52400*	52448*	52529
52349	52404	52449	

Totals : L. & Y. 218, F.R. 5

0-6-0   3F

*Introduced 1912. Hughes L. & Y. Class 28, superheated development of Class 27.

Remainder. Introduced 1913. Rebuilds of Class 27.

Weight : Loco. 46 tons 10 cwt.

Pressure : 180 lb. Su.

Cyls. : $20\frac{1}{2}'' \times 26''$.

Dr. Wheels : $5' \ 1''$.   T.E. : 27,405 lb.

Joy Valve Gear, P.V.

52549*	52557	52561	52575
52551*	52558	52569	52576
52554*	52559	52572	52579

52580	52587	52592	52615
52581	52588	52598	52616
52582	52590	52608	52619
52583			

Total 25

0-8-0   7F

Introduced 1912. L. & Y. Cl. 31. **Super-
heated** development of Class 30.
Weight : Loco. 66 tons 4 cwt.
Pressure : 180 lb. Su.
Cyls. : 21½″ × 26″.
Dr. Wheels : 4′ 6″.   T.E. : 34,055 lb.
Joy Valve Gear, P.V

52857	52870	52945

Total 3

2-8-0   7F

Introduced 1914. Fowler design for
S. & D.J. with 4′ 9″ boiler (some
rebuilt from 1925 series).
*Introduced 1925. Fowler design with
5′ 3″ boiler.
(All taken into L.M.S. stock, 1930).
Weight : Loco. { 64 tons 15 cwt.
                       { 68 tons 11 cwt.*
Pressure : 190 lb. Su.
Cyls. : (O) 21″ × 28″
Dr. Wheels : 4′ 8½″.   T.E. : 35,295 lb.
Walschaerts Valve Gear P.V.

53800	53803	53806*	53809
53801	53804	53807*	53810
53802	53805	53808*	

Total 11

IMPORTANT NOTE

A careful reading of the notes
on page 9 is essential to
understand the use of reference marks in this book.

4-4-0 " Ben " Class   2P

Introduced 1898. Drummond Highland
" Small Ben," later rebuilt with C.R.
boiler.
Weight : Loco. 46 tons 17 cwt.
Pressure : 180 lb.
Cyls. : 18¼″ × 26″.
Dr. Wheels : 6′ 0″.   T.E. : 18,400 lb

54398 Ben Alder
54399 Ben Wyvis

Total 2

4-4-0   3P

Introduced 1910. McIntosh Caledonian
" Dunalastair IV Superheater " or
" 139 " class.
*Introduced 1915. Superheated re-
build of McIntosh Caledonian " Dun-
alastair IV " or " 140 " class (origin-
ally introduced 1904).
Weight : Loco. 61 tons 5 cwt.
Pressure : 180 lb. Su.
Cyls. : 20¼″ × 26″.
Dr. Wheels : 6′ 6″.   T.E. : 20,915 lb.
P.V.

54438*	54445	54451	54456
54439*	54446	54452	54457
54440	54447	54453	54458
54441	54448	54454	54459
54443	54449	54455	54460
54444	54450		

Total 22

4-4-0   3P

Introduced 1916. Pickersgill Cale-
donian " 113 " and " 928 " classes.
Weight : Loco. 61 tons 5 cwt.
Pressure : 180 lb. Su.
Cyls. : 20″ × 26″.
Dr. Wheels : 6′ 6″.   T.E. : 20,400 lb.
P.V.

54461	54465	54469	54473
54462	54466	54470	54474
54463	54467	54471	54475
54464	54468	54472	54476

Total 16

4-4-0   3P

Introduced 1920. Pickersgill Caledonian " 72 " class.

Weight : Loco. 61 tons 5 cwt.

Pressure : 180 lb. Su.

Cyls. : $20\frac{1}{2}'' \times 26''$.

Dr. Wheels : 6' 6". T.E.: 21,435 lb. P.V.

54477	54485	54493	54501
54478	54486	54494	54502
54479	54487	54495	54503
54480	54488	54496	54504
54481	54489	54497	54505
54482	54490	54498	54506
54483	54491	54499	54507
54484	54492	54500	54508

Total 32

4-6-0   4MT

Introduced 1925. Post-Grouping development of Caledonian " 60 " Class.

Weight : Loco. 74 tons 15 cwt.

Pressure : 180 lb.

Cyls. : (O) $20\frac{1}{2}'' \times 26''$.

Dr. Wheels : 6' 1". T.E. : 22,900 lb. P.V.

54634	54638	54640	54648
54635	54639	54647	54649
54636			

Total 9

4-6-0   4MT

Introduced 1916. Pickersgill Caledonian " 60 " Class.

Weight : Loco. 75 tons 0 cwt.

Pressure : 180 lb. Su.

Cyls. : (O) $20'' \times 26''$.

Dr. Wheels : 6' 1". T.E. : 21,795 lb. P.V.

54650   54654

Total 2

0-4-4T   1P

Introduced 1905. Drummond Highland design.

Weight : 35 tons 15 cwt.

Pressure : 150 lb.

Cyls. : $14'' \times 20''$.

Dr. Wheels : 4' 6".   T.E. : 9,255 lb.

55051   55053

Total 2

0-4-4T   2P

*Introduced 1895. McIntosh Caledonian " 19 " class, with railed coal bunkers.
Remainder. Introduced 1897. McIntosh " 92 " class, developed from " 29 " class with larger tanks and highsided coal bunkers (both classes originally fitted for condensing on Glasgow underground system).

Weight : $\begin{cases} 53 \text{ tons } 16 \text{ cwt.}^* \\ 53 \text{ tons } 19 \text{ cwt.} \end{cases}$

Pressure : 180 lb.

Cyls. : $18'' \times 26''$.

Dr. Wheels : 5' 9".   T.E. : 18,680 lb.

55119*	55126	55138	55143
55121*	55132	55139	55144
55122*	55134	55140	55145
55124*	55135	55141	55146
55125	55136	55142	

Total 19

0-4-4T   2P

Introduced 1900. McIntosh Caledonian " 439 " or " Standard Passenger " class.
*Introduced 1915. Pickersgill locos. with detail alterations.

Weight : $\begin{cases} 53 \text{ tons } 19 \text{ cwt.} \\ 57 \text{ tons } 12 \text{ cwt.}^* \end{cases}$

Pressure : 180 lb.

Cyls. : $18'' \times 26''$.

Dr. Wheels : 5' 9".   T.E. : 18,680 lb.

55160	55179	55202	55220
55161	55181	55203	55221
55162	55182	55204	55222
55164	55185	55206	55223
55165	55186	55207	55224
55166	55187	55208	55225
55167	55188	55209	55226
55168	55189	55210	55227*
55169	55193	55211	55228*
55170	55194	55212	55229*
55171	55195	55213	55230*
55172	55196	55214	55231*
55173	55197	55215	55232*
55174	55198	55216	55233*
55175	55199	55217	55234*
55176	55200	55218	55235*
55177	55201	55219	55236*
55178			

Total 69

0-4-4T   2P

Introduced 1922. Pickersgill Caledonian " 431 " class (developed from " 439 " class) with cast-iron front buffer beam for banking.
Weight : 57 tons 17 cwt.
Pressure : 180 lb.
Cyls. : $18\frac{1}{2}'' \times 26''$.
Dr. Wheels : 5' 9".   T.E. : 19,200 lb.

55237	55238	55239	55240

Total 4

0-4-4T   2P

Introduced 1925. Post-Grouping development of Caledonian " 439 " class.
Weight : 59 tons 12 cwt.
Pressure : 180 lb.
Cyls. : $18\frac{1}{2}'' \times 26''$.
Dr. Wheels : 5' 9".   T.E. : 19,200 lb.

55260	55263	55266	55268
55261	55264	55267	55269
55262	55265		

Total 10

4-6-2T   4P

Introduced 1917. Pickersgill Caledonian " 944 " class.
Weight : 91 tons 13 cwt.
Pressure : 180 lb. Su. Cyls. : (O) $19\frac{1}{2}'' \times 26''$.
Dr. Wheels : 5' 9".   T.E. : 21,920 lb.
P.V.

55350	55353	55360	55361
55352	55359		

Total 6

0-4-0ST   0F

Introduced 1885. Drummond and McIntosh Caledonian " Pugs."
Weight : 27 tons 7 cwt.
Pressure : 160 lb. Cyls. : (O) $14'' \times 20''$.
Dr. Wheels : 3' 8".   T.E. : 12,115 lb.

56011	56027	56030	56035
56020	56028	56031	56038
56025	56029	56032	56039

Total 12

0-6-0T   2F

Introduced 1911. McIntosh Caledonian dock shunters, " 498 " class.
Weight : 47 tons 15 cwt.
Pressure : 160 lb. Cyls. : (O) $17'' \times 22''$.
Dr. Wheels : 4' 0".   T.E. : 18,015 lb.

56151	56157	56163	56169
56152	56158	56164	56170
56153	56159	56165	56171
56154	56160	56166	56172
56155	56161	56167	56173
56156	56162	56168	

Total 23

0-6-0T   3F

Introduced 1895. McIntosh Caledonian " 29 " and " 782 " classes (56231-9 originally condensing).
Weight : 47 tons 15 cwt.
Pressure : 160 lb. Cyls. : $18'' \times 26''$.
Dr. Wheels : 4' 6".   T.E. : 21,215 lb.

56230	56236	56242	56248
56231	56237	56243	56249
56232	56238	56244	56250
56233	56239	56245	56251
56234	56240	56246	56252
56235	56241	56247	56253

56254	56286	56316	56346	57243	57292	57353	57416
56255	56287	56317	56347	57244	57295	57354	57417
56256	56288	56318	56348	57245	57296	57355	57418
56257	56289	56319	56349	57246	57299	57356	57419
56258	56290	56320	56350	57247	57300	57357	57423
56259	56291	56321	56352	57249	57302	57359	57424
56260	56292	56322	56353	57250	57303	57360	57426
56261	56293	56323	56354	57251	57306	57361	57429
56262	56294	56324	56355	57252	57307	57362	57430
56263	56295	56325	56356	57253	57309	57363	57431
56264	56296	56326	56357	57254	57311	57364	57432
56265	56297	56327	56358	57255	57312	57365	57433
56266	56298	56328	56359	57256	57314	57366	57434
56267	56299	56329	56360	57257	57315	57367	57435
56268	56300	56330	56361	57258	57317	57368	57436
56269	56301	56331	56362	57259	57318	57369	57437
56271	56302	56332	56363	57260	57319	57370	57438
56272	56303	56333	56364	57261	57320	57372	57439
56273	56304	56334	56365	57262	57321	57373	57441
56274	56305	56335	56366	57263	57322	57375	57443
56275	56306	56336	56367	57264	57323	57377	57444
56276	56307	56337	56368	57265	57324	57378	57445
56277	56308	56338	56369	57266	57325	57383	57446
56278	56309	56339	56370	57267	57326	57384	57447
56279	56310	56340	56371	57268	57328	57385	57448
56280	56311	56341	56372	57269	57329	57386	57450
56281	56312	56342	56373	57270	57331	57387	57451
56282	56313	56343	56374	57271	57332	57388	57454
56283	56314	56344	56375	57272	57334	57389	57455
56284	56315	56345	56376	57273	57335	57392	57456
56285				57274	57336	57394	57457
			Total 145	57275	57337	57395	57458
				57276	57338	57396	57459
				57277	57339	57397	57460
				57278	57340	57398	57461
				57279	57341	57404	57462
				57280	57344	57405	57463
				57282	57345	57407	57464
				57284	57346	57410	57465
				57285	57347	57411	57468
				57287	57348	57412	57470
				57288	57349	57413	57472
				57289	57350	57414	57473
				57291	57352		

0-6-0   2F

Introduced 1883. Drummond Caledonian "Standard Goods"; later additions by Lambie and McIntosh.
*Rebuilt with L.M.S. boilers.
Weight : Loco·{ 41 tons 6 cwt.
                 { 42 tons 4 cwt.*
Pressure : 180 lb.
Cyls. : $18'' \times 26''$.
Dr. Wheels : 5′ 0″.   T.E. : 21,480 lb

57230	57234	57237	57240
57232	57235	57238	57241
57233	57236	57239	57242

Total 185

0-6-0   3F

Introduced 1899. McIntosh Caledonian "812" Nos. (57550-57628) and "652" (remainder) classes.
Weight : Loco. 45 tons 14 cwt.
Pressure : 180 lb.
Cyls. : 18½″×26″.
Dr. Wheels : 5′ 0″.   T.E. : 22,690 lb.

57550	57575	57599	57623
57552	57576	57600	57625
57553	57577	57601	57626
57554	57579	57602	57627
57555	57580	57603	57628
57556	57581	57604	57630
57557	57582	57605	57631
57558	57583	57607	57632
57559	57585	57608	57633
57560	57586	57609	57634
57562	57587	57611	57635
57563	57588	57612	57637
57564	57589	57613	57638
57565	57590	57614	57640
57566	57591	57615	57642
57568	57592	57617	57643
57569	57593	57618	57644
57570	57594	57619	57645
57571	57595	57620	
57572	57596	57621	
57573	57597	57622	

Total 81

0-6-0   3F

Introduced 1918. Pickersgill Caledonian "294" class (superheated) and "670" classes.
Weight : Loco. 50 tons 13 cwt.
Pressure : 180 lb. Su.
Cyls. : 18½″×26″.
Dr. Wheels : 5′ 0″.   T.E. : 22,690 lb.
P.V.

57650	57661	57670	57682
57651	57663	57671	57684
57652	57665	57672	57686
57653	57666	57673	57688
57654	57667	57674	57689
57655	57668	57679	57690
57658	57669	57681	57691
57659			

Total 29

0-6-0   3F

Introduced 1900. Drummond Highland design, later rebuilt with Caledonian boilers.
Weight : Loco. 43 tons 10 cwt.
Pressure : 175 lb.
Cyls. : 18½″×26″.
Dr. Wheels : 5′ 0″.   T.E. : 21,470 lb.

57695   57698

Total 2

4-6-0   4MT

Introduced 1918. Cumming Highland "Clan Goods" Class.
Weight : Loco. 56 tons 9 cwt.
Pressure : 175 lb. Su.
Cyls. : (O) 20½″×26″.
Dr. Wheels : 5′ 3″.   T.E. : 25,800 lb.
Walschaerts Valve Gear, P.V.

57951 | 57954 | 57955 | 57956

Total 4

0-4-4T   1P

Introduced 1875. Johnson Midland design, later rebuilt with Belpaire boiler.
Weight : 53 tons 4 cwt.
Pressure : 140 lb.
Cyls. : 18″×24″.
Dr. Wheels : 5′ 7″.   T.E. : 13,810 lb.
(Former L.M.S. number in brackets)

58038   (1261)   **Total 1**

0-4-4T   1P

Introduced 1881. Johnson Midland design.
*Rebuilt with Belpaire boiler.
†Locos. with increased boiler pressure.
Weight : 53 tons 4 cwt.
Pressure : {140 lb. / 150 lb.†
Cyls. : 18″×24″.   T.E. : {14,460 lb. / 15,490 lb.†
Dr. Wheels : 5′ 4″.
(Former L.M.S. numbers in brackets)

†Nos. 58040-59 LOCOS. WITH 140 lb. PRESSURE.

58040	(1273)	58051	(1330)
58042	(1278)	58052*	(1337)
58045*	(1295)	58053*	(1340)
58046*	(1298)	58054*	(1341)
58047	(1303)	58056*	(1344)
58050*	(1324)	58058*	(1350)

†Nos. 58060-91 LOCOS. WITH 150 lb. PRESSURE.

58060*	(1357)	58076*	(1396)
58062*	(1360)	58077*	(1397)
58063*	(1365)	58080*	(1411)
58065*	(1367)	58083*	(1420)
58066*	(1368)	58084*	(1421)
58067*	(1370)	58085*	(1422)
58068*	(1371)	58086*	(1423)
58069*	(1373)	58087*	(1424)
58070*	(1375)	58088*	(1425)
58071	(1377)	58089	(1426)
58072	(1379)	58090*	(1429)
58073*	(1382)	58091*	(1430)
58075*	(1390)		

Total 37

2-4-0T   1P

Introduced 1877. Webb L.N.W. design.
Weight : 38 tons 4 cwt.
Pressure : 150 lb.
Cyls. : 17″×20″.
Dr. Wheels : 4′ 8½″.   T.E. : 13,045 lb.
Allan Straight link gear.

(Former L.M.S. number in brackets)

58092 (26428)   Total 1

0-10-0

Introduced 1919. Fowler Midland banker for Lickey incline.
Weight : Loco. 73 tons 13 cwt.
Pressure : 180 lb. Su.
Cyls. (4) : 16¾″×28″.
Dr. Wheels : 4′ 7½″.   T.E. : 43,315 lb.
Walschaerts Valve Gear.
(Former L.M.S. number in brackets)
58100 (22290)   Total 1

0-6-0   2F

Introduced 1868. Kirtley Midland double-framed design with round top boiler(Survivor built 1870).
Weight : Loco. 37 tons 12 cwt.
Pressure : 160 lb.
Cyls. : 18″×24″.
Dr. Wheels : 5′ 3″.   T.E. : 16,785 lb.
(Former L.M.S. number in brackets)

58110 (22630)

Total 1

0-6-0   2F

*Introduced 1875. Johnson Midland 4′ 11″ design, with round top boiler.
†Introduced 1917. Rebuilt with Belpaire boiler.
‡Introduced 1878. Johnson Midland 5′ 3″ design, with round top boiler.
§Introduced 1917. Rebuilt with Belpaire boiler.
Weight : Loco. Various.
37 tons 12 cwt. to 40 tons 3 cwt.
Pressure : 160 lb.
Cyls. : 18″×26″.
Dr. Wheels : { 4′ 11″* / 4′ 11″† / 5′ 3″‡ / 5′ 3″§
T.E. : { 19,420 lb.* / 19,420 lb.† / 18,185 lb.‡ / 18,185 lb.§

(Former L.M.S. numbers in brackets)

58114†	(22900)	58130†	(22932)
58115†	(22901)	58131†	(22933)
58116†	(22902)	58132†	(22934)
58117†	(22904)	58133†	(22935)
58118†	(22907)	58135†	(22944)
58119†	(22911)	58136†	(22945)
58120†	(22912)	58137†	(22946)
58121†	(22913)	58138†	(22947)
58122†	(22915)	58139†	(22950)
58123†	(22918)	58140†	(22951)
58124†	(22920)	58142†	(22954)
58125†	(22921)	58143†	(22955)
58126†	(22924)	58144†	(22958)
58127†	(22926)	58145†	(22959)
58128†	(22929)	58146†	(22963)
58129‡	(22931)	58147†	(22965)

58148† (22967)	58196§ (3044)	58254§ (3270)	58285§ (3539)
58149† (22968)	58197§ (3045)	58257§ (3372)	58286§ (3543)
58151† (22970)	58198§ (3047)	58258§ (3377)	58287§ (3545)
58152† (22971)	58199§ (3048)	58259§ (3385)	58288§ (3551)
58153† (22974)	58200§ (3049)	58260§ (3420)	58289§ (3559)
58154† (22975)	58201§ (3051)	58261§ (3423)	58290§ (3561)
58156† (22977)	58203§ (3054)	58264§ (3445)	58291§ (3564)
58157† (22978)	58204§ (3058)	58265§ (3451)	58293§ (3571)
58158† (22982)	58206§ (3062)	58268§ (3479)	58295§ (3603)
58159† (22983)	58207§ (3064)	58269§ (3485)	58296§ (3617)
58160† (22984)	58209§ (3071)	58271§ (3492)	58298§ (3648)
58161† (2987)	58211§ (3074)	58272§ (3493)	58299§ (3655)
58162† (2988)	58212§ (3078)	58273§ (3503)	58300§ (3688)
58163† (2989)	58213§ (3084)	58274‡ (3508)	58302§ (3691)
58164† (2990)	58214§ (3090)	58276§ (3512)	58303§ (3696)
58165† (2992)	58215§ (3094)	58277§ (3516)	58304§ (3703)
58166† (2993)	58216§ (3095)	58278§ (3517)	58305§ (3707)
58167† (2994)	58217§ (3096)	58279§ (3525)	58306§ (3725)
58168† (2995)	58218§ (3098)	58280§ (3526)	58308§ (3738)
58169† (2996)	58219§ (3099)	58281§ (3527)	58309§ (3739)
58170† (2997)	58220§ (3101)	58283§ (3536)	58310§ (3764)
58171† (2998)	58221§ (3103)		
58172† (2999)	58224§ (3113)		**Total 166**
58173† (23000)	58225§ (3118)		
58174† (23001)	58226§ (3119)		
58175† (23002)	58228§ (3127)		
58176† (23003)	58229* (3130)		
58177† (23005)	58230† (3134)	**0-6-0**	**2F**
58178† (23006)	58231† (3138)		
58179† (23007)	58232† (3140)	Introduced 1873. Webb L.N.W. " Coal	
58180† (23008)	58233† (3144)	Engines."	
58181† (23009)	58234† (3149)	Weight : Loco. 32 tons 0 cwt.	
58182† (23010)	58235† (3150)	Pressure : 150 lb.	
58183† (23011)	58236* (3151)	Cyls. : 17″×24″.	
58184† (23012)	58237† (3154)	Dr. Wheels : 4′ 5½″. T.E. : 16,530 lb.	
58185† (23013)	58238† (3156)	(Former L.M.S. numbers in brackets)	
58186† (23014)	58240* (3161)		
58187† (23018)	58241† (3164)	58321 (28091)	58336 (28172)
58188§ (3023)	58242† (3166)	58322 (28093)	58340 (28205)
58189§ (3027)	58244† (3171)	58323 (28100)	58343 (28227)
58190§ (3031)	58245† (3173)	58326 (28106)	58346 (28239)
58191§ (3035)	58246* (3175)	58327 (28107)	58347 (28245)
58192§ (3037)	58247* (3176)	58328 (28115)	58350 (28251)
58193§ (3038)	58248† (3177)	58330 (28128)	58352 (28256)
58194§ (3039)	58249§ (3190)	58332 (28141)	58354 (28263)
58195§ (3042)	58252§ (3262)	58333 (28152)	58360 (28312)
		58335 (28166)	
			Total 19

0-6-0   2F

Introduced 1887. Webb L.N.W. " 18 "
   Goods (" Cauliflowers ") many later
   rebuilt with Belpaire boilers.
Weight : Loco. 36 tons 10 cwt.
Pressure : 150 lb.
Cyls. : 18″×24″.
Dr. Wheels : 5′ 2½″.   T.E. : 15,865 lb.
Joy Valve Gear.
(Former L.M.S. numbers in brackets)

58362	(28318)	58398	(28515)
58363	(28333)	58400	(28525)
58365	(28337)	58409	(28548)
58368	(28345)	58412	(28553)
58375	(28408)	58413	(28555)
58376	(28417)	58415	(28559)
58377	(28428)	58418	(28580)
58378	(28430)	58419	(28583)
58381	(28450)	58420	(28585)
58382	(28451)	58421	(28589)
58383	(28457)	58426	(28611)
58389	(28492)	58427	(28616)
58393	(28507)	58429	(28619)
58394	(28509)	58430	(28622)
58396	(28512)		

Total 29

0-6-2T   2F

Introduced 1882. Webb L.N.W. " Coal
   Tanks."
Weight : 43 tons 15 cwt.
Pressure : 150 lb.
Cyls. : 17″×24″.
Dr. Wheels : 4′ 5½″.   T.E. : 16,530 lb.
(Former L.M.S. numbers in brackets)

58880	(27553)	58910	(7741)
58887	(27596)	58911	(7746)
58888	(27602)	58913	(7752)
58889	(27603)	58915	(7757)
58891	(27621)	58919	(7773)
58892	(27625)	58921	(7782)
58895	(27654)	58924	(7791)
58899	(7692)	58925	(7794)
58900	(7699)	58926	(7799)
58902	(7710)	58932	(7822)
58903	(7711)	58933	(7829)
58904	(7720)	58935	(7833)
58908	(7737)		

Total 25

FORMER L.M.S.
SERVICE LOCOS.

0-6-0T   2F

Introduced 1879. Park North London
   design (oldest survivor built 1881).
Weight : 45 tons 10 cwt.
Pressure : 160 lb.
Cyls. : (O) 17″×24″.
Dr. Wheels : 4′ 4″.   T.E. : 18,140 lb.
(Former L.M.S. numbers in brackets)

58850	(27505)	58857	(27517)
58851	(27509)	58858	(27520)
58852	(27510)	58859	(27522)
58853	(27512)	58860	(27527)
58854	(27513)	58861	(27528)
58855	(27514)	58862	(27530)
58856	(27515)	58863	(27532)

Total 14

0-6-0ST   2F

Introduced 1870. Webb version of
   Ramsbottom " Special Tank " (oldest
   survivor built 1875).
Weight : 34 tons 10 cwt.
Pressure : 140 lb.
Cyls. : 17″×24″.
Dr. Wheels : 4′ 5½″.   T.E. : 17,005 lb.

3323 (L.N.W. No) Crewe Loco.
       Works
C.D.3 Wolverton Carriage
       Works
C.D.6   ,,   ,,   ,,
C.D.7   ,,   ,,   ,,
C.D.8 "Earlestown" Wolverton
       Carriage Works

Service Locos.

0-6-0ST   2F

Introduced 1891. Aspinall rebuild o
L. & Y. Barton Wright class 23
0-6-0 tender loco. (introduced 1876).
Weight : 43 tons 17 cwt.
Pressure : 140 lb.
Cyls. : 17½″ × 26″.
Dr. Wheels : 4′ 6″.   T.E. 17,545 lb.

51304
51305
51324 ⎬ Horwich Loco. Works
51368
51394

(see p. 54 for *remainder of class*)

0-4-0   Diesel

Introduced 1936. Fowler diesel.
Weight : 21 tons 5 cwt.
Departmental Locomotives :

| E.D.1 | E.D.3 | E.D.5 |
| E.D.2 | E.D.4 | E.D.6 |

Total 6

(E.D.1. renumbered from E.D.2.)

0-4 0 Diesel

18″ gauge.
Introduced 1930. Hudswell Clarke
47½ h.p. design for Crewe works,
transferred to Horwich in 1935.
Departmental locomotive :—
ZM9

0-4-0   Battery

Introduced 1914.
Weight : 18 tons.
Midland design, for West India Docks.
41550   **Total 1**
Introduced 1917. North Staffordshire
design, now used at Oakamoor
(Electrical Engineer's dept.).
Weight : 17 tons.

Unnumbered

Total 1

HISTORIC LOCOMOTIVES PRESERVED IN STORE

Type	Originating Company	Pre-Grouping No.	L.M.S. No.	Name	Place of Preservation
4-2-2	M.R.	118	(673)	—	Derby
2-2-2	L.N.W.	(49)	—	Columbine	York Museum
2-2-2	L.N.W.	3020	—	Cornwall	Crewe
2-4-0	L.N.W.	790	(5031)	Hardwicke	Crewe
*0-4-0T	L.N.W.	—	—	Pet	Crewe
0-4-0	F.R.	3	—	Coppernob	Horwich
0-4-2	Liverpool & Manchester	—	—	Lion	Crewe
4-2-2	C.R.	123	(14010)	—	S t.Rollox
4-6-0	H.R.	103	(17916)	—	St. Rollox

The un-bracketed numbers are the ones at present carried by the locos.
*18in. gauge works shunter.

THE ABC OF BRITISH RAILWAYS LOCOMOTIVES

EDITED BY A. F. COOK

PART 4 - Nos. 60001-90774

EASTERN, NORTH EASTERN,
SCOTTISH REGION, EX-W.D. &
B.R. STANDARD STEAM
LOCOMOTIVES

LONDON :

Ian Allan Ltd

FOREWORD

THIS booklet lists all British Railways locomotives numbered between 60000 and 90774. This series of numbers includes all Eastern, North Eastern and Scottish (ex-L.N.E.R.) Region steam locomotives, i.e. steam locomotives of the former L.N.E.R., new British Railways standard locomotives and ex-Ministry of Supply locos. Under the general British Railways renumbering scheme, the numbers of L.N.E.R. steam locomotives were increased by 60000, with the exception of Classes W1 and L1. A later scheme involved the renumbering of all ex-M.o.S. locomotives in the 90000 series, and there have also been minor amendments to Classes B16 and D31 to make way for new locomotives.

Former L.N.E.R. electric, diesel electric and petrol locomotives have been renumbered in the 20000 and 15000 series, and details of them will be found in ABC of British Railways Locomotives, Part 2 (Nos. 10000-39999).

NOTES ON THE USE OF THIS BOOK

In the lists of locomotives which follow :

1. Many of the classes listed are sub-divided, the sub-divisions being denoted in some cases by " Parts " shown thus : D16/3. At the head of each class will be found a list of such sub-divisions, if any, usually arranged in order of introduction. Each part is given there a reference mark by which its relevant dimensions, if differing from other parts, and the locos in the list it comprises, may be identified. Any other differences between locomotives are also indicated, with reference marks, below the details of the class's introduction. For further remarks on the classification of ex-L.N.E.R. locos, see the note on p. 64.

2. The lists of dimensions at the head of each class show locomotives fitted with two inside cylinders, Stephenson gear and slide valves, unless otherwise stated, e.g. (O) = two outside cylinders, P.V. = piston valves.

3. The following method is used to denote superheated locomotives, the letters being inserted, where applicable, after the boiler pressure details : Su = All engines superheated.

SS = Some engines superheated.

4. The date on which the first locomotive of a class was built is denoted by " Introduced." If the oldest locomotive still running was built at a later date, that also is indicated.

5. The numbers of locomotives in service have been checked to March 24th, 1951.

6. S denotes Service (Departmental) locomotive. This reference letter is introduced only for the reader's guidance and is not borne by the locomotive concerned.

NUMERICAL LIST OF ENGINES

4-6-2   8P   Class A4

*Introduced 1935. Gresley streamlined design.
†‡Inside cylinder reduced to 17″.
‡§Non-corridor tender (remainder corridor).
**Kylchap blast pipe and double chimney.
Weights : Loco. 102 tons 19 cwt.
Tender { 64 tons 19 cwt.
{ 60 tons 7 cwt.‡§
Pressure : 250 lb. Su.
Cyls.: { (3) 18½″ × 26″.
{ (2) 18¼″ × 26″. (1) 17″ × 26″†
Driving Wheels : 6′ 8″.
T.E.: { 35,455 lb.
{ 33,616 lb.†
Walschaerts gear and derived motion P.V.

60001 § Sir Ronald Matthews
60002 § Sir Murrough Wilson
60003 † Andrew K. McCosh
60004 § William Whitelaw
60005 §**Sir Charles Newton
60006 * Sir Ralph Wedgwood
60007 * Sir Nigel Gresley
60008 * Dwight D. Eisenhower
60009 * Union of South Africa
60010 * Dominion of Canada
60011 * Empire of India
60012 † Commonwealth of Australia
60013 * Dominion of New
60014 † Silver Link   [Zealand
60015 * Quicksilver
60016 * Silver King
60017 * Silver Fox
60018 § Sparrow Hawk
60019 § Bittern
60020 ‡ Guillemot
60021 § Wild Swan
60022 ** Mallard
60023 § Golden Eagle
60024 * Kingfisher
60025 * Falcon
60026 * Miles Beevor
60027 * Merlin
60028 * Walter K. Whigham
60029 * Woodcock

60030 § Golden Fleece
60031 † Golden Plover
60032 § Gannet
60033 ** Seagull
60034 ** Lord Faringdon

Total 34

4-6-2   7P   Class A3

A3 Introduced 1927. Development of Gresley G.N. 180 lb. Pacific (introduced 1922, L.N.E.R. A1, later A10) with 220 lb. pressure (prototype and others rebuilt from A10). Some have G.N.-type tender† with coal rails, remainder L.N.E.R. pattern.
*Kylchap blast pipe and double chimney.
Weights : Loco. 96 tons 5 cwt.
Tender { 56 tons 6 cwt.†
{ 57 tons 18 cwt.
Pressure : 220 lb. Su. Cyls.: 19″ × 26″
Driving Wheels: 6′ 8″ T.E.: 32,910 lb.
Walschaerts gear and derived motion, P.V.

60035 Windsor Lad
60036 Colombo
60037 Hyperion
60038 Firdaussi
60039 Sandwich
60040 Cameronian
60041 Salmon Trout
60042 Singapore
60043 Brown Jack
60044 Melton
60045 Lemberg
60046 Diamond Jubilee
60047 Donovan
60048 Doncaster
60049 Galtee More
60050 Persimmon
60051 Blink Bonny
60052 Prince Palatine
60053 Sansovino
60054 Prince of Wales
60055 Woolwinder
60056 Centenary
60057 Ormonde
60058 Blair Athol

3

60059	Tracery
60060	The Tetrarch
60061	Pretty Polly
60062	Minoru
60063	Isinglass
60064	Tagalie
60065	Knight of Thistle
60066	Merry Hampton
60067	Ladas
60068	Sir Visto
60069	Sceptre
60070	Gladiateur
60071	Tranquil
60072	Sunstar
60073	St. Gatien
60074	Harvester
60075	St. Frusquin
60076	Galopin
60077	The White Knight
60078	Night Hawk
60079	Bayardo
60080	Dick Turpin
60081	Shotover
60082	Neil Gow
60083	Sir Hugo
60084	Trigo
60085	Manna
60086	Gainsborough
60087	Blenheim
60088	Book Law
60089	Felstead
60090	Grand Parade
60091	Captain Cuttle
60092	Fairway
60093	Coronach
60094	Colorado
60095	Flamingo
60096	Papyrus
60097*	Humorist
60098	Spion Kop
60099	Call Boy
60100	Spearmint
60101	Cicero
60102	Sir Frederick Banbury
60103	Flying Scotsman
60104	Solario
60105	Victor Wild
60106	Flying Fox

60107	Royal Lancer
60108	Gay Crusader
60109	Hermit
60110	Robert the Devil
60111	Enterprise
60112	St. Simon

Total 78

4-6-2 8P **Class A1**

A1/1* Introduced 1945. Thompson rebuild of A10.

A1 Peppercorn development of A1/1 for new construction.

A1† Fitted with roller bearings.

Weights : Loco. $\begin{cases} 101 \text{ tons.*} \\ 104 \text{ tons 2 cwt.} \end{cases}$ Tender 60 tons 7 cwt.

Pressure : 250 lb. Su.

Cyls.: (3) 19″ × 26″

Driving Wheels : 6′ 8″ T.E.: 37,400 lb.

Walschaerts gear, P.V.

60113*	Great Northern
60114	W. P. Allen
60115	Meg Merrilies
60116	Hal o' the Wynd
60117	Bois Roussel
60118	Archibald Sturrock
60119	Patrick Stirling
60120	Kittiwake
60121	Silurian
60122	Curlew
60123	H. A. Ivatt
60124	Kenilworth
60125	Scottish Union
60126	Sir Vincent Raven
60127	Wilson Worsdell
60128	Bongrace
60129	Guy Mannering
60130	Kestrel
60131	Osprey
60132	Marmion
60133	Pommern
60134	Foxhunter
60135	Madge Wildfire
60136	Alcazar
60137	Redgauntlet
60138	Boswell

60139	Sea Eagle
60140	Balmoral
60141	Abbotsford
60142	Edward Fletcher
60143	Sir Walter Scott
60144	King's Courier
60145	Saint Mungo
60146	Peregrine
60147	North Eastern
60148	Aboyeur
60149	Amadis
60150	Willbrook
60151	Midlothian
60152	Holyrood
60153†	Flamboyant
60154†	Bon Accord
60155†	Borderer
60156†	Great Central
60157†	Great Eastern
60158	Aberdonian
60159	Bonnie Dundee
60160	Auld Reekie
60161	North British
60162	Saint Johnstoun

Total 50

————

4-6-2 7MT (A2/1:6MT) Class A2

A2/2* Introduced 1943. Original Thompson Pacific, rebuilt from Gresley Class P2 2-8-2 (introduced 1934).
Weight : Loco. 101 tons 10 cwt.
Pressure : 225 lb. Su.
Cyls.: (3) 20″ × 26″
Driving Wheels : 6′ 2″ T.E.: 40,320 lb.

A2/1† Introduced 1944. Development of Class A2/2, incorporating Class V2 2-6-2 type boiler.
Weight : Loco. 98 tons.
Pressure : 225 lb. Su.
Cyls.: (3) 19″ × 26″
Driving Wheels : 6′ 2″ T.E.: 36,385 lb.

A2/3‡ Introduced 1946. Development of Class A2/2 for new construction.
Weight : Loco. 101 tons 10 cwt.
Pressure : 250 lb. Su.
Cyls.: (3) 19″ × 26″
Driving Wheels : 6′ 2″ T.E.: 40,430 lb.

A2§ Introduced 1947. Peppercorn development of Class A2/3 with shorter wheelbase. (No. 60539 built with double blast pipe.)

A2** Rebuilt with double blastpipe and multiple valve regulator.
Weight : Loco. 101 tons.
Pressure : 250 lb. Su.
Cyls.: (3) 19″ × 26″
Driving Wheels : 6′ 2″ T.E.: 40,430 lb.
Tender weight (all parts): 60 tons 7 cwt. (except Nos. 60509-10, 52 tons).
Walschaerts gear, P.V.

60500‡	Edward Thompson
60501*	Cock o' the North
60502*	Earl Marischal
60503*	Lord President
60504*	Mons Meg
60505*	Thane of Fife
60506*	Wolf of Badenoch
60507*	Highland Chieftain
60508†	Duke of Rothesay
60509†	Waverley
60510†	Robert the Bruce
60511‡	Airborne
60512‡	Steady Aim
60513‡	Dante
60514‡	Chamossaire
60515‡	Sun Stream
60516‡	Hycilla
60517‡	Ocean Swell
60518‡	Tehran
60519‡	Honeyway
60520‡	Owen Tudor
60521‡	Watling Street
60522‡	Straight Deal
60523‡	Sun Castle
60524‡	Herringbone
60525§	A. H. Peppercorn
60526**	Sugar Palm
60527§	Sun Chariot
60528§	Tudor Minstrel
60529**	Pearl Diver
60530§	Sayajirao
60531§	Bahram
60532**	Blue Peter
60533**	Happy Knight
60534§	Irish Elegance
60535§	Hornet's Beauty
60536§	Trimbush

60537§ Bachelor's Button
60538**Velocity
60539§ Bronzino

Totals :
Class A2   15   Class A2/2   6
Class A2/1   4   Class A2/3   15

———————

4-6-4   8P   Class W1

Introduced 1937. Rebuilt from Gresley
  experimental high-pressure 4-cyl.
  compound with water-tube boiler,
  introduced 1929.
Weights : Loco. 107 tons 17 cwt.
               Tender 60 tons 7 cwt.
Pressure : 250 lb. Su.
Cyls.: (3) 20″ × 26″
Driving Wheels : 6′ 8″ T.E. 41,435 lb.
Walschaerts gear and derived motion,
  P.V.

60700   **Total 1**

———————

2-6-2   6MT   Class V2

Introduced 1936. Gresley design.
Weights : Loco.   93 tons 2 cwt.
               Tender 52 tons.
Pressure : 220 lb. Su.
Cyls.: (3) 18½″ × 26″
Driving Wheels : 6′ 2″ T.E.: 33,730 lb.
Walschaerts gear and derived motion,
  P.V.

60800   Green Arrow
60801
60802
60803
60804
60805
60806
60807
60808
60809   The Snapper, The East
        Yorkshire Regiment,
        The Duke of York's
        Own
60810
60811

60812
60813
60814
60815
60816
60817
60818
60819
60820
60821
60822
60823
60824
60825
60826
60827
60828
60829
60830
60831
60832
60833
60834
60835   The Green Howard,
        Alexandra, Princess of
        Wales's Own Yorkshire
        Regiment
60836
60837
60838
60839
60840
60841
60842
60843
60844
60845
60846
60847   St. Peter's School, York,
            A.D. 627
60848
60849
60850
60851
60852
60853
60854
60855

60856			
60857			
60858			
60859			
60860	Durham School		
60861			
60862			
60863			
60864			
60865			
60866			
60867			
60868			
60869			
60870			
60871			
60872	King's Own Yorkshire Light Infantry		
60873	Coldstreamer		
60874	60902	60930	60958
60875	60903	60931	60959
60876	60904	60932	60960
60877	60905	60933	60961
60878	60906	60934	60962
60879	60907	60935	60963
60880	60908	60936	60964
60881	60909	60937	60965
60882	60910	60938	60966
60883	60911	60939	60967
60884	60912	60940	60968
60885	60913	60941	60969
60886	60914	60942	60970
60887	60915	60943	60971
60888	60916	60944	60972
60889	60917	60945	60973
60890	60918	60946	60974
60891	60919	60947	60975
60892	60920	60948	60976
60893	60921	60949	60977
60894	60922	60950	60978
60895	60923	60951	60979
60896	60924	60952	60980
60897	60925	60953	60981
60898	60926	60954	60982
60899	60927	60955	60983
60900	60928	60956	
60901	60929	60957	

Total 184

4-6-0   5MT   Class B1

Introduced 1942. Thompson design.
Weights : Loco.   71 tons 3 cwt.
             Tender 52 tons.
Pressure : 225 lb. Su.
Cyls.: (O) 20″ × 26″
Driving Wheels : 6′ 2″ T.E.: 26,880 lb.
Walschaerts gear, P.V.

61000	Springbok
61001	Eland
61002	Impala
61003	Gazelle
61004	Oryx
61005	Bongo
61006	Blackbuck
61007	Klipspringer
61008	Kudu
61009	Hartebeeste
61010	Wildebeeste
61011	Waterbuck
61012	Puku
61013	Topi
61014	Oribi
61015	Duiker
61016	Inyala
61017	Bushbuck
61018	Gnu
61019	Nilghai
61020	Gemsbok
61021	Reitbok
61022	Sassaby
61023	Hirola
61024	Addax
61025	Pallah
61026	Ourebi
61027	Madoqua
61028	Umseke
61029	Chamois
61030	Nyala
61031	Reedbuck
61032	Stembok
61033	Dibatag
61034	Chiru
61035	Pronghorn
61036	Ralph Assheton
61037	Jairou
61038	Blacktail
61039	Steinbok
61040	Roedeer

61041-61245

61041	61079	61116	61153	61199
61042	61080	61117	61154	61200
61043	61081	61118	61155	61201
61044	61082	61119	61156	61202
61045	61083	61120	61157	61203
61046	61084	61121	61158	61204
61047	61085	61122	61159	61205
61048	61086	61123	61160	61206
61049	61087	61124	61161	61207
61050	61088	61125	61162	61208
61051	61089	61126	61163	61209
61052	61090	61127	61164	61210
61053	61091	61128	61165	61211
61054	61092	61129	61166	61212
61055	61093	61130	61167	61213
61056	61094	61131	61168	61214
61058	61095	61132	61169	61215 William Henton Carver
61059	61096	61133	61170	61216
61060	61097	61134	61171	61217
61061	61098	61135	61172	61218
61062	61099	61136	61173	61219
61063	61100	61137	61174	61220
61064	61101	61138	61175	61221 Sir Alexander Erskine-Hill
61065	61102	61139	61176	
61066	61103	61140	61177	61222
61067	61104	61141	61178	61223
61068	61105	61142	61179	61224
61069	61106	61143	61180	61225
61070	61107	61144	61181	61226
61071	61108	61145	61182	61227
61072	61109	61146	61183	61228
61073	61110	61147	61184	61229
61074	61111	61148	61185	61230
61075	61112	61149	61186	61231
61076	61113	61150	61187	61232
61077	61114	61151	61188	61233
61078	61115	61152		61234
				61235
61189 Sir William Gray				61236
61190				61237 Geoffrey H. Kitson
61191				61238 Leslie Runciman
61192				61239
61193				61240 Harry Hinchliffe
61194				61241 Viscount Ridley
61195				61242 Alexander Reith Gray
61196				61243 Sir Harold Mitchell
61197				61244 Strang Steel
61198				61245 Murray of Elibank

61246	Lord Balfour of Burleigh		
61247	Lord Burghley		
61248	Geoffrey Gibbs		
61249	FitzHerbert Wright		
61250	A. Harold Bibby		
61251	Oliver Bury		

61252	61292	61332	61372
61253	61293	61333	61373
61254	61294	61334	61374
61255	61295	61335	61375
61256	61296	61336	61376
61257	61297	61337	61377
61258	61298	61338	61378
61259	61299	61339	61379
61260	61300	61340	61380
61261	61301	61341	61381
61262	61302	61342	61382
61263	61303	61343	61383
61264	61304	61344	61384
61265	61305	61345	61385
61266	61306	61346	61386
61267	61307	61347	61387
61268	61308	61348	61388
61269	61309	61349	61389
61270	61310	61350	61390
61271	61311	61351	61391
61272	61312	61352	61392
61273	61313	61353	61393
61274	61314	61354	61394
61275	61315	61355	61395
61276	61316	61356	61396
61277	61317	61357	61397
61278	61318	61358	61398
61279	61319	61359	61399
61280	61320	61360	61400
61281	61321	61361	61401
61282	61322	61362	61402
61283	61323	61363	61403
61284	61324	61364	61404
61285	61325	61365	61405
61286	61326	61366	61406
61287	61327	61367	61407
61288	61328	61368	61408
61289	61329	61369	61409
61290	61330	61370	
61291	61331	61371	

N.B.—Locomotives of this class are still being delivered.

4-6-0   6MT   Class B16

B16/1 Introduced 1920. Raven N.E. design with inside Stephenson gear.
B16/2* Introduced 1937. Gresley rebuild of B16/1 with outside Walschaerts gear and derived motion for inside cylinder.
B16/3† Introduced 1944. Thompson rebuild of B16/1 with three Walschaerts gears.

Weights : Loco. { 77 tons 14 cwt.
79 tons 4 cwt.*
78 tons 19 cwt.†
Tender 46 tons 12 cwt.
Pressure : 180 lb. Su.
Cyls.: (3) 18½″ × 26″
Driving Wheels : 5′ 8″ T.E.: 30,030 lb. P.V.

61410	61428	61446	61464†
61411	61429	61447	61465
61412	61430	61448†	61466
61413	61431	61449†	61467†
61414	61432	61450	61468†
61415	61433	61451	61469
61416	61434†	61452	61470
61417†	61435*	61453†	61471
61418†	61436	61454†	61472†
61419	61437*	61455*	61473
61420†	61438*	61456	61474
61421*	61439†	61457*	61475*
61422	61440	61458	61476†
61423	61441	61459	61477
61424	61442	61460	61478
61425	61443	61461†	
61426	61444†	61462	
61427	61445	61463†	

Totals : Class B16/1 45
Class B16/2 7
Class B16/3 17

4-6-0   4P   Class B12

B12/1* Introduced 1911. S. D. Holden G.E. design with small Belpaire boiler.
B12/3 Introduced 1932. Gresley rebuild of B12/1 with large round-topped boiler and long-travel valves.
B12/1† Introduced 1943. Rebuild of B12/1 with small round-topped boiler, retaining original valves.
(B12/2 was a development of B12/1 with Lentz valves, since rebuilt to B12/3.)

9

Weights : Loco. $\begin{cases} 63 \text{ tons.*†} \\ 69 \text{ tons 10 cwt.} \end{cases}$
          Tender 39 tons 6 cwt.
Pressure : 180 lb. Su. Cyls.: 20″ × 28″
Driving Wheels : 6′ 6″ T.E.: 21,970 lb.
P.V.

61501*	61525	61549	61567
61502*	61526†	61550	61568
61503*	61528*	61552*	61569
61505†	61530	61553	61570
61507†	61532†	61554	61571
61508†	61533	61555	61572
61511†	61535	61556	61573
61512	61537	61557	61574
61513*	61538	61558	61575
61514	61539*	61559	61576
61515	61540	61560*	61577
61516	61541	61561	61578
61519	61542	61562	61579
61520	61543*	61563*	61580
61521*	61545	61564	
61523	61546	61565	
61524†	61547	61566	

Totals : Class B12/1 18
          Class B12/3 47

Classes
4-6-0   4P   **B2 & B17**

B17/1[1] Introduced 1928. Gresley design for G.E. section with G.E.-type tenders.

B17/6[2] Introduced 1947. B17/1 fitted with 100A (B1 type) boiler.

B17/4[3] Introduced 1936. Locos with L.N.E.R. 4,200-gallon tenders.

B17/6[4] Introduced 1943. B17/4 fitted with 100A (B1 type) boiler.

B17/5[5] Introduced 1937. Rebuild of B17/4 with streamlined casing.

B17/5[6] B17/5 fitted with 100A boiler. (B17/2 and B17/3 were variants of B17/1 now included in that part.)

Weights : Loco. $\begin{cases} 77 \text{ tons } 5 \text{ cwt.}[1] \\ 77 \text{ tons } 5 \text{ cwt.}[2] \\ 77 \text{ tons } 5 \text{ cwt.}[3] \\ 77 \text{ tons } 5 \text{ cwt.}[4] \\ 80 \text{ tons } 10 \text{ cwt.}[5] \\ 80 \text{ tons } 10 \text{ cwt.}[6] \end{cases}$

Tender $\begin{cases} 39 \text{ tons } 6 \text{ cwt.}[1] \\ 39 \text{ tons } 6 \text{ cwt.}[2] \\ 52 \text{ tons.}[3] \\ 52 \text{ tons.}[4] \\ 52 \text{ tons } 13 \text{ cwt.}[5] \end{cases}$

Pressure : $\begin{cases} 180 \text{ lb.}[1] \\ 225 \text{ lb.}[2] \\ 180 \text{ lb.}[3] \\ 225 \text{ lb.}[4] \\ 180 \text{ lb.}[5] \\ 225 \text{ lb.}[6] \end{cases}$ Su.

Cyls.: (3) $17\frac{1}{4}$″ × 26″
Driving Wheels : 6′ 8″

T.E.: $\begin{cases} 22,485 \text{ lb.}[1] \\ 28,555 \text{ lb.}[2] \\ 22,485 \text{ lb.}[3] \\ 28,555 \text{ lb.}[4] \\ 22,485 \text{ lb.}[5][6] \end{cases}$

Walschaerts gear and derived motion, P.V.

B2[7] Introduced 1945. Thompson 2-cyl. rebuild of B17, with 100A boiler and ex-N.E. tender.

B2[8] Introduced 1945, with L.N.E.R. tender.

Weights : Loco.   73 tons 10 cwt.
          Tender$\begin{cases} 46 \text{ tons } 12 \text{ cwt.}[7] \\ 52 \text{ tons.}[8] \end{cases}$

Pressure : 225 lb. Su.
Cyls.: (O) 20″ × 26″
Driving Wheels : 6′ 8″ T.E.: 24,865 lb.
Walschaerts gear and derived motion, P.V.

61600[2]	Sandringham
61601[1]	Holkham
61602[1]	Walsingham
61603[7]	Framlingham
61604[1]	Elveden
61605[2]	Lincolnshire Regiment
61606[2]	Audley End
61607[7]	Blickling
61608[1]	Gunton
61609[1]	Quidenham
61610[1]	Honingham Hall
61611[1]	Raynham Hall
61612[1]	Houghton Hall
61613[1]	Woodbastwick Hall
61614[7]	Castle Hedingham
61615[8]	Culford Hall
61616[7]	Fallodon
61617[7]	Ford Castle
61618[1]	Wynyard Park
61619[1]	Welbeck Abbey
61620[1]	Clumber
61621[1]	Hatfield House
61622[2]	Alnwick Castle
61623[2]	Lambton Castle

61624¹	Lumley Castle
61625¹	Raby Castle
61626¹	Brancepeth Castle
61627³	Aske Hall
61628²	Harewood House
61629¹	Naworth Castle
61630²	Tottenham Hotspur
61631¹	Serlby Hall
61632⁸	Belvoir Castle
61633²	Kimbolton Castle
61634¹	Hinchingbrooke
61635²	Milton
61636¹	Harlaxton Manor
61637¹	Thorpe Hall
61638²	Melton Hall
61639⁷	Norwich City
61640¹	Somerleyton Hall
61641³	Gayton Hall
61642²	Kilverstone Hall
61643¹	Champion Lodge
61644⁷	Earlham Hall
61645¹	The Suffolk Regiment
61646²	Gilwell Park
61647³	Helmingham Hall
61648⁸	Arsenal
61649³	Sheffield United
61650²	Grimsby Town
61651²	Derby County
61652⁴	Darlington
61653³	Huddersfield Town
61654⁴	Sunderland
61655³	Middlesbrough
61656³	Leeds United
61657²	Doncaster Rovers
61658²	The Essex Regiment
61659⁶	East Anglian
61660³	Hull City
61661³	Sheffield Wednesday
61662³	Manchester United
61663³	Everton
61664²	Liverpool
61665⁴	Leicester City
61666⁴	Nottingham Forest
61667³	Bradford
61668²	Bradford City
61669⁴	Barnsley
61670⁵	City of London
61671⁸	Royal Sovereign

61672⁸ West Ham United

Totals : Class B2 10
Class B17/1 24
Class B17/4 15
Class B17/5 2
Class B17/6 22

4-6-0 Class B13

Introduced 1899 (Survivor built 1906). Worsdell N.E. design later rebuilt to counter-pressure loco for loco testing purposes. Now maintained at Rugby Testing Plant.
Pressure : 160 lb. Cyls.: (O) 20″ × 26″
Driving Wheels: 6′ 1¼″ T.E.: 19,310 lb. P.V.

61699S Total 1

2-6-2 5MT Class V4

Introduced 1941. Gresley design.
Weights : Loco. 70 tons 8 cwt.
Tender 42 tons 15 cwt.
Pressure : 250 lb. Su.
Cyls.: (3) 15″ × 26″
Driving Wheels : 5′ 8″ T.E.: 27,420 lb.
Walschaerts gear and derived motion, P.V.

61700 Bantam Cock
61701 Total 2

2-6-0 4MT Class K2

K2/2 Introduced 1914. Gresley G.N. design.
† K2/2 fitted with side-window cab in Scottish Region.
K2/1* Introduced 1931. Rebuilt from small-boilered K1 (introduced 1912).
‡ K2/1 with side-window cab.
Weights : Loco. 64 tons 8 cwt.
Tender 43 tons 2 cwt.
Pressure : 180 lb. Su.
Cyls.: (O) 20″ × 26″
Driving Wheels : 5′ 8″ T.E.: 23,400 lb.
Walschaerts gear, P.V.

61720*	61727*	61734	61741
61721*	61728*	61735	61742
61722*	61729‡	61736	61743
61723*	61730	61737	61744
61724*	61731	61738	61745
61725*	61732	61739	61746
61726*	61733	61740	61747

61748	61752	61756	61760
61749	61753	61757	61761
61750	61754	61758	61762
61751	61755	61759	61763

61764† Loch Arkaig

61765	61767	61769	61771
61766	61768	61770	

61772† Loch Lochy
61773

61774† Loch Garry
61775† Loch Treig

61776†	61778	61780
61777	61779†	

61781† Loch Morar
61782† Loch Eil
61783† Loch Sheil

61784† | 61785† | 61786†

61787† Loch Quoich
61788† Loch Rannoch
61789† Loch Laidon
61790† Loch Lomond
61791† Loch Laggan

61792† | 61793†

61794† Loch Oich

Totals : Class K2/1 9
Class K2/2 66

Classes
2-6-0 6MT K3 & K5

K3/2 Introduced 1924. Development of Gresley G.N. design, built to L.N.E.R. loading gauge.

K3/3* Introduced 1929. Differ in details only, such as springs, from K3/2.

‡ K3/2 fitted with ex-G.N. tender. (K3/1 were ex-G.N. locos (introduced 1920), with G.N. cabs, and K3/4, K3/5 and K3/6 were variations of K3/2, differing in weight and details. These locos have now been modified to K3/2.)

Weights : Loco. 72 tons 12 cwt.
Tender { 52 tons.
{ 43 tons 2 cwt.‡
Pressure : 180 lb. Su.
Cyls. : (3) 18½″ × 26″
Driving Wheels : 5′ 8″ T.E. : 30,030 lb.
Walschaerts gear and derived motion, P.V.

K5† Introduced 1945. Thompson 2-cyl. rebuild of K3.
Weights : Loco. 71 tons 5 cwt.
Tender 52 tons.
Pressure : 225 lb. Su.
Cyls. : (O) 20″ × 26″
Driving Wheels : 5′ 8″ T.E. : 29,250 lb
Walschaerts gear, P.V.

61800	61842	61884*	61926
61801	61843	61885*	61927
61802	61844	61886*	61928
61803	61845	61887*	61929
61804	61846	61888*	61930
61805	61847	61889*	61931
61806	61848	61890	61932
61807	61849	61891	61933
61808	61850	61892	61934
61809	61851	61893	61935
61810	61852	61894	61936
61811	61853	61895	61937
61812‡	61854‡	61896	61938
61813	61855‡	61897	61939
61814	61856‡	61898	61940
61815	61857‡	61899	61941
61816	61858‡	61900	61942
61817	61859‡	61901	61943
61818	61860	61902	61944
61819	61861	61903	61945
61820	61862	61904	61946
61821	61863†	61905	61947
61822	61864	61906	61948
61823	61865	61907	61949
61824	61866	61908	61950
61825	61867	61909	61951
61826	61868	61910	61952
61827	61869	61911	61953
61828	61870*	61912	61954
61829	61871*	61913	61955
61830	61872*	61914	61956
61831	61873*	61915	61957
61832	61874*	61916	61958
61833	61875*	61917	61959
61834	61876*	61918	61960
61835	61877*	61919	61961
61836	61878*	61920	61962
61837	61879*	61921	61963
61838	61880*	61922	61964
61839	61881*	61923	61965
61840	61882*	61924	61966
61841‡	61883*	61925	61967

61968	61975	61982	61989
61969	61976	61983	61990
61970	61977	61984	61991
61971	61978	61985	61992
61972	61979	61986	
61973	61980	61987	
61974	61981	61988	

Totals : Class K3/2 172
Class K3/3 20
Class K5 1

62045	62052	62059	62066
62046	62053	62060	62067
62047	62054	62061	62068
62048	62055	62062	62069
62049	62056	62063	62070
62050	62057	62064	
62051	62058	62065	

Totals : Class K1 70
Class K1/1 1
Class K4 5

2-6-0 6MT K1 & K4

K4* Introduced 1937. Gresley loco for West Highland line.
Weights : Loco. 68 tons 8 cwt.
Tender 44 tons 4 cwt.
Pressure : 200 lb. Su.
Cyls.: (3) 18½″ × 26″
Driving Wheels : 5′ 2″ T.E.: 36,600 lb.
Walschaerts gear and derived motion, P.V.
K1/1† Introduced 1945. Thompson 2-cyl. loco. Rebuilt from K4.
K1 Introduced 1949. Peppercorn development of Thompson K1/1 (No. 61997) for new construction, with increased length.
Weights : Loco. 66 tons 17 cwt.
Tender 44 tons 4 cwt.
Pressure : 225 lb. Su.
Cyls.: (O) 20″ × 26″
Driving Wheels : 5′ 2″ T.E.: 32,080 lb.
Walschaerts gear, P.V.

61993* Loch Long
61994* The Great Marquess
61995* Cameron of Locheil
61996* Lord of the Isles
61997† MacCailin Mor
61998* MacLeod of MacLeod

62001	62012	62023	62034
62002	62013	62024	62035
62003	62014	62025	62036
62004	62015	62026	62037
62005	62016	62027	62038
62006	62017	62028	62039
62007	62018	62029	62040
62008	62019	62030	62041
62009	62020	62031	62042
62010	62021	62032	62043
62011	62022	62033	62044

4-4-0 1P Class D3

Introduced 1896. Ivatt G.N. design. Survivor rebuilt with large boiler and later with side-window cab for working officers' saloons.
Weights : Loco. 45 tons 14 cwt.
Tender 38 tons 10 cwt.
Pressure : 175 lb. Cyls.: 17½″ × 26″
Driving Wheels : 6′ 8″ T.E.: 14,805 lb.

62000 **Total 1**

4-4-0 1P Class D2

Introduced 1897. Ivatt G.N. design.
Weights : Loco. 45 tons 10 cwt.
Tender 40 tons 18 cwt.
Pressure : 175 lb.
Cyls.: 17½″ × 26″
Driving Wheels : 6′ 8″
T.E.: 14,805 lb.

62172 **Total 1**

4-4-0 2P Class D41

Introduced 1893. Pickersgill and Johnson G.N.o.S. design.
Weights : Loco. 45 tons.
Tender 37 tons 8 cwt.
Pressure : 165 lb. Cyls.: 18″ × 26″
Driving Wheels : 6′ 1″ T.E.: 16,185 lb.

62225	62231	62246	62255
62228	62232	62248	62256
62229	62241	62251	
62230	62242	62252	

Total 14

13

4-4-0 2P Class D40

Introduced 1899. Pickersgill G.N.o.S. design.
* Introduced 1920. Heywood superheated locos.
Weights : Loco. { 46 tons 7 cwt.
48 tons 13 cwt.*
Tender 37 tons 8 cwt.
Pressure : 165 lb. SS. Cyls.: 18″ × 26″
Driving Wheels : 6′ 1″ T.E.: 16,185 lb.

62260	62264	62268	62271
62261	62265	62269	62272
62262	62267	62270	

62273* George Davidson
62274* Benachie
62275* Sir David Stewart
62276* Andrew Bain
62277* Gordon Highlander
62278* Hatton Castle
62279* Glen Grant

Total 18

4-4-0 2P Class D31

Introduced 1890 Holmes N.B. design. (Rebuilt from 1918.)
Weights : Loco. 46 tons 8 cwt.
Tender 33 tons 9 cwt.
Pressure : 175 lb. Cyls.: 18½″ × 26″
Driving Wheels : 6′ 6″ T.E.: 16,515 lb.

62281 Total 1

4-4-0 2P Class D20

D20/1 Introduced 1899. W. Worsdell N.E. design. Since superheated.
D20/2* Introduced 1936. D20/1 rebuilt with long-travel valves.
† Locos with tender rebuilt with J39-type tank.
Weights : Loco. { 54 tons 2 cwt.
55 tons 9 cwt.*
Tender { 41 tons 4 cwt.
43 tons.*
Pressure : 175 lb. Su. Cyls.: 19″ × 26″
Driving Wheels : 6′ 10″ T.E.: 17,025 lb. P.V.

62343	62349*	62354	62360*
62344	62351	62355	62362
62345	62352	62358†	62365
62347	62353	62359	62370

62371*	62378	62384	62391
62372	62379	62386†	62392
62373	62380	62387	62395
62374	62381	62388	62396
62375*	62383	62389	62397†

Totals : Class D20/1 32
Class D20/2 4

4-4-0 3P Class D29

Introduced 1909. Reid N.B. " Scott " class, later superheated.
Weights : Loco. 54 tons 4 cwt.
Tender 46 tons.
Pressure : 190 lb. Su. Cyls.: 19″ × 26″
Driving Wheels : 6′ 6″ T.E.: 19,435 lb. P.V.

62410 Ivanhoe
62411 Lady of Avenel

Total 2

4-4-0 3P Class D30

D30/2 Introduced 1914. Development of D30/1, introduced 1912 (Reid N.B. " Scott " class) with detail differences.
Weights : Loco. 57 tons 16 cwt.
Tender 46 tons 13 cwt.
Pressure : 165 lb. Su. Cyls.: 20″ × 26″
Driving Wheels : 6′ 6″ T.E.: 18,700 lb. P.V.

62418 The Pirate
62419 Meg Dods
62420 Dominie Sampson
62421 Laird o' Monkbarns
62422 Caleb Balderstone
62423 Dugald Dalgetty
62424 Claverhouse
62425 Ellangowan
62426 Cuddie Headrigg
62427 Dumbiedykes
62428 The Talisman
62429 The Abbot
62430 Jingling Geordie

62431	Kenilworth
62432	Quentin Durward
62434	Kettledrummle
62435	Norna
62436	Lord Glenvarloch
62437	Adam Woodcock
62438	Peter Poundtext
62439	Father Ambrose
62440	Wandering Willie
62441	Black Duncan
62442	Simon Glover

Total 24

4-4-0   **3P**   **Class D32**

Introduced 1906. Reid N.B. "Intermediate" class. Since superheated.
Weights : Loco. 53 tons 14 cwt.
          Tender 40 tons.
Pressure : 180 lb. Su. Cyls.: 19″ × 26″
Driving Wheels : 6′ 0″ T.E.: 19,945 lb.
P.V.

62451   **Total 1**

4-4-0   **3P**   **Class D33**

Introduced 1909. Later Reid N.B. "Intermediate" class. Since superheated.
Weights : Loco. 54 tons 3 cwt.
          Tender 44 tons 11 cwt.
Pressure : 180 lb. Su. Cyls.: 19″ × 26″
Driving Wheels : 6′ 0″ T.E.: 19,945 lb.
P.V.

62457	62460	62462	62466
62459	62461	62464	

Total 7

4-4-0   **3P**   **Class D34**

Introduced 1913. Reid N.B. "Glen" class
Weights : Loco. 57 tons 4 cwt.
          Tender 46 tons 13 cwt.
Pressure : 165 lb. Su. Cyls.: 20″ × 26″
Driving Wheels : 6′ 0″ T.E.: 20,260 lb.
P.V.

62467	Glenfinnan
62468	Glen Orchy
62469	Glen Douglas
62470	Glen Roy

62471	Glen Falloch
62472	Glen Nevis
62474	Glen Croe
62475	Glen Beasdale
62477	Glen Dochart
62478	Glen Quoich
62479	Glen Sheil
62480	Glen Fruin
62482	Glen Mamie
62483	Glen Garry
62484	Glen Lyon
62485	Glen Murran
62487	Glen Arklet
62488	Glen Aladale
62489	Glen Dessary
62490	Glen Fintaig
62492	Glen Garvin
62493	Glen Gloy
62494	Glen Gour
62495	Glen Luss
62496	Glen Loy
62497	Glen Mallie
62498	Glen Moidart

Total 27

Classes
4-4-0   **2P**   **D15 & D16**

D15[1] Introduced 1904. Belpaire boiler development of original J. Holden (G.E.) "Claud Hamilton" class, some rebuilt from D14.
D16/2[2] Introduced 1923. Hill "Super Claud"—D15 with larger boiler, some rebuilt from D15.
D16/3[3] Introduced 1933. Gresley rebuild of D15 with larger round-topped boiler and modified footplating.
D16/3[4] Introduced 1933. Rebuild of D15 with larger round-topped boiler, modified footplating and 8″ piston valves.
D16/3[5] Introduced 1936. Rebuild of D15 with larger round-topped boiler, modified footplating and 9¼″ piston valves.
D16/3[6] Introduced 1938. Rebuild of D16/2 with round-topped boiler, but retaining original footplating and slide valves.
D16/3[7] Introduced 1939. Rebuild of D16/2 with round-topped boiler and modified footplating, retaining slide valves.

15

(At grouping the remaining locos of the "Claud Hamilton" class retaining small round-topped boilers were classified D14. Saturated locos of D15 were originally classified D15, superheated locos with short smokeboxes D15/1 and superheated locos with extended smokeboxes D15/2. All the remaining locos were converted to D15/2 and then known simply as D15. D16/1 were the original D16 locos with short smokeboxes.)

Weights : Loco. { 52 tons 4 cwt.[1]
54 tons 18 cwt.[2]
55 tons 18 cwt. (all D16/3)
Tender 39 tons 5 cwt.
Pressure : 180 lb. Su. Cyls. : 19″ × 26″
Driving Wheels : 7′ 0″ T.E. : 17,095 lb.

62501[1]	62532[5]	62564[6]	62593[3]
62502[1]	62533[3]	62565[6]	62596[6]
62505[1]	62534[3]	62566[3]	62597[3]
62506[1]	62535[5]	62567[3]	62598[3]
62507[1]	62536[5]	62568[4]	62599[5]
62509[1]	62538[1]	62569[6]	62601[6]
62510[3]	62539[1]	62570[6]	62603[2]
62511[3]	62540[3]	62571[3]	62604[3]
62513[3]	62541[3]	62572[3]	62605[6]
62514[3]	62542[6]	62573[6]	62606[6]
62515[3]	62543[6]	62574[3]	62607[6]
62516[3]	62544[6]	62575[3]	62608[3]
62517[3]	62545[3]	62576[5]	62609[4]
62518[3]	62546[4]*	62577[2]	62610[3]
62519[3]	62548[3]	62578[6]	62611[6]
62520[1]	62549[3]	62579[3]	62612[6]
62521[3]	62551[3]	62580[6]	62613[6]
62522[3]	62552[6]	62581[5]	62614[7]
62523[3]	62553[6]	62582[3]	62615[6]
62524[3]	62554[6]	62584[6]	62616[6]
62525[3]	62555[6]	62585[3]	62617[6]
62526[3]	62556[6]	62586[3]	62618[6]
62527[3]	62557[6]	62587[4]	62619[6]
62528[1]	62558[6]	62588[4]	62620[6]
62529[3]	62559[3]	62589[6]	
62530[3]	62561[3]	62590[2]	
62531[3]	62562[6]	62592[6]	

Totals : Class D15   9
Class D16/2   3
Class D16/3 93

* Named *Claud Hamilton*.

4-4-0   3P   Class D10

Introduced 1913. Robinson G.C. "Director" class.
Weights : Loco.   61 tons.
Tender 48 tons 6 cwt.
Pressure : 180 lb. Su. Cyls. : 20″ × 26″
Driving Wheels : 6′ 9″ T.E. : 19,645 lb. P.V.

62650   Prince Henry
62651   Purdon Viccars
62652   Edwin A. Beazley
62653   Sir Edward Fraser
62654   Walter Burgh Gair
62655   The Earl of Kerry
62656   Sir Clement Royds
62657   Sir Berkeley Sheffield
62658   Prince George
62659   Worsley-Taylor

Total 10

4-4-0   3P   Class D11

D11/1* Introduced 1920. Robinson G.C. "Large Director," development of D10.
D11/2 Introduced 1924. Post-grouping locos built to Scottish loading gauge. From 1938 the class has been rebuilt with long-travel valves.
Weights : Loco.   61 tons 3 cwt.
Tender 48 tons 6 cwt.
Pressure : 180 lb. Su. Cyls. : 20″ × 26″
Driving Wheels : 6′ 9″ T.E. : 19,645 lb. P.V.

62660*   Butler-Henderson
62661*   Gerard Powys Dewhurst
62662*   Prince of Wales
62663*   Prince Albert
62664*   Princess Mary
62665*   Mons
62666*   Zeebrugge
62667*   Somme
62668*   Jutland
62669*   Ypres
62670*   Marne
62671   Bailie MacWheeble
62672   Baron of Bradwardine
62673   Evan Dhu
62674   Flora MacIvor
62675   Colonel Gardiner
62676   Jonathan Oldbuck
62677   Edie Ochiltree

Top to bottom : Class A1 4-6-2 No. 60141 Abbotsford ; Class A2/2 4-6-2 No. 60506 Wolf of Badenoch ; Class A3 4-6-2 No. 60055 Woolwinder ; Class A2 4-6-2 No. 60539 Bronzino.

[C. C. B. Herbert, J. Davenport, J. P. Wilson (2)

Top to bottom : Class V2 2-6-2 No. 60813 (with shovel - shaped smoke deflector); Class B1 4-6-0 No. 61407 ; Class B16/1 4-6-0 No. 61447 ; Class B16/3 4-6-0 No. 61434.

[J. F. Aylard (2),
C. C. B. Herbert,
W. J. V. Anderson]

Right : Class B2
4 - 6 - 0 No. 61603
Framlingham.

Below : Class B17/1
4 - 6 - 0 No. 61611
Raynham Hall.

[F. W. Day,
R. E. Vincent

Above : Class B12/3
4-6-0 No. 61538.

Right : Class B12/1
4-6-0 No. 1511
(new No. 61511).

[E. Treacy,
M. H. Margerison

Above left : Class K2/2 2-6-0 No. 61760. *Above right :* Class K3/2 2-6-0 No. 61807. *Below left :* Class K4 2-6-0 No. 61995 *Cameron c/ Locheil.* *Below right :* Class K1 2-6-0 No. 62015.

[P. ,H. Wells, H. C. Casserley, P. Ransome-Wallis, S. E. Teasdale

Top to bottom : Class
E4 2-4-0s Nos. 62794
(with ex-D15 class
tender) and 62784
(with cut down
chimney and side
window cab) ; Class
O2/4 2-8-0 No. 63947
(this engine has since
been rebuilt to
O2/3) : Class O1 2-8-0
No. 63619.

[H. Gordon Tidey,
M. P. Mileham,
R. E. Vincent (2)

Above left : Class D49/1 4-4-0 No. 62708 Argyllshire.   Above right : Class D49/2 4-4-0 No. 62740 The Bedale.   Below left : Class D10 4-4-0 No. 62659 Worsley-Taylor.   Below right : Class D11/1 4-4-0 No. 62660 Butler-Henderson.

J. Davenport, W. S. Garth, H. C. Casserley, A. F. Cook

Top to bottom : Class
D15 4-4-0 No. 62507
(with cut away
frames); Class D16/3
4-4-0s Nos. 62620
and 62575 (with cut
away frames) ; Class
D20/1 4-4-0 No.
62374.

[*T. G. Hepburn,
H. C. Casserley,
P. H. Wells,
P. L. Melvill*

Above left : Class D29 4-4-0 No. 62411 Lady of Avenel. Above right : Class D33 4-4-0 No. 62461. Below left : Class D40 4-4-0 No. 62271. Below right : Class D41 4-4-0 No. 62241.
[P. L. Melvill, W. J. V. Anderson, J. Davenport, H. N. A. Shelton

62678	Luckie Mucklebackit
62679	Lord Glenallan
62680	Lucy Ashton
62681	Captain Craigengelt
62682	Haystoun of Bucklaw
62683	Hobbie Elliott
62684	Wizard of the Moor
62685	Malcolm Graeme
62686	The Fiery Cross
62687	Lord James of Douglas
62688	Ellen Douglas
62689	Maid of Lorn
62690	The Lady of the Lake
62691	Laird of Balmawhapple
62692	Allan-Bane
62693	Roderick Dhu
62694	James Fitzjames

Totals : Class D11/1 11
Class D11/2 24

4-4-0 4P Class D49

D49/1*† Introduced 1927. Gresley design with piston valves, Walschaerts gear and derived motion.
D49/2‡§ Introduced 1928. Development of D49/1 with Lentz Rotary Cam poppet valves.
D49/4ø Introduced 1942. Rebuild of D49/2 with two inside cyls, of D11 pattern, Stephenson gear and piston valves.
(D49/3 comprised locos 62720-4 as built with Lentz Oscillating Cam poppet valves. From 1938 these locos were converted to D49/1. 62751-75 have larger valves than the earlier D49/2, and were at first classified D49/4.)
* Fitted with ex-G.C. tender.
†§Fitted with ex-N.E. tender.
The remainder (†ø) have L.N.E.R. tenders.

Weights : Loco. { 66 tons.*† / 64 tons 10 cwt.‡§ / 62 tons.ø
Tender { 48 tons 6 cwt.* / 44 tons 2 cwt.†§ / 52 tons.‡ø
Pressure : 180 lb. Su.
Cyls. { (3) 17″ × 26″*†‡§ / 20″ × 26″ø
Driving Wheels : 6′ 8″
T.E. { 21,555 lb.*†‡§ / 19,890 lb.ø

62700*	Yorkshire
62701*	Derbyshire
62702*	Oxfordshire
62703†	Hertfordshire
62704*	Stirlingshire
62705*	Lanarkshire
62706*	Forfarshire
62707*	Lancashire
62708*	Argyllshire
62709*	Berwickshire
62710*	Lincolnshire
62711*	Dumbartonshire
62712*	Morayshire
62713*	Aberdeenshire
62714*	Perthshire
62715*	Roxburghshire
62716*	Kincardineshire
62717*	Banffshire
62718*	Kinross-shire
62719*	Peebles-shire
62720†	Cambridgeshire
62721*	Warwickshire
62722*	Huntingdonshire
62723†	Nottinghamshire
62724†	Bedfordshire
62725*	Inverness-shire
62726*	The Meynell
62727§	The Quorn
62728*	Cheshire
62729*	Rutlandshire
62730*	Berkshire
62731*	Selkirkshire
62732*	Dumfries-shire
62733*	Northumberland
62734*	Cumberland
62735*	Westmorland
62736‡	The Bramham Moor
62737‡	The York and Ainsty
62738‡	The Zetland
62739‡	The Badsworth
62740‡	The Bedale
62741‡	The Blankney
62742‡	The Braes of Derwent
62743‡	The Cleveland
62744‡	The Holderness
62745‡	The Hurworth
62746‡	The Middleton
62747‡	The Percy
62748‡	The Southwold

62749‡	The Cottesmore
62750‡	The Pytchley
62751‡	The Albrighton
62752‡	The Atherstone
62753‡	The Belvoir
62754‡	The Berkeley
62755‡	The Bilsdale
62756‡	The Brocklesby
62757‡	The Burton
62758‡	The Cattistock
62759‡	The Craven
62760‡	The Cotswold
62761‡	The Derwent
62762‡	The Fernie
62763‡	The Fitzwilliam
62764‡	The Garth
62765‡	The Goathland
62766‡	The Grafton
62767‡	The Grove
62768ø	The Morpeth
62769‡	The Oakley
62770‡	The Puckeridge
62771‡	The Rufford
62772‡	The Sinnington
62773‡	The South Durham
62774‡	The Staintondale
62775‡	The Tynedale

Totals : Class D49/1 34
Class D49/2 41
Class D49/4 1

2-4-0   **1MT**   **Class E4**

Introduced 1891. J. Holden G.E. design.
* Fitted with side-window cab.
Weights : Loco.   40 tons 6 cwt.
          Tender 30 tons 13 cwt.
Pressure : 160 lb.   Cyls.: 17½″ × 24″
Driving Wheels : 5′ 8″   T.E. : 14,700 lb.

62780	62785	62790	62795*
62781*	62786	62791	62796
62782	62787	62792	62797*
62783	62788*	62793*	
62784*	62789	62794	

Total 18

0-8-0   **5F**   **Class Q4**

Q4/1* Introduced 1902. Robinson G.C. design. Saturated locos with slide valves.
Q4/2† Introduced 1914. Superheated rebuild, retaining slide valves.
Q4/2‡ Introduced 1914. Rebuilt with superheater and piston valves.
Weights : Loco. { 62 tons 8 cwt.*
                  63 tons.†
                  64 tons 1 cwt.‡
          Tender 48 tons 6 cwt.
Pressure : 180 lb. SS.
Cyls.: (O) { 19″ × 26″*†
            21″ × 26″‡
Driving Wheels : 4′ 8″
T.E.: { 25,645 lb.*†
        31,325 lb.‡

63202*	63225‡	63235†	63240†
63204*	63227*‡	63236†	63243†
63223†			

Totals: Class Q4/1   3
Class Q4/2   6

0-8-0   **6F**   **Class Q5**

Q5/1 (Slide valve). Introduced 1901. Worsdell N.E. design.
Q5/1* (Piston valve). Introduced 1903.
Weights : Loco.   58 tons 8 cwt.
          Tender 40 tons 8 cwt.
Pressure : 175 lb.   Cyls.: (O) 20″ × 26″
Driving Wheels: 4′ 7½″   T.E.:28,000 lb.

63259	63284*	63311	63319
63267	63303	63314	63326
63270*			

Total 9

0-8-0   **6F**   **Class Q6**

Introduced 1913. Raven N.E. design.
* Some locos are fitted with tenders from withdrawn B15 locos.
Weights : Loco.   65 tons 18 cwt.
          Tender { 44 tons 2 cwt.
                   44 tons.*
Pressure : 180 lb. Su.
Cyls.: (O) 20″ × 26″
Driving Wheels: 4′ 7½″   T.E.: 28,800 lb. P.V.

63340	63347	63354	63361
63341	63348	63355	63362
63342	63349	63356	63363
63343	63350	63357	63364
63344	63351	63358	63365
63345	63352	63359	63366
63346	63353	63360	63367

63368	63391	63414	63437
63369	63392	63415	63438
63370	63393	63416	63439
63371	63394	63417	63440
63372	63395	63418	63441
63373	63396	63419	63442
63374	63397	63420	63443
63375	63398	63421	63444
63376	63399	63422	63445
63377	63400	63423	63446
63378	63401	63424	63447
63379	63402	63425	63448
63380	63403	63426	63449
63381	63404	63427	63450
63382	63405	63428	63451
63383	63406	63429	63452
63384	63407	63430	63453
63385	63408	63431	63454
63386	63409	63432	63455
63387	63410	63433	63456
63388	63411	63434	63457
63389	63412	63435	63458
63390	63413	63436	63459

Total 120

0-8-0   7F   Class Q7

Introduced 1919. Raven N.E. design.
Weights : Loco.   71 tons 12 cwt.
     Tender 44 tons 2 cwt.
Pressure : 180 lb. Su.
Cyls.: (3) $18\frac{1}{2}" \times 26"$
Driving Wheels: $4' 7\frac{1}{4}"$ T.E.: 36,965 lb. P.V.

63460	63464	63468	63472
63461	63465	63469	63473
63462	63466	63470	63474
63463	63467	63471	**Total 15**

2-8-0   8F   Class O3

Introduced 1913. Gresley G.N. design.
Weights : Loco.   76 tons 4 cwt.
     Tender 43 tons 2 cwt.
Pressure : 180 lb. Su.
Cyls.: (O) $21" \times 28"$
Driving Wheels: $4' 8"$ T.E.: 33,735 lb.
Walschaerts gear, P.V.

63475	63478	63481	63484
63476	63479	63482	63485
63477	63480	63483	63488

Total 12

2-8-0   8F(O1) 7F(O4)   Classes O1 & O4

O4/1 Introduced 1911. Robinson G.C. design with small Belpaire boiler, steam and vacuum brakes and water scoop.
O4/3 Introduced 1917. Ex-R.O.D. locos with steam brake only and no scoop. Taken into L.N.E.R. stock from 1924.
O4/2 Introduced 1925. O4/3 with cab and boiler mountings reduced to Scottish loading gauge.
O4/5 Introduced 1932. Rebuilt with shortened O2-type boiler and separate smokebox saddle.
O4/6 Introduced 1924. Rebuilt from O5, retaining higher cab (63912-20 with side-windows).
O4/7 Introduced 1939. Rebuilt with shortened O2-type boiler, retaining G.C. smokebox.
O4/8 Introduced 1944. Rebuilt with 100A(B1) boiler, retaining original cylinders.
(O4/4 were rebuilds with O2 boilers, since rebuilt again ; O5 was a G.C. development of O4 with larger Belpaire boiler.)

Weights : Loco. { 73 tons 4 cwt.[1] / 73 tons 4 cwt.[3] / 73 tons 4 cwt.[2] / 74 tons 13 cwt.[6] / 73 tons 4 cwt.[8] / 73 tons 1 cwt.[8] / 72 tons 10 cwt.[7] }
Tender { 48 tons 6 cwt. (with scoop) / 47 tons 6 cwt. (without scoop) }
Pressure : 180 lb. Su.
Cyls.: (O) $21" \times 26"$
Driving Wheels : $4' 8"$ T.E.: 31,325 lb. P.V.

O1 Introduced 1944. Thompson rebuild with 100A boiler, Walschaerts valve gear and new cylinders.
Weights : Loco.   73 tons 6 cwt.
Tender as O4.
Pressure : 225 lb. Su.
Cyls.: (O) $20" \times 26"$
Driving Wheels : $4' 8"$ T.E.: 35,520 lb.
Walschaerts gear, P.V.

63570[6]	63579[8]	63588[8]
63571[8]	63580[1]	63589[8]
63572[1]	63581[1]	63590[8]
63573[1]	63582[6]	63591[8]
63574[1]	63583[1]	63592[8]
63575[7]	63584[1]	63593[1]
63576[1]	63585[1]	63594[8]
63577[1]	63586[1]	63595[8]
63578[8]	63587[1]	63596[8]

27

635 97-63920

63597[1]	63645[2]	63693[1]	63741[2]	63789[8]	63836[7]	63877[2]
63598[1]	63646[8]	63694[2]	63742[2]	63790[2]	63837[2]	63878[2]
63599[1]	63647[3]	63695[2]	63743[1]	63791[2]	63838[8]	63879[8]
63600[6]	63648[3]	63696[2]	63744[2]	63792[8]	63839[6]	63880[6]
63601[1]	63649[2]	63697[2]	63745[4]	63793[2]	63840[2]	63881[2]
63602[1]	63650[8]	63698[1]	63746[8]	63794[2]	63841[2]	63882[7]
63603[6]	63651[7]	63699[6]	63747[8]	63795[8]	63842[2]	63883[2]
63604[1]	63652[8]	63700[1]	63748[6]	63796[8]	63843[6]	63884[6]
63605[1]	63653[7]	63701[2]	63749[6]	63797[1]	63845[2]	63885[2]
63606[6]	63654[1]	63702[2]	63750[2]	63798[2]	63846[2]	63886[8]
63607[1]	63655[6]	63703[2]	63751[2]	63799[1]	63847[3]	63887[8]
63608[1]	63656[2]	63704[3]	63752[8]	63800[2]	63848[6]	63888[2]
63609[1]	63657[2]	63705[6]	63753[2]	63801[2]	63849[2]	63889[2]
63610[8]	63658[1]	63706[2]	63754[2]	63802[7]	63850[2]	63890[8]
63611[1]	63659[2]	63707[1]	63755[8]	63803[8]	63851[4]	63891[6]
63612[1]	63660[1]	63708[6]	63756[2]	63804[2]	63852[2]	63893[7]
63613[7]	63661[6]	63709[3]	63757[1]	63805[1]	63853[7]	63894[6]
63614[1]	63662[6]	63710[1]	63758[6]	63806[8]	63854[8]	63895[2]
63615[6]	63663[8]	63711[8]	63759[2]	63807[2]	63855[2]	63897[2]
63616[6]	63664[1]	63712[8]	63760[8]	63808[8]	63856[8]	63898[2]
63617[1]	63665[2]	63713[2]	63761[6]	63809[1]	63857[6]	63899[2]
63618[1]	63666[2]	63714[2]	63762[1]	63812[2]	63858[2]	63900[2]
63619[8]	63667[2]	63715[2]	63763[2]	63813[3]	63859[2]	63901[8]
63620[1]	63668[2]	63716[2]	63764[2]	63816[4]	63860[6]	63902[5]
63621[1]	63669[6]	63717[2]	63765[2]	63817[8]	63861[2]	63904[5]
63622[1]	63670[8]	63718[2]	63766[2]	63818[7]	63862[2]	63905[5]
63623[1]	63671[1]	63719[1]	63767[2]	63819[7]	63863[8]	63906[5]
63624[1]	63672[2]	63720[2]	63768[8]	63821[2]	63864[2]	63907[5]
63625[1]	63673[6]	63721[2]	63769[2]	63822[2]	63865[8]	63908[5]
63626[1]	63674[3]	63722[1]	63770[6]	63823[2]	63867[8]	63911[5]
63627[1]	63675[6]	63723[1]	63771[2]	63824[6]	63868[8]	63912[5]
63628[4]	63676[8]	63724[2]	63772[6]	63827[7]	63869[8]	63913[5]
62639[2]	63677[1]	63725[8]	63773[8]	63828[7]	63870[2]	63914[5]
63630[8]	63678[8]	63726[4]	63774[2]	63829[2]	63872[8]	63915[5]
63631[1]	63679[2]	63727[1]	63775[8]	63832[2]	63873[2]	63917[5]
63632[1]	63680[3]	63728[2]	63776[2]	63833[2]	63874[8]	63920[5]
63633[7]	63681[2]	63729[2]	63777[8]	63835[2]	63876[6]	
63634[6]	63682[2]	63730[3]	63778[1]			
63635[1]	63683[1]	63731[2]	63779[2]			
63636[2]	63684[1]	63732[2]	63780[8]			
63637[2]	63685[2]	63733[2]	63781[2]			
63638[2]	63686[2]	63734[2]	63782[2]			
63639[2]	63687[8]	63735[2]	63783[2]			
63640[1]	63688[2]	63736[1]	63784[8]			
63641[2]	63689[8]	63737[2]	63785[7]			
63642[2]	63690[3]	63738[7]	63786[6]			
63643[6]	63691[2]	63739[2]	63787[2]			
63644[3]	63692[1]	63740[8]	63788[4]			

Totals :

Class	O1	58
Class	O4/1	69
Class	O4/2	11
Class	O4/3	116
Class	O4/5	6
Class	O4/6	13
Class	O4/7	40
Class	O4/8	16

2-8-0   8F   Class O2

O2/1* Introduced 1921. Development of experimental Gresley G.N. 3-cyl. loco (L.N.E.R. 3921). Subsequently rebuilt with side-window cab, and reduced boiler mountings.
O2/2† Introduced 1924. Development of O2/1 with detail differences.
O2/3 Introduced 1932. Development of O2/2 with side-window cab and reduced boiler mountings.
O2/4‡ Introduced 1943. Rebuilt with 100A (B1 type) boiler and smokebox extended backwards (3924 retaining G.N. tender).

Weights : Loco. $\begin{cases} 75 \text{ tons } 16 \text{ cwt.*†} \\ 78 \text{ tons } 13 \text{ cwt.} \\ 74 \text{ tons } 2 \text{ cwt.‡} \end{cases}$
Tender $\begin{cases} 43 \text{ tons } 2 \text{ cwt. (63922-46)} \\ 52 \text{ tons (63947-87)} \end{cases}$
Pressure : 180 lb. Su.
Cyls. : (3) $18\frac{1}{2}'' \times 26''$
Driving Wheels : 4′ 8″ T.E. : 36,470 lb.
Walschaerts gear and derived motion, P.V.

63922*	63939†	63956	63973
63923*	63940†	63957	63974
63924‡	63941†	63958	63975
63925*	63942†	63959	63976
63926*	63943†	63960	63977
63927*	63944†	63961	63978
63928*	63945†	63962‡	63979
63929*	63946†	63963	63980
63930*	63947	63964	63981
63931*	63948	63965	63982
63932‡	63949	63966	63983
63933†	63950‡	63967	63984
63934†	63951	63968	63985
63935†	63952	63969	63986
63936†	63953	63970	63987
63937†	63954	63971	
63938†	63955	63972	

Totals : Class O2/4   4
Class O2/1   9
Class O2/2 14
Class O2/3 39

IMPORTANT NOTE
A careful reading of the notes on page 2 is essential to understand the use of reference marks in this book.

0-6-0   2F   Classes J3 & J4

J4* Introduced 1896. Ivatt G.N. development of standard Stirling 0-6-0.
J3 Introduced 1912. Larger boilered rebuild of J4 (some rebuilt from Stirling domeless locos, oldest survivor built 1892).

Weights : Loco. $\begin{cases} 41 \text{ tons } 5 \text{ cwt.}^\bullet \\ 42 \text{ tons } 12 \text{ cwt.} \end{cases}$
Tender $\begin{cases} 34 \text{ tons } 18 \text{ cwt.}^\bullet \\ 38 \text{ tons } 10 \text{ cwt.} \end{cases}$
Pressure : 175 lb.   Cyls.: $17\frac{1}{4}'' \times 26''$
Driving Wheels : 5′ 2″ T.E.: 19,105 lb.

64105	64119	64131	64148
64112*	64122	64132	64150
64114	64123	64133	64151
64116	64124	64140	64153
64117	64125	64141	64158
64118	64129	64142	64160*

Totals : Class J3 22
Class J4 2

0-6-0   3F   Class J6

Introduced 1911. Gresley G.N. design.
Weights : Loco. 50 tons 10 cwt.
Tender 43 tons 2 cwt.
Pressure : 170 lb. Su. Cyls.: $19'' \times 26''$
Driving Wheels : 5′ 2″ T.E.: 21,875 lb.
P.V.

64170	64188	64206	64224
64171	64189	64207	64225
64172	64190	64208	64226
64173	64191	64209	64227
64174	64192	64210	64228
64175	64193	64211	64229
64176	64194	64212	64230
64177	64195	64213	64231
64178	64196	64214	64232
64179	64197	64215	64233
64180	64198	64216	64234
64181	64199	64217	64235
64182	64200	64218	64236
64183	64201	64219	64237
64184	64202	64220	64238
64185	64203	64221	64239
64186	64204	64222	64240
64187	64205	64223	64241

64242	64252	64262	64272
64243	64253	64263	64273
64244	64254	64264	64274
64245	64255	64265	64275
64246	64256	64266	64276
64247	64257	64267	64277
64248	64258	64268	64278
64249	64259	64269	64279
64250	64260	64270	64271
64251	64261	64271	

Total 110

0-6-0 3F Class J11

Introduced 1901. Robinson G.C. design.
Parts 1 and 4 have 3,250 gallon
tenders ; Parts 2 and 5 4,000 gallon.
Parts 1 and 2 have high boiler
mountings ; Parts 4 and 5 low. All
Parts 4 and 5 are superheated, and
some of Parts 1 and 2. There are
frequent changes between these parts
J11/3* Introduced 1942. Rebuilt with
long-travel piston valves and boiler
higher pitched.

Weights: Loco. $\begin{cases} 51 \text{ tons } 19 \text{ cwt. (Sat.)} \\ 52 \text{ tons } 2 \text{ cwt. (Su.)} \\ 53 \text{ tons } 6 \text{ cwt.*} \end{cases}$

Tender $\begin{cases} 44 \text{ tons } 3 \text{ cwt. (3,250 gall.)} \\ 48 \text{ tons } 6 \text{ cwt. (4,000 gall.)} \end{cases}$

Pressure : 180 lb. SS. Cyls.: $18\frac{1}{2}" \times 26"$
Driving Wheels : 5' 2" T.E.: 21,960 lb.

64280	64300	64320	64340
64281	64301	64321	64341
64282	64302	64322	64342
64283*	64303	64323	64343
64284*	64304*	64324*	64344
64285	64305	64325	64345
64286	64306	64326	64346*
64287	64307	64327	64347
64288	64308	64328	64348
64289	64309	64329	64349
64290	64310	64330	64350
64291	64311	64331	64351
64292	64312	64332*	64352*
64293	64313	64333*	64353
64294	64314*	64334	64354*
64295	64315	64335	64355
64296	64316*	64336	64356
64297	64317*	64337	64357
64298	64318*	64338	64358
64299	64319	64339	64359*

64360	64384	64408	64432
64361	64385	64409	64433
64362*	64386*	64410	64434
64363	64387	64411	64435
64364*	64388	64412	64436
64365	64389	64413	64437
64366	64390	64414	64438
64367	64391	64415	64439*
64368	64392	64416	64440
64369	64393	64417*	64441*
64370	64394	64418*	64442*
64371	64395	64419	64443
64372	64396	64420*	64444
64373*	64397	64421	64445
64374	64398	64422	64446
64375*	64399	64423	64447
64376	64400	64424	64448
64377	64401	64425	64449
64378	64402*	64426	64450*
64379*	64403	64427*	64451
64380	64404	64428	64452
64381	64405	64429	64453
64382	64406*	64430	
64383	64407	64431	

Totals : Class J11/3 30
Class J11 (other parts) 144

0-6-0 3F Class J35

J35/5* Introduced 1906. Reid N.B.
design with piston valves.
J35/4 Introduced 1908. Slide valves.
(Parts 1, 2 and 3 were variations of
Parts 4 and 5 before superheating.)

Weights : Loco. $\begin{cases} 51 \text{ tons.*} \\ 50 \text{ tons } 15 \text{ cwt.} \end{cases}$

Tender $\begin{cases} 38 \text{ tons } 1 \text{ cwt.*} \\ 37 \text{ tons } 15 \text{ cwt.} \end{cases}$

Pressure : 180 lb. Su. Cyls.: $18\frac{1}{2}" \times 26"$
Driving Wheels : 5' 0" T.E.: 22,080 lb.

64460*	64473*	64484	64494
64461*	64474*	64485	64495
64462*	64475*	64486	64496
64463*	64476*	64487	64497
64464*	64477*	64488	64498
64466*	64478	64489	64499
64468*	64479	64490	64500
64470*	64480	64491	64501
64471*	64482	64492	64502
64472*	64483	64493	64504

64505	64514	64522	64530
64506	64515	64523	64531
64507	64516	64524	64532
64509	64517	64525	64533
64510	64518	64526	64534
64511	64519	64527	64535
64512	64520	64528	
64513	64521	64529	

Totals : Class J35/4 55
Class J35/5 15

0-6-0 4F Class J37

Introduced 1914. Reid N.B. design. Superheated development of J35.
Weights : Loco. 54 tons 14 cwt.
Tender 40 tons 19 cwt.
Pressure : 180 lb. Su. Cyls.: 19½" × 26"
Driving Wheels : 5' 0" T.E.: 25,210 lb.
P.V.

64536	64562	64588	64614
64537	64563	64589	64615
64538	64564	64590	64616
64539	64565	64591	64617
64540	64566	64592	64618
64541	64567	64593	64619
64542	64568	64594	64620
64543	64569	64595	64621
64544	64570	64596	64622
64545	64571	64597	64623
64546	64572	64598	64624
64547	64573	64599	64625
64548	64574	64600	64626
64549	64575	64601	64627
64550	64576	64602	64628
64551	64577	64603	64629
64552	64578	64604	64630
64553	64579	64605	64631
64554	64580	64606	64632
64555	64581	64607	64633
64556	64582	64608	64634
64557	64583	64609	64635
64558	64584	64610	64636
64559	64585	64611	64637
64560	64586	64612	64638
64561	64587	64613	64639

Total 104

0-6-0 4F Class J19

Introduced 1912. S. Holden G.E. design rebuilt with round-topped boiler from 1934.
* Rebuilt with 19" cyls. and 180 lb. pressure.
† Rebuilt with 19" cyls. and 160 lb. pressure.
Weights : Loco. 50 tons 7 cwt.
Tender 38 tons 5 cwt.
Pressure { 170 lb. Su. / 180 lb. Su.* / 160 lb. Su.† }
Cyls.: { 20" × 26" / 19" × 26"*† }
Driving Wheels : 4' 11"
T.E.: { 27,430 lb. / 26,215 lb.* / 23,300 lb.† }
P.V.

64640	64649	64658	64667
64641	64650	64659	64668
64642	64651	64660	64669
64643	64652	64661	64670
64644	64653	64662	64671*
64645	64654	64663	64672†
64646	64655	64664*	64673
64647	64656	64665	64674
64648	64657	64666	

Total 35

0-6-0 6F Class J20

J20* Introduced 1920. Hill G.E. design with Belpaire boiler.
J20/1 Introduced 1943. Rebuilt with B12/1 type round-topped boiler.
Weights : Loco. 54 tons 15 cwt.
Tender 38 tons 5 cwt.
Pressure : 180 lb. Su. Cyls.: 20" × 28"
Driving Wheels: 4' 11" T.E.: 29,045 lb.
P.V.

64675*	64682	64588	64694
64676*	64683*	64689*	64695
64677	64684	64690	64696*
64678	64685	64691	64697
64679	64686	64692	64698*
64680	64687*	64693	64699
64681			

Totals : Class J20 7
Class J20/1 18

0-6-0   4F   Class J39

Introduced 1926. Gresley design.
J39/1 Standard 3,500 gallon tender.
J39/2* Standard 4,200 gallon tender.
J39/3† Various ex-N.E. tenders (3,940 gallon on 64843-5, 4,125 gallon on 64855-9).
Weights : Loco. 57 tons 17 cwt.
Tender { 44 tons 4 cwt. } and others { 52 tons 13 cwt.* }
Pressure : 180 lb. Su. Cyls.: 20″ × 26″
Driving Wheels : 5′ 2″ T.E.: 25,665 lb P.V.

64700	64738	64776	64814
64701	64739	64777	64815
64702	64740	64778	64816
64703	64741	64779	64817
64704	64742	64780	64818
64705	64743	64781	64819
64706	64744	64782	64820*
64707	64745	64783	64821*
64708	64746	64784*	64822*
64709	64747	64785*	64823
64710	64748	64786*	64824
64711	64749	64787*	64825
64712	64750	64788*	64826
64713	64751	64789*	64827
64714	64752	64790*	64828
64715	64753	64791*	64829
64716	64754	64792*	64830
64717	64755	64793*	64831
64718	64756	64794*	64832
64719	64757	64795*	64833
64720	64758	64796	64834
64721	64759	64797	64835
64722	64760	64798	64836
64723	64761	64799	64837
64724	64762	64800	64838*
64725	64763	64801	64839*
64726	64764	64802	64840*
64727	64765	64803	64841*
64728	64766	64804	64842†
64729	64767	64805	64843†
64730	64768	64806	64844†
64731	64769	64807	64845†
64732	64770	64808	64846
64733	64771	64809	64847
64734	64772	64810	64848
64735	64773	64811	64849
64736	64774	64812	64850
64737	64775	64813	64851

64852	64887*	64922*	64957*
64853	64888*	64923*	64958*
64854	64889*	64924*	64959*
64855†	64890*	64925*	64960*
64856†	64891*	64926*	64961*
64857†	64892*	64927*	64962*
64858†	64893*	64928*	64963*
64859†	64894*	64929*	64964*
64860	64895*	64930*	64965*
64861	64896*	64931*	64966*
64862	64897*	64932*	64967*
64863	64898*	64933	64968*
64864	64899*	64934	64969*
64865	64900*	64935	64970*
64866	64901*	64936	64971†
64867	64902*	64937	64972†
64868	64903*	64938	64973†
64869	64904*	64939	64974†
64870	64905*	64940	64975†
64871	64906*	64941	64976†
64872*	64907*	64942	64977†
64873*	64908*	64943	64978†
64874*	64909*	64944	64979†
64875*	64910*	64945*	64980†
64876*	64911*	64946*	64981†
64877*	64912*	64947*	64982†
64878*	64913*	64948*	64983†
64879*	64914*	64949*	64984†
64880*	64915*	64950*	64985†
64881*	64916*	64951*	64986†
64882*	64917*	64952*	64987†
64883*	64918*	64953*	64988†
64884*	64919*	64954*	
64885*	64920*	64955*	
64886*	64921*	64956*	

Totals : Class J39/1   156
Class J39/2   106
Class J39/3   27

0-6-0   2MT   Class J1

Introduced 1908. Ivatt G.N. design.
Weights : Loco. 46 tons 14 cwt.
Tender 43 tons 2 cwt.
Pressure : 175 lb. Cyls.: 18″ × 26″
Driving Wheels : 5′ 8″ T.E.: 18,430 lb.

65002	65005	65008	65013
65003	65006	65009	65014
65004	65007	65010	**Total 11**

0-6-0 2MT Class J2

Introduced 1912. Ivatt/Gresley G.N. design.
Weights : Loco. 50 tons 10 cwt.
             Tender 43 tons 2 cwt.
Pressure : 170 lb. Su. Cyls.: 19″ × 26″
Driving Wheels : 5′ 8″ T.E.: 19,945 lb. P.V.

65015	65017	65019	65022
65016	65018	65020	65023

Total 8

0-6-0 2F Class J21

Introduced 1886. T. W. Worsdell N.E. design. Majority built as 2-cyl. compounds and later rebuilt as simple locos.
* Saturated with Joy's gear and slide valves.
† Rebuilt with superheater, Stephenson gear and piston valves.
‡ Rebuilt with piston valves, superheater removed, 24″ piston stroke.
Weights : Loco. { 42 tons 1 cwt.*
                  43 tons 15 cwt.†
                  42 tons 9 cwt.‡
             Tender 36 tons 19 cwt.
Pressure : 160 lb. SS.
Cyls.: { 18″ × 24″*
         19″ × 24″†‡
T.E.: { 17,265 lb.*
        19,240 lb.†‡
Driving Wheels : 5′ 1¼″

65025‡	65061†	65080‡	65099‡
65028†	65062†	65082†	65100‡
65030‡	65064†	65088†	65102‡
65033‡	65067‡	65089†	65103†
65035‡	65068†	65090†	65105‡
65038†	65070‡	65091†	65110†
65039‡	65075†	65092†	65117‡
65040†	65076‡	65095†	65118‡
65042‡	65077†	65097†	65119†
65047†	65078†	65098†	65122*

Total 40

0-6-0 2F Class J10

J10/2* Introduced 1892. Parker M.S. & L. design with small tenders.
J10/4† Introduced 1896. Pollitt development of J10/2 with larger bearings and larger tenders.
J10/6 Introduced 1901. Robinson locos with larger bearings and small tenders.
Weights : Loco. 41 tons 6 cwt.
             Tender { 37 tons 6 cwt.
                      43 tons.†
Pressure : 160 lb. Cyls.: 18″ × 26″
Driving Wheels : 5′ 1″ T.E.: 18,780 lb.

65126*	65148†	65169†	65189
65130*	65149†	65170†	65190
65131	65151†	65171†	65191
65132†	65153†	65172	65192
65133†	65154†	65173	65193
65134†	65155†	65175	65194
65135†	65156†	65176	65196
65136†	65157†	65177	65197
65137†	65158†	65178†	65198
65138†	65159†	65179	65199
65139	65160†	65180	65200
65140†	65161†	65181	65201
65141†	65162	65182	65202
65142†	65163	65183	65203
65143†	65164†	65184	65204
65144†	65165†	65185	65205
65145†	65166†	65186	65208
65146†	65167†	65187	65209
65147†	65168	65188	

Totals : Class J10/2 2
Class J10/4 35
Class J10/6 38

0-6-0 2F Class J36

Introduced 1888. Holmes N.B. design.
Weights : Loco. 41 tons 19 cwt.
             Tender 33 tons 9 cwt.
Pressure : 165 lb. Cyls.: 18½″ × 26″
Driving Wheels : 5′ 0″ T.E.: 19,690 lb.

65210	65218	65227	65233*
65211	65221	65228	65234
65213	65222*	65229	65235*
65214	65224*	65230	65236*
65216*	65225	65231	65237
65217*	65226*	65232	

*Names
65216 Byng 65217 French 65222 Somme
65224 Mons 65226 Haig   65233 Plumer
     65235 Gough 65236 Horne

65238-65519

65238	65261	65293	65320
65239	65264	65295	65321
65240	65265	65296	65322
65241	65266	65297	65323
65242	65267	65300	65324
65243*	65268*	65303	65325
65244	65270	65304	65327
65245	65271	65305	65329
65246	65273	65306	65330
65247	65275	65307	65331
65248	65276	65308	65333
65249	65277	65309	65334
65250	65278	65310	65335
65251	65280	65311	65338
65252	65281	65312	65339
65253*	65282	65213	65340
65254	65283	65314	65241
65255	65285	65315	65342
65257	65286	65316	65343
65258	65287	65317	65344
65259	65288	65318	65345
65260	65290	65319	65346

Total 111

* Names 65243 Maude   65253 Joffre
65268 Allenby

0-6-0   **2F**   **Class J15**

Introduced 1883. Worsdell G.E. design,
modified by J. Holden. (Oldest
survivor built 1886.)
* Fitted with side-window cab for
Colne Valley line.
Weights : Loco.   37 tons 2 cwt.
Tender 30 tons 13 cwt.
Pressure : 160 lb.   Cyls.: 17½″ × 24″
Driving Wheels: 4′ 11″ T.E.: 16,940 lb.

65355	65382	65401	65422
65356	65384	65404	65424*
65359	65388	65405*	65425
65361	65389	65406	64526
65362	65390	65407	65430
65366	65391*	65408	65432*
65370	65396	65417	65433
65378	65398	65420	65434

65435	65448	65459	65470
65438*	65449	65460	65471
65439	65450	65461	65472
65440	65451	65462	65473
65441	65452	65463	65474
65442	65453	65464	65475
65443	65454	65465	65476
65444	65455	65466	65477
65445	65456	65467	65478
65446	65457	65468	65479
65447	65458	65469	

Total 75

0-6-0   **3F**   **Class J5**

Introduced 1909. Ivatt G.N. design.
* Rebuilt with superheater.
Weights : Loco.   47 tons 6 cwt.
Tender 43 tons 2 cwt.
Pressure: { 175 lb.
170 lb. Su.*
Cyls.: 18″ × 26″
Driving Wheels : 5′ 2″
T.E.: { 20,210 lb.
19,630 lb.*

65480*	65485	65490	65495
65481	65486	65491	65496
65482	65487	65492	65497
65483	65488	65493	65498
65484	65489*	65494	65499

Total 20

0-6-0   **4F**   **Class J17**

Introduced 1901. J. Holden G.E.
design. Many rebuilt from round-top
boiler J16, introduced 1900.
* Fitted with small tender.
Weights : Loco.   45 tons 8 cwt.
Tender { 30 tons 12 cwt.*
38 tons 5 cwt.
Pressure : 180 lb. Su. Cyls.: 19″ × 26″
Driving Wheels: 4′ 11″ T.E.: 24,340 lb.

65500*	65505*	65510*	65515*
65501*	65506*	65511*	65516*
65502*	65507*	65512*	65517*
65503*	65508*	65513*	65518*
65504*	65509	65514*	65519*

34

65520	65538	65557	65575
65521	65539	65558	65576
65522	65540	65559	65577
65523	65541	65560	65578
65524	65542	65561	65579
65525	65543	65562	65580
65526	65544	65563	65581
65527	65545	65564	65582
65528*	65546	65565	65583
65529	65547	65566	65584
65530	65548	65567	65585
65531	65549	65568	65586
65532	65551	65569	65587
65533	65552	65570	65588
65534	65553	65571*	65589
65535	65554	65572	
65536	65555	65573	
65537	65556	65574	

Total 89

IMPORTANT NOTE

A careful reading of the notes on page 2 is essential to understand the use of reference marks in this book.

0-6-0   3F   Class J24

Introduced 1894.
* W. Worsdell N.E. design, saturated with slide valves.
† Rebuilt with superheater and piston valves.
‡ Rebuilt with piston valves, superheater removed.
Weights : Loco. { 38 tons 10 cwt.*
{ 39 tons 11 cwt.†‡
Tender 36 tons 19 cwt.
Pressure : 160 lb. SS.
Cyls.: { 18″ × 24″*
{ 18½″ × 24″†‡
Driving Wheels : 4′ 7¼″
T.E. { 19,140 lb.*
{ 20,220 lb.†‡

65601*	65615*	65619*	65640*
65614*	65617†	65623*	65644‡

Total 8

0-6-0   3F   Class J25

Introduced 1898. W. Worsdell N.E. design.
* Original design, saturated with slide valves.
† Rebuilt with superheater and piston valves.
‡ Rebuilt with piston valves, superheater removed.
Weights : Loco. { 39 tons 11 cwt.*
{ 41 tons 14 cwt.†
{ 40 tons 17 cwt.‡
Tender 36 tons 19 cwt.
Pressure : 160 lb. SS. Cyls.: 18½″ × 26″
Driving Wheels : 4′ 7¼″ T.E.: 21,905 lb.

65645†	65667*	65689*	65708*
65647*	65670*	65690*	65710*
65648*	65671*	65691*	65712*
65650*	65672*	65692‡	65713*
65653*	65673‡	65693*	65714*
65654‡	65675*	65694*	65716*
65655*	65676*	65695*	65717†
65656*	65677‡	65696*	65718*
65657*	65679*	65697*	65720*
65660*	65680*	65698*	65723*
65661*	65683‡	65699*	65726*
65662†	65685*	65700*	65727*
65663*	65686*	65702‡	65728*
65664*	65687*	65705*	
65666*	65688*	65706†	

Total 58

0-6-0   4F   Class J26

Introduced 1904. W. Worsdell N.E. design.
Weights : Loco. 46 tons 16 cwt.
Tender 36 tons 19 cwt.
Pressure : 180 lb. Cyls.: 18½″ × 26″
Driving Wheels : 4′ 7¼″ T.E.: 24,640 lb.

65730	65740	65750	65760
65731	65741	65751	65761
65732	65742	65752	65762
65733	65743	65753	65763
65734	65744	65754	65764
65735	65745	65755	65765
65736	65746	65756	65766
65737	65747	65757	65767
65738	65748	65758	65768
65739	65749	65759	65769

65770-67187

65770	65773	65776	65778
65771	65774	65777	65779
65772	65775		

Total 50

0-6-0   4F   Class J27

ntroduced 1906. W. Worsdell N.E. design developed from J26.
* Introduced 1921. Raven locos superheated with piston valves.
† Introduced 1943. Piston valves, superheater removed.
Weights : Loco. { 47 tons Sat.
49 tons 10 cwt. Su.
Tender 36 tons 19 cwt.
Pressure : 180 lb. SS. Cyls.: 18½″ × 26″
Driving Wheels: 4′ 7¼″ T.E.: 24,640 lb.

65780	65809	65838	65867†
65781	65810	65839	65868†
65782	65811	65840	65869*
65783	65812	65841	65870†
65784	65813	65842	65871*
65785	65814	65843	65872*
65786	65815	65844	65873†
65787	65816	65845	65874*
65788	65817	65846	65875†
65789	65818	65847	65876†
65790	65819	65848	65877†
65791	65820	65849	65878*
65792	65821	65850	65879†
65793	65822	65851	65880*
65794	65823	65852	65881*
65795	65824	65853	65882†
65796	65825	65854	65883*
65797	65826	65855	65884†
65798	65827	65856	65885*
65799	65828	65857	65886*
65800	65829	65858	65887*
65801	65830	65859	65888†
65802	65831	65860†	65889*
65803	65832	65861†	65890*
65804	65833	65862†	65891†
65805	65834	65863*	65892*
65806	65835	65864†	65893*
65807	65836	65865†	65894*
65808	65837	65866*	

Total 115

0-6-0   6F   Class J38

Introduced 1926. Gresley design. Predecessor of J39, with 4′ 8″ wheels, boiler 6″ longer than J39 and smokebox 6″ shorter.
* Rebuilt with J39 boiler.
Weights : Loco. 58 tons 19 cwt.
Tender 44 tons 4 cwt.
Pressure : 180 lb. Su. Cyls.: 20″ × 26″
Driving Wheels : 4′ 8″ T.E.: 28,415 lb. P.V.

65900	65909	65918*	65927*
65901	65910	65919	65928
65902	65911	65920	65929
65903*	65912	65921	65930
65904	65913	65922	65931
65905	65914	65923	65932
65906*	65915	65924	65933
65907	65916	65925	65934
65908*	65917*	65926*	

Total 35

2-4-2T   IP   Class F3

Introduced 1893. J. Holden G.E. design. (Oldest survivor built 1895.)
Weight : 58 tons 12 cwt.
Pressure : 160 lb. Cyls.: 17½″ × 24″
Driving Wheels : 5′ 8″ T.E.: 14,710 lb.

67127   **Total 1**

2-4-2T   IP   Class F4

Introduced 1884. Worsdell G.E. design, modified by J. Holden. (Oldest survivor built 1906.)
* Push-and-pull fitted.
Weight : 53 tons 19 cwt.
Pressure : 160 lb. Cyls.: 17½″ × 24″
Driving Wheels : 5′ 4″ T.E.: 15,620 lb.

67151*	67158	67171	67184
67152	67162	67174	67186
67153	67163	67175	67187
67154	67164	67176	
67155	67166	67178	
67157	67167	67182	

Total 21

36

2-4-2T 2P Class F5

Introduced 1911. S. D. Holden design.
(Rebuilt from F4, oldest survivor originally built 1903.)
* Introduced 1949. Push-and-pull fitted.
Weight : 53 tons 19 cwt.
Pressure : 180 lb.   Cyls.: 17½" × 24"
Driving Wheels : 5' 4" T.E.: 17,570 lb.

67188	67196	67204	67212
67189	67197	67205	67213
67190	67198	67206	67214
67191	67199	67207	67215
67192	67200*	67208	67216
67193*	67201	67209	67217
67194	67202*	67210	67218
67195	67203*	67211	67219

Total 32

2-4-2T 2P Class F6

Introduced 1911. S. D. Holden design, development of F4 with higher pressure and larger tanks.
Weight : 56 tons 9 cwt.
Pressure : 180 lb.   Cyls.: 17½" × 24"
Driving Wheels : 5' 4" T.E.: 17,570 lb.

67220	67225	67230	67235
67221	67226	67231	67236
67222	67227	67232	67237
67223	67228	67233	o7238
67224	67229	67234	67239

Total 20

0-4-4T 2P Class G5

Introduced 1894. W. Worsdell N.E. design.
* Push-and-pull fitted.
† Push-and-pull fitted and rebuilt with larger tanks.
Weight : 54 tons 4 cwt.
Pressure : 160 lb.   Cyls.: 18" × 24"
Driving Wheels : 5' 1¼" T.E.: 17,265 lb.

67240	67246	67252	67258
67241	67247	67253*	67259
67242	67248	67254	67260
67243	67249	67255	67261*
67244	67250*	67256	67262
67245	67251	67257	67263

67264	67286*	67309	67330
67265	67287	67310	67331
67266	67288	67311*	67332
67267	67289	67312	67333
67268	67290	67313	67334
67269	67291	67314	67335
67270	67292	67315	67336
67271	67293	67316	67337*
67272	67294	67317	67338
67273*	67295	67318	67339*
67274	67296	67319	67340†
67275	67297*	67320	67341
67276	67298	67321	67342
67277	67300	67322*	67343
67278	67301	67323*	67344
67279*	67302	67324	67345
67280*	67303	67325	67346
67281*	67304	67326	67347
67282*	67305*	67327	67348
67283	67307	67328	67349
67284	67308	67329	

Total 107

4-4-2T 2P Class C12

Introduced 1898. Ivatt G.N. design.
*†Boiler pressure reduced to 170 lb.
†‡Push-and-pull fitted.
Weight : 62 tons 6 cwt.
Pressure: { 175 lb. / 170 lb.*†
Cyls.: 18" × 26"
Driving Wheels : 5' 8"
T.E.: { 18,425 lb. / 17,900 lb.*†

67350	67364	67376	67389
67352	67365	67379	67390
67353	67366	67380	67391
67354*	67367	67381	67392
67356‡	67368	67382	67393
67357	67369	67383	67394
67360	67371	67384	67395
67361	67372	67385	67397
67362	67374†	67386‡	67398*
67263†	67375	67387‡	

Total 39

4-4-2T 2P Class C13

Introduced 1903. Robinson G.C.
design, later rebuilt with superheater.
* Push-and-pull fitted.
Weight : 66 tons 13 cwt.
Pressure : 160 lb. Su. Cyls.: 18" × 26"
Driving Wheels : 5' 7" T.E.: 17,100 lb.

67400	67410	67420*	67430
67401	67411	67421*	67431
67402	67412	67422	67432
67403	67413	67423	67433*
67404	67414	67424	67434
67405	67415	67425	67435
67406	67416*	67426	67436*
67407	67417*	67427	67437
67408	67418*	67428	67438*
67409	67419	67429	67439

Total 40

4-4-2T 2P Class C14

Introduced 1907. Robinson G.C. design,
later superheated, development of
C13. With detail differences.
Weight : 71 tons.
Pressure : 160 lb. Su. Cyls.: 18" × 26"
Driving Wheels : 5' 7" T.E.: 17,100 lb.

67440	67443	67446	67449
67441	67444	67447	67450
67442	67445	67448	67451

Total 12

4-4-2T 2P Class C15

Introduced 1911. Reid N.B. design.
* Push-and-pull fitted.
Weight : 68 tons 15 cwt.
Pressure : 175 lb. Cyls.: 18" × 26"
Driving Wheels : 5' 9" T.E.: 18,160 lb.

67452	67460*	67468	67475
67453	67461	67469	67476
67454	67462	67470	67477
67455	67463	67471	67478
67456	67464	67472	67479
67457	67465	67473	67480
67458	67466	67474	67481
67459	67467		

Total 30

4-4-2T 2P Class C16

Introduced 1915. Reid N.B. design,
superheated development of C15.
* Superheater removed.
Weight : 72 tons 10 cwt.
Pressure : 165 lb. SS. Cyls.: 19" × 26"
Driving Wheels : 5' 9" T.E.: 19,080 lb.
P.V.

67482	67488	67493	67498
67483*	67489	67494	67499
67484	67490	67495	67500
67485	67491	67496	67501
67486	67492	67497	67502
67487			

Total 21

Classes
2-6-2T 4MT V1 & V3

V1 Introduced 1930. Gresley design.
V3* Introduced 1939. Development of
V1 with higher pressure (locos num-
bered below 67682 rebuilt from V1).
Weights : { 84 tons.
{ 86 tons 16 cwt.*
Pressure : { 180 lb. Su.
{ 200 lb. Su.*
Cyls.: (3) 16" × 26"
Driving Wheels : 5' 8"
T.E.: { 22,465 lb.
{ 24,960 lb.*
Walschaerts gear, derived motion, P.V.

67600	67619	67638	67657
67601	67620	67639	67658
67602	67621	67640	67659
67603	67622	67641	67660
67604	67623	67642	67661
67605	67624	67643	67662
67606	67625	67644	67663
67607	67626	67645	67664
67608	67627	67646	67665
67609	67628	67647	67666
67610	67629	67648	67667
67611	67630	67649	67668
67612	67631	67650	67669*
67613	67632	67651	67670
67614	67633	67652	67671
67615	67634*	67653	67672*
67616	67635	67654	67673
67617	67636	67655	67674
67618	67637	67656	67675*

67676	67680	67684*	67688*
67677	67681	67685*	67689*
67678	67682*	67686*	67690*
67679	67683*	67687*	67691*

Totals : Class V1 78
Class V3 14

2-6-4T 4MT Class L1

Introduced 1945. Thompson design.
Weight : 89 tons 9 cwt.
Pressure : 225 lb. Cyls.: (O) 20″ × 26″
Driving Wheels : 5′ 2″ T.E.: 32,080 lb.
Walschaerts gear, P.V.

67701	67726	67751	67776
67702	67727	67752	67777
67703	67728	67753	67778
67704	67729	67754	67779
67705	67730	67755	67780
67706	67731	67756	67781
67707	67732	67757	67782
67708	67733	67758	67783
67709	67734	67759	67784
67710	67735	67760	67785
67711	67736	67761	67786
67712	67737	67762	67787
67713	67738	67763	67788
67714	67739	67764	67789
67715	67740	67765	67790
67716	67741	67766	67791
67717	67742	67767	67792
67718	67743	67768	67793
67719	67744	67769	67794
67720	67745	67770	67795
67721	67746	67771	67796
67722	67747	67772	67797
67723	67748	67773	67798
67724	67749	67774	67799
67725	67750	67775	67800

Total 100

0-6-0ST 4F Class J94

Introduced 1943. Riddles M.o.S. design.
(Bought from M.o.S. 1946.)
Weight : 48 tons 5 cwt.
Pressure : 170 lb. Cyls.: 18″ × 26″
Driving Wheels : 4′ 3″ T.E.: 23,870 lb.

68006	68008	68010	68012
68007	68009	68011	68013

68014	68031	68048	68065
68015	68032	68049	68066
68016	68033	68050	68067
68017	68034	68051	68068
68018	68035	68052	68069
68019	68036	68053	68070
68020	68037	68054	68071
68021	68038	68055	68072
68022	68039	68056	68073
68023	68040	68057	68074
68024	68041	68058	68075
68025	68042	68059	68076
68026	68043	68060	68077
68027	68044	68061	68078
68028	68045	68062	68079
68029	68046	68063	68080
68030	68047	68064	

Total 75

0-4-0T (Tram Locos) 0F Class Y6

Introduced 1883. Worsdell G.E. design.
(Oldest survivor built 1897.)
Weight : 21 tons 5 cwt.
Pressure : 140 lb. Cyls.: 11″ × 15″
Driving Wheels : 3′ 1″ T.E.: 5,835 lb.

| 68082 | 68083 | Total 2 |

0-4-0T 0F Class Y7

Introduced 1888. T. W. Worsdell N.E.
design. (Survivors built 1923.)
Weight : 22 tons 14 cwt.
Pressure : 140 lb. Cyls.: 14″ × 20″
Driving Wheels: 3′ 6¼″ T.E.: 11,040 lb.

| 68088S | 68089 | Total 2 |

0-4-0T 0F Class Y8

Introduced 1890. T. W. Worsdell N.E.
design.
Weight : 15 tons 10 cwt.
Pressure : 140 lb. Cyls.: 11″ × 15″
Driving Wheels : 3′ 0″ T.E.: 6,000 lb.

| 68091 | Total 1 |

39

0-4-0ST   oF   Class Y9

Introduced 1882. Holmes N.B. design.
* Locos running permanently attached
to wooden tenders.
Weights : Loco.   27 tons 16 cwt.
         Tender   6 tons.*
Pressure : 130 lb. Cyls.: (O) 14″ × 20″
Driving Wheels :   3′ 8″   T.E.: 9,845 lb.

68092	68101	68110	68119*
68093*	68102	68111	68120*
68094*	68103*	68112*	68121*
68095	68104	68113	68122*
68096	68105	68114*	68123
68097	68106*	68115	68124
68098	68107*	68116*	
68099*	68108*	68117*	
68100	68109*	68118*	

Total 33

0-4-0T   oF   Class Y4

Introduced 1913. Hill G.E. design.
Weight : 38 tons 1 cwt.
Pressure : 180 lb. Cyls.: (O) 17″ × 20″
Driving Wheels: 3′ 10″ T.E.: 19,225 lb.
Walschaerts gear.

68125	68127	68128	68129S
68126			**Total 5**

0-4-0T   Unclass   Class Y1

Sentinel Wagon Works design. Single-
speed Geared Sentinel Locomotives.
The four parts of this class differ in
details, including size of boiler and
fuel capacity.
Y1/1* Introduced 1925.
Y1/2† Introduced 1927.
Y1/3** Introduced 1926.
Y1/4‡ Introduced 1927.
§ Sprocket gear ratio 9 : 25 (remainder
11 : 25).
Weights : { 20 tons 17 cwt.*
           19 tons 16 cwt.†
           14 tons.**
           19 tons 7 cwt.‡
Pressure : 275 lb. Su. Cyls.: 6¾″ × 9″
Driving Wheels : 2′ 6″
T.E.: { 7,260 lb.
      8,870 lb. §
Poppet valves.

68130S*	68132S*	68136S*
68131S*	68133S*	68137†

68138†	68144†§	68150†§
68139**	68145†§	68151†§
68140†	68146†§	68152S*
68141†	68147†§	68153S†
68142†	68148†§	
68143†§	68149†§	

Totals :   Class Y1/1   5
           Class Y1/2   15
           Class Y1/3   1
           Class Y1/4   1

0-4-0T   Unclass   Class Y3

Sentinel Wagon Works design. Two-
speed Geared Sentinel Locos.
Introduced 1927.
* Sprocket gear ratio 15 : 19 (re-
mainder 19 : 19).
Weight : 20 tons 16 cwt.
Pressure : 275 lb. Su. Cyls.: 6¾″ × 9″
Driving Wheels : 2′ 6″
T.E.: { Low Gear : 12,600 lb.
       High Gear :   4,705 lb.
       Low Gear : 15,960 lb.*
       High Gear :   5,960 lb.*
Poppet valves.

68154	68162	68172	68180*
68155	68163	68173S	68181*
68156	68164	68174	68182*
68157	68165	68175	68183*
68158	68166S	68176	68184
68159	68168	68177S	68185
68160	68169	68178S	
68161	68171	68179	

Total 30

0-4-0T   Unclass   Class Y10

Sentinel Wagon Works design. Double-
ended Two-speed Geared Sentinel
Loco.
Introduced 1930.
Weight : 23 tons 19 cwt.
Pressure : 275 lb. Su. Cyls.: 6¾″ × 9″
Driving Wheels : 3′ 2″
T.E.: { Low Gear : 11,435 lb.
       High Gear :   7,965 lb.
Poppet valves.

68186	**Total 1**

Top to bottom :
Class J11 0-6-0
No. 64438; Class
J37 0-6-0 No.
64562 ; Class J36
0-6-0 No. 65240 ;
Class J10/4 0-6-0
No. 65133.

[B. Canning,
H.C.Casserley (3)

Top : Class J38 0-6-0 No. 65914.   Above : Class J19 0-6-0 No. 64649.
Below : Class J17 0-6-0 No. 65579.   Bottom : Class J15 0-6-0 No. 65466.
[H. C. Casserley, R. E. Vincent (2), J. F. Aylard

Top : Class J4 (ex-M. & G.N.) 0-6-0 No. 64160. *Above :* Class J6 0-6-0 No. 64269.
Below : Class J27 0-6-0 No. 65869. *Bottom :* Class J21 0-6-0 No. 65119.
[*H. C. Casserley (2), J. F. Aylard, E. D. Bruton*

This page. Above left : Class J70 0-6-0T No. 68222. Below left : Class Z5 0-4-2T No. 68192. Above : Class N15/1 0-6-2T No. 69222. Below : Class N8 0-6-2T No. 69371.

[H. Shelton, H. C. Casserley (2), J. F. Aylard

Facing page. Top left : Class C15 4-4-2T No. 67458. Top right : Class F5 2-4-2T No. 67193. Bottom left : Class C13 4-4-2T No. 67436. Bottom right : Class F6 2-4-2T No. 67223.

[H. C. Casserley, F. Day, J. Davenport, R. Vincent

Top to bottom : Class N2/2 0-6-2T No. 69505 ; Class N2/4 0-6-2T No. 69587 ; Class N7/3 0-6-2T No. 69647 ; Class N1 0-6-2T No. 69434

[F. W. Day,
H. C. Casserley (2)
J. F. Aylard

Right : Class J50/3
0-6-0T No. 68954.
Below : Class J52/2
0-6-0ST No. 68888.

[*H. C. Casserley* (2)

Right : Class J72
0-6-0T No.68709.
Below : Class
Q1/1 0-8-0T No.
69927.

[*H. C. Casserley*
(2)

Above : Class J88 0-6-0T No. 68330.   Above right : Class J66
0-6-0T No. 68378.   Below : Class J69/1 0-6-0T No. 68552.
Below right : Class J68 0-6-0T No. 68659.
[H. C. Casserley (2), F. W. Day, J. F. Aylard

0-4-2T   OF   Class Z4

Introduced 1915. Manning-Wardle design of G.N. of S.
Weight : 25 tons 17 cwt.
Pressure : 160 lb. Cyls.: (O) 13″ × 20″
Driving Wheels : 3′ 6″ T.E.: 10,945 lb.

68190	68191	**Total 2**

0-4-2T   OF   Class Z5

Introduced 1915. Manning-Wardle design of G.N. of S.
Weight : 30 tons 18 cwt.
Pressure : 160 lb. Cyls.: (O) 14″ × 20″
Driving Wheels : 4′ 0″ T.E.: 11,105 lb.

68192	68193	**Total 2**

0-6-0ST   OF   Class J62

Introduced 1897. Pollitt M.S. & L. design.
Weight : 30 tons 17 cwt.
Pressure : 150 lb. Cyls.: (O) 13″ × 20″
Driving Wheels : 3′ 6″ T.E.: 10,260 lb.

68200	**Total 1**

0-6-0T   OF   Class J63

Introduced 1906. Robinson G.C. design.
Weight : 37 tons 9 cwt.
Pressure : 150 lb. Cyls.: (O) 13″ × 20″
Driving Wheels : 3′ 6″ T.E.: 10,260 lb.

68204	68206	68208	68210
68205	68207	68209	

Total 7

0-6-0T   OF   Class J65

Introduced 1889. J. Holden G.E. design.
Weight : 36 tons 11 cwt.
Pressure : 160 lb.   Cyls.: 14″ × 20″
Driving Wheels : 4′ 0″ T.E.: 11,105 lb.

68211	68214	**Total 2**

0-6-0T (Tram Locos)   OF   Class J70

Introduced 1903. J. Holden G.E. design.
Weight : 27 tons 1 cwt.
Pressure : 180 lb. Cyls.: (O) 12″ × 15″
Driving Wheels : 3′ 1″ T.E.: 8,930 lb.
Walschaerts gear.

68216	68220	68223	68226
68217	68221	68224	
68219	68222	68225	

Total 10

0-6-0T   OF   Class J71

Introduced 1886. T. W. Worsdell N.E. design.
*†Altered cylinder dimensions.
Weight : 37 tons 12 cwt.
Pressure : 140 lb. Dr. Wheels : 4′ 7¼″
Cyls.: { 16″ × 22″ / 16¾″ × 22″* / 18″ × 22″† } T.E.: { 12,130 lb. / 13,300 lb. / 15,355 lb.† }

68230*	68252*	68273	68296
68231	68253*	68275	68297
68232	68254	68276	68298
68233	68255	68278	68299
68234*	68256	68279	68300
68235	68258*	68280*	68301
68236	68259*	68281	68302*
68238	68260	68282	68303*
68239	68262	68283	68304*
68240	68263	68284	68305*
68242	68264	68286*	68306*
68244	68265	68287*	68307*
68245	68266	68289*	68308*
68246*	68267	68290	68309*
68247	68268	68291	68311*
68248	68269	68292	68312†
68249	68270	68293*	68313*
68250*	68271	68294	68314
68251	68272	68295	68316*

Total 76

IMPORTANT NOTE
A careful reading of the notes on page 2 is essential to understand the use of reference marks in this book.

68320-68481

0-6-0T 0F Class J88

Introduced 1904. Reid N.B. design with short wheelbase.
Weight : 38 tons 14 cwt.
Pressure : 130 lb. Cyls.: (O) 15″ × 22″
Driving Wheels : 3′ 9″ T.E.: 12,155 lb.

68320	68329	68338	68347
68321	68330	68339	68348
68322	68331	68340	68349
68323	68332	68341	68350
68324	68333	68342	68351
68325	68334	68343	68352
68326	68335	68344	68353
68327	68336	68345	68354
68328	68337	68346	

Total 35

0-6-0T 3F Class J73

Introduced 1891. W. Worsdell N.E. design.
Weight : 46 tons 15 cwt.
Pressure : 160 lb. Cyls.: 19″ × 24″
Driving Wheels : 4′ 7¼″ T.E. 21,320 lb.

68355	68358	68361	68363
68356	68359	68362	68364
68357	68360		

Total 10

0-6-0T 2F Class J66

Introduced 1886. J. Holden G.E. design.
Weight : 40 tons 6 cwt.
Pressure : 160 lb. Cyls.: 16½″ × 22″
Driving Wheels : 4′ 0″ T.E.: 16,970 lb.

68370S	68375	68378	68383
68371	68376	68380	68385
68373	68377	68382	68388
68374			

Total 13

0-6-0T 2F Class J77

Introduced 1899. W. Worsdell N.E. rebuild of Fletcher 0-4-4T originally built 1874-84.
* Darlington rebuilds with square-cornered cab roof (remainder York rebuilds with rounded cab).
Weight : 43 tons.
Pressure : 160 lb. Cyls.: 17″ × 22″
Driving Wheels : 4′ 1¼″ T.E.: 17,560 lb.

68391	68405*	68420*	68430
68392*	68406	68421	68431
68393*	68407	68422	68432*
68395*	68408	68423	68433
68397*	68409	68424	68434
68398	68410	68425	68435
68399	68412*	68426	68436
68401	68413	68427	68437
68402	68414	68428	68438
68404*	68417	68429	68440*

Total 40

> **IMPORTANT NOTE**
> A careful reading of the notes on page 2 is essential to understand the use of reference marks in this book.

0-6-0T 2F Class J83

Introduced 1900. Holmes N.B. design.
Weight : 45 tons 5 cwt.
Pressure : 150 lb. Cyls.: 17″ × 26″
Driving Wheels : 4′ 6″ T.E.: 17,745 lb.

68442	68452	68463	68473
68443	68453	68464	68474
68444	68454	68465	68475
68445	68455	68466	68476
68446	68456	68467	68477
68447	68457	68468	68478
68448	68458	68469	68479
68449	68459	68470	68480
68450	68460	68471	68481
68451	68461	68472	

Total 39

Classes

0-6-0T $\begin{array}{c} \text{2F (J67)} \\ \text{3F (J69)} \end{array}$ J67 & J69

J67/1* Introduced 1890. J. Holden G.E. design with 160 lb. pressure.

J69/1† Introduced 1902. Development of J67 with 180 lb. pressure, larger tanks and larger firebox (some rebuilt from J67).

J67/2‡ Introduced 1937. Rebuild of J69 with 160 lb. boiler and small firebox.

J69/2§ Introduced 1950. J67/1 rebuilt with 180 lb. boiler and large firebox.

Weights: $\begin{cases} 40 \text{ tons.*‡} \\ 40 \text{ tons 9 cwt.†§} \end{cases}$

Pressure: $\begin{cases} 160 \text{ lb.*‡} \\ 180 \text{ lb.†§} \end{cases}$

Cyls.: 16½" × 22"
Driving Wheels : 4' 0"
T.E.: $\begin{cases} 16,970 \text{ lb.*‡} \\ 19,090 \text{ lb.†§} \end{cases}$

68490§	68522§	68554†	68588*
68491†	68523*	68555†	68589*
68492*	68524†	68556†	68590*
68493†	68525†	68557†	68591†
68494†	68526†	68558†	68592*
68495†	68527†	68559†	68593*
68496*	68528†	68560†	68594*
68497*	68529‡	68561†	68595*
68498*	68530†	68562†	68196*
68499†	68531‡	68563†	68597‡
68500†	68532†	68565†	68598†
68501*	68533†	68566†	68599†
68502†	68534*	68567†	68600†
68503†	68535†	68568†	68601†
68504†	68536§	68569†	68602†
68505†	68537†	68570†	68603†
68507†	68538†	68571†	68605*
68508†	68540†	68572‡	68606*
68509*	68541†	68573†	68607*
68510§	68542†	68574†	68608*
68511*	68543†	68575†	68609‡
68512§	68544†	68576†	68610‡
68513*	68545†	68577†	68611*
68514*	68546†	68578†	68612†
68515*	68547‡	68579†	68613†
68516*	68548†	68581†	68616*
68517*	68549†	68583*	68617†
68518*	68550†	68584*	68618†
68519§	68551†	68585†	68619†
68520§	68552†	68586†	68621†
68521*	68553†	68587†	68623†

68625†	68629†	68632†	68635†
68626†	68630†	68633†	68636†
68628‡	68631†		

Totals : Class J67/1   29
              Class J67/2   10
              Class J69/1   90
              Class J69/2   5

0-6-0T   3F   Class J68

Introduced 1912. Hill G.E. development of J69 with side-window cab.
Weight : 42 tons 9 cwt.
Pressure : 180 lb.   Cyls.: 16½" × 22"
Driving Wheels : 4' 0"   T.E.: 19,090 lb.

68638	68646	68654	68662
68639	68647	68655	68663
68640	68648	68656	68664
68641	68649	68657	68665
68642	68650	68658	68666
68643	68651	68659	
68644	68652	68660	
68645	68653	68661	

Total 29

0-6-0 Crane Tank
0F   Class J92

Introduced 1891. J. Holden G.E. rebuild of Ruston & Proctor 0-6-0T (originally built 1868).
Weight : 40 tons 8 cwt.
Pressure : 140 lb.   Cyls.: 16" × 22"
Driving Wheels : 4' 0"   T.E.: 13,960 lb.

68667S	68668S

Total 2

0-6-0T   2F   Class J72

Introduced 1898. W. Worsdell N.E. design.
* Altered cylinder dimensions.
Weight : 38 tons 12 cwt.
Pressure : 140 lb.   Cyls.: $\begin{cases} 17" \times 24" \\ 18" \times 24"* \end{cases}$
Driving Wheels : 4' 1¼"
T.E.: $\begin{cases} 16,760 \text{ lb.} \\ 18,790 \text{ lb.*} \end{cases}$

68670	68675	68680	68685*
68671	68676	68681	68686
68672	68677	68682	68687
68673	68678	68683	68688
68674	68679	68684	68689

68690	68707	68723	68739	68829	68845**S**	68861	68877
68691	68708	68724	68740	68830	68846	68862	68878
68692	68709	68725	68741	68831	68847	68863	68879
68693	68710	68726	68742	68832	68848	68864	68880
68694	68711	68727	68743	68833	68849	68865	68881
68695	68712	68728	68744	68834	68850	68866	68882
68696	68713	68729	68745	68835	68851	68867	68883
68697	68714	68730	68746	68836	68852	68868	68884
68698	68715	68731	68747	68837	68853	68869	68885
68699	68716	68732	68748	68838	68854	68870	68886
68700	68717	68733	68749	68839	68855	68871	68887
68701	68718	68734	68750	68840‡	68856	68872	68888
68702	68719	68735	68751	68841	68857	68873	68889
68703	68720	68736	68752	68842	68858	68874	
68704	68721	68737	68753	68843	68859	68875	
68705	68722	68738	68754	68844	68860‡	68876‡	
68706							

(Class continued with No. 69001)

Totals : Class J52/1 44
Class J52/2 85

0-6-0ST   3F   Class J52

J52/2 Introduced 1897. Ivatt standard G.N. saddletank with domed boiler.
J52/1* Introduced 1922. Rebuild of Stirling domeless saddletank (introduced 1892)—non-condensing.
J52/1† Introduced 1922. Condensing rebuild of Stirling locos.
‡ J52/2 with boiler pressure raised to 175 lb.
Weight : 51 tons 14 cwt.
Pressure: { 170 lb.   Cyls.: 18″ × 26″
           { 175 lb.‡
Driving Wheels: 4′ 8″ T.E.: { 21,735 lb.
                            { 22,370 lb.‡

68757†	68776†	68794‡	68812
68758†	68777†	68795†	68813
68759†	68778†	68796†	68814
68760†	68779*	68797*	68815
68761†	68780*	68798*	68816**S**
68762*	68781†	68799*	68817
68764*	68783†	68800*	68818
68765*	68784†	68802*	68819
68766*	68785†	68803*	68820
68768*	68786*	68804*	68821
68769*	68787†	68805	68822
68770*	68788†	68806	68823
68771*	68789†	68807	68824
68772*	68790*	68808	68825
68773†	68791†	68809	68826
68774†	68792*	68810	68827
68775*	68793†	68811	68828

0-6-0T   4F   Class J50

J50/2* Introduced 1922. Gresley G.N. design (68900-19 rebuilt from smaller J51, built 1915-22).
J50/3† Introduced 1926. Post-grouping development with detail differences.
J50/1‡ Introduced 1929. Rebuilt from smaller J51, built 1913-4.
J50/4§ Introduced 1937. Development of J50/3 with larger bunker.
Weights : { 56 tons 6 cwt.‡
          { 58 tons 3 cwt.†§
          { 57 tons.*
Pressure : 175 lb.   Cyls.: 18½″ × 26″
Driving Wheels : 4′ 8″ T.E.: 23,635 lb.

68890‡	68906*	68922*	68938*
68891‡	68907*	68923*	68939*
68892‡	68908*	68924*	68940†
68893‡	68909*	68925*	68941†
68894‡	68910*	68926*	68942†
68895‡	68911*	68927*	68943†
68896‡	68912*	68928*	68944†
68897‡	68913*	68929*	68945†
68898‡	68914*	68930*	68946†
68899‡	68915*	68931*	68947†
68900*	68916*	68932*	68948†
68901*	68917*	68933*	68949†
68902*	68918*	68934*	68950†
68903*	68919*	68935*	68951†
68904*	68920*	68936*	68952†
68905*	68921*	68937*	68953†

68954†	68964†	68974†	68984§
68955†	68965†	68975†	68985§
68956†	68966†	68976†	68986§
68957†	68967†	68977†	68987§
68958†	68968†	68978§	68988§
68959†	68969†	68979§	68989§
68960†	68970†	68980§	68990§
68961†	68971†	68981§	68991§
68962†	68972†	68982§	
68963†	68973†	68983§	

Totals : Class J50/1 10
Class J50/2 40
Class J50/3 38
Class J50/4 14

0-6-0T 2F Class J72
(Continued from 68754)

69001	69008	69015	69022
69002	69009	69016	69023
69003	69010	69017	69024
69004	69011	69018	69025
69005	69012	69019	69026
69006	69013	69020	69027
69007	69014	69021	69028

N.B.—Locomotives of this class are still being delivered.

2-6-4T 5F Class L3
Introduced 1914. Robinson G.C. design.
* Altered cylinder dimensions.
Weight : 97 tons 9 cwt.
Pressure: 180 lb. Su. Cyls⋅ $\{21'' \times 26''$ / $20'' \times 26''*$
Driving Wheels: 5′ 1″ T.E.:$\{28,760$ lb. / $26,085$ lb.*

69050	69055	69062	69065
69051	69060	69064	69069
69052	69061*		Total 10

0-6-2T 3F Class N10
Introduced 1902. W. Worsdell N.E. design.
Weight : 57 tons 14 cwt.
Pressure : 160 lb. Cyls.: $18\frac{1}{2}'' \times 26''$
Driving Wheels: 4′ 7¼″ T.E.: 21,905 lb.

69090	69095	69100	69106
69091	69096	69101	69107
69092	69097	69102	69108
69093	69098	69104	69109
69094	69099	69105	Total 19

0-6-2T 4F Class N13
Introduced 1913. Stirling H. & B. design.
Pressure : 175 lb. Cyls.: $18'' \times 26''$
Driving Wheels : 4′ 6″ T.E.: 23,205 lb.

69111	69114	69116	69118
69112	69115	69117	69119
69113			

Total 9

0-6-2T 4MT Class N14
Introduced 1909 Reid N.B. design.
Pressure : 175 lb. Cyls.: $18'' \times 26''$
Driving Wheels : 4′ 6″ T.E.: 23,205 lb

69120	69125

Total 2

0-6-2T 4MT Class N15
N15/2* Introduced 1910. Reid N.B. design developed from N14. Cowlairs incline banking locos.
N15/1 Introduced 1910. Development of N15/2 with smaller bunker for normal duties.
Weights:$\{62$ tons 1 cwt.* / 60 tons 18 cwt.
Pressure : 175 lb. Cyls.: $18'' \times 26''$
Driving Wheels : 4′ 6″ T.E.: 23,205 lb.

69126*	69147	69168	69189
69127*	69148	69169	69190
69128*	69149	69170	69191
69129*	69150	69171	69192
69130*	69151	69172	69193
69131*	69152	69173	69194
69132	69153	69174	69195
69133	69154	69175	69196
69134	69155	69176	69197
69135	69156	69177	69198
69136	69157	69178	69199
69137	69158	69179	69200
69138	69159	69180	69201
69139	69160	69181	69202
69140	69161	69182	69203
69141	69162	69183	69204
69142	69163	69184	69205
69143	69164	69185	69206
69144	69165	69186	69207
69145	69166	69187	69208
69146	69167	69188	69209

69210	69214	69218	69222
69211	69215	69219	69223
69212	69216	69220	69224
69213	69217	69221	

Totals : **Class N15/1 93**
Class N15/2 6

0-6-2T 2MT Class N4

N4/2 Introduced 1889. Parker M.S. & L. design.
N4/4* Introduced 1892. Development of N4/2 with larger bunker.
N4/1 and N4/3 were N4/2 and N4/4 with longer chimney.
Weights: $\begin{cases} 61 \text{ tons } 10 \text{ cwt.} \\ 61 \text{ tons } 19 \text{ cwt.*} \end{cases}$
Pressure : 160 lb.   Cyls. : 18″ × 26″
Driving Wheels : 5′ 1″ T.E. : 18,780 lb. Joy gear.

69225	69230	69234	69240
69227	69231	69235	69242*
69228	69232	69236	69244*
69229	69233	69239	69246*

Totals : **Class N4/2 13**
Class N4/4 3

0-6-2T 2MT Class N5

N5/2 Introduced 1891. Parker M.S. & L. design developed from N4.
N5/3* Introduced 1915. N5/2 rebuilt with larger tanks, bunker and cyls. (N5/1 was N5/2 with longer chimney.)
Weights: $\begin{cases} 62 \text{ tons } 7 \text{ cwt.} \\ 64 \text{ tons } 13 \text{ cwt.*} \end{cases}$
Pressure : 160 lb. Cyls.: $\begin{cases} 18″ × 26″ \\ 18\frac{1}{4}″ × 26″* \end{cases}$
Driving Wheels : 5′ 1″ T.E.: $\begin{cases} 18,780 \text{ lb.} \\ 19,840 \text{ lb.*} \end{cases}$

69250	69262	69273	69284
69252	69263	69274	69285
69253	69264	69275	69286
69254	69265	69276	69287
69255	69266	69277	69288
69256	69267	69278	69289
69257	69268	69279	69290
69258	69269	69280	69291
69259	69270	69281	69292
69260	69271	69282	69293
69261	69272	69283	69294

69295	69314	69333	69352
69296	69315	69334	69353
69297	69316	69335	69354
69298	69317	69336	69355
69299	69318	69337	69356
69300	69319	69338	69357
69301	69320	69339	69358
69302	69321	69340	69359
69303	69322	69341	69360
69304	69323	69342	69361
69305	69324	69343	69362
69306	69325	69344	69363
69307	69326	69345	69364
69308	69327	69346	69365
69309	69328	69347	69366
69310	69329	69348	69367
69311*	69330	69349	69368
69312	69331	69350	69369
69313	69332	69351	69370

Totals : **Class N5/2 119**
Class N5/3 1

0-6-2T 3MT Class N8

* Introduced 1886. T. W. Worsdell N.E. design, saturated with Joy's gear and slide valves (majority rebuilt from compounds).
† Rebuilt with superheater, Stephenson gear and piston valves, 24″ piston stroke.
‡ As † but with 26″ stroke.
§ Rebuilt with Stephenson gear and piston valves, superheater removed, 24″ stroke.
¶ As § but with 26″ piston stroke.
Weights: $\begin{cases} 56 \text{ tons } 5 \text{ cwt.*§¶} \\ 58 \text{ tons } 14 \text{ cwt.†‡} \end{cases}$
Pressure : 160 lb. SS.
Cyls.: $\begin{cases} 18″ × 24″* \\ 19″ × 24″†§ \\ 19″ × 26″‡¶ \end{cases}$
Driving Wheels : 5′ 1¼″
T.E.: $\begin{cases} 17,265 \text{ lb.*} \\ 19,235 \text{ lb.†§} \\ 20,840 \text{ lb.‡¶} \end{cases}$

69371†	69379†	69385†	69389*
69377†	69381¶	69386‡	69390†
69378§	69382¶	69387‡	69391†

69392*	69394†	69398†	69401‡
69393†	69395†	69400¶	

Total 19

0-6-2T 3MT Class N9

Introduced 1893. T. W. Worsdell N.E. design.
Weight : 56 tons 10 cwt.
Pressure : 160 lb. Cyls.: 19″ × 26″
Driving Wheels: 5′ 1¼″ T.E.: 20,840 lb.

69423	69426	69427	69429
69424			

Total 5

0-6-2T 2MT Class N1

* Introduced 1907. Ivatt G.N. design, prototype of class.
†‡§¶ Introduced 1907. Standard design with shorter tanks and detail differences.
§¶ Rebuilt with superheater and reduced pressure.
‡¶ Fitted with condensing gear.
Weights: { 64 tons 14 cwt.*
{ 65 tons 17 cwt.
Pressure: { 175 lb.
{ 170 lb. Su.§¶
Cyls.: 18″ × 26″
Driving Wheels: 5′ 8″
T.E.: { 18,430 lb.
{ 17,900 lb.§¶

69430*	69445‡	69459†	69473†
69431‡	69446†	69460‡	69474†
69432‡	69447†	69461‡	69475‡
69433‡	69448†	69462‡	69476‡
69434‡	69449†	69463‡	69477‡
69435¶	69450‡	69464¶	69478¶
69436§	69451‡	69465‡	69479¶
69437¶	69452§	69466‡	69480‡
69439¶	69453‡	69467‡	69481‡
69440†	69454†	69468‡	69482¶
69441‡	69455‡	69469‡	69483§
69442‡	69456‡	69470‡	69484‡
69443†	69457‡	69471‡	69485‡
69444†	69458‡	69472§	

Total 55

0-6-2T 3MT Class N2

N2/2* Introduced 1925. Post-grouping development of Gresley ex-G.N. N2/1, introduced 1920, which class is now included in N2/2. Condensing gear and small chimney.

N2/2† Condensing gear removed.

N2/3‡ Introduced 1925. Locos built non-condensing, originally fitted with large chimney. Some now with small chimney.

N2/4§ Introduced 1928. Development of N2/2, slightly heavier. Condensing gear and small chimney.
(The small chimneys are to suit the Metropolitan loading gauge, for working to Moorgate St. Condensing gear has been removed from or added to certain locos transferred from or to the London area.)

Weights: { 70 tons 5 cwt.*†
{ 70 tons 8 cwt.‡
{ 71 tons 9 cwt.§
Pressure : 170 lb. Su. Cyls.: 19″ × 26″
Driving Wheels : 5′ 8″ T.E.: 19,945 lb. P.V.

69490*	69515†	69540*	69565‡
69491*	69516†	69541*	69566‡
69492*	69517*	69542*	69567‡
69493*	69518†	69543*	69568§
69494*	69519†	69544*	69569§
69495*	69520*	69545*	69570§
69496*	69521*	69546*	69571§
69497*	69522*	69547*	69572§
69498*	69523*	69548*	69573§
69499*	69524*	69549*	69574§
69500*	69525*	69550*	69575§
69501*	69526*	69551†	69576§
69502†	69527*	69552*	69577§
69503†	69528*	69553†	69578§
69504*	69529*	69554*	69579§
69505*	69530*	69555*	69580§
69506*	69531*	69556§	69581§
69507†	69532*	69557†	69582§
69508†	69533*	69558†	69583§
69509†	69534*	69559*	69584§
69510†	69535*	69560†	69585§
69511†	69536*	69561*	69586§
69512*	69537*	69562‡	69587§
69513*	69538*	695o3†	69588§
69514†	69539*	69564‡	69589§

69590§	69592§	69594‡	69596‡
69591§	69593§	69595‡	

Totals : Class N2/2 70
Class N2/3 9
Class N2/4 28

0-6-2T 3MT Class N7

N7/1[1] Introduced 1925. Post-grouping development of Hill G.E. design with detail differences.

N7/2[2] Introduced 1926. Development of N7/1 with long-travel valves.

N7/3[3] Introduced 1927. Doncaster-built version of N7/2 with round-topped boiler.

N7/4[4] Introduced 1940. Pre-grouping N7 (G.E.) rebuilt with round-topped boiler, retaining short-travel valves.

N7/3[5] Introduced 1943. N7/1 rebuilt with round-topped boiler, retaining short-travel valves.

N7/3[6] Introduced 1943. N7/2 rebuilt with round-topped boiler.

Weights:
$\begin{cases} 63 \text{ tons: } 13 \text{ cwt.}[1] \\ 64 \text{ tons } 17 \text{ cwt.}[2] \\ 64 \text{ tons.}[3] \\ 61 \text{ tons } 16 \text{ cwt.}[4] \\ 64 \text{ tons.}[5] \\ 64 \text{ tons.}[6] \end{cases}$

Pressure : 180 lb. Su. Cyls.: 18″ × 24″
Driving Wheels: 4′ 10″ T.E.: 20,515 lb.
Walschaerts gear, P.V.

69600[1]	69618[4]	69636[5]	69654[1]
69601[4]	69619[4]	69637[1]	69655[5]
69602[4]	69620[4]	69638[5]	69656[5]
69603[4]	69621[4]	69639[5]	69657[1]
69604[4]	69622[5]	69640[5]	69658[1]
69605[4]	69623[1]	69641[1]	69659[1]
69606[4]	69624[1]	69642[1]	69660[5]
69607[4]	69625[5]	69643[5]	69661[1]
69608[4]	69626[1]	69644[5]	69662[5]
69609[4]	69627[1]	69645[1]	69663[5]
69610[4]	69628[1]	69646[1]	69664[5]
69611[4]	69629[1]	69647[5]	69665[1]
69612[4]	69630[5]	69648[5]	69666[5]
69613[4]	69631[1]	69649[5]	69667[5]
69614[4]	69632[5]	69650[5]	69608[1]
69615[4]	69633[5]	69651[5]	69669[5]
69616[4]	69634[1]	69652[5]	69670[1]
69617[4]	69635[5]	69653[1]	69671[5]

69672[2]	69688[2]	69704[3]	69720[3]
69673[6]	69689[2]	69705[3]	69721[3]
69674[2]	69690[2]	69706[3]	69722[3]
69675[6]	69691[6]	69707[3]	69723[3]
69676[6]	69692[6]	69708[3]	69724[3]
69677[6]	69693[6]	69709[3]	69725[3]
69678[6]	69694[2]	69710[3]	69726[3]
69679[6]	69695[2]	69711[3]	69727[3]
69680[6]	69696[6]	69712[3]	69728[3]
69681[6]	69697[6]	69713[3]	69729[3]
69682[6]	69698[2]	69714[3]	69730[3]
69683[2]	69699[6]	69715[3]	69731[3]
69684[6]	69700[2]	69716[3]	69732[3]
69685[6]	69701[6]	69717[3]	69733[3]
69686[6]	69702[3]	69718[3]	
69687[6]	69703[3]	69719[3]	

Totals : Class N7/1 23
Class N7/2 11
Class N7/3 78
Class N7/4 22

4-6-2T 5F Class A7

Introduced 1910. Raven N.E. design, later rebuilt with superheater and reduced pressure.
* Saturated.
Weight : 87 tons 10 cwt.
Pressure: $\begin{cases} 160 \text{ lb. Su.} \\ 180 \text{ lb.*} \end{cases}$
Cyls.: (3) $16\frac{1}{2}$″ × 26″
Driving Wheels: 4′ $7\frac{1}{4}$″
T.E.: $\begin{cases} 26,140 \text{ lb.} \\ 29,405 \text{ lb.*} \end{cases}$
P.V.

69770	69775*	69780	69785
69771	69776	69781	69786
69772	69777	69782	69787*
69773	69778*	69783	69788
69774	69779	69784	69789

Total 20

4-6-2T 4P Class A6

Introduced 1915. Raven N.E. design. (Rebuild of Worsdell Class "W" 4-6-0T, introduced 1907.) Later superheated.
* Saturated.
Weights: $\begin{cases} 79 \text{ tons.} \\ 78 \text{ tons.*} \end{cases}$
Pressure : 175 lb. SS. Cyls.: 19″ × 26″
Driving Wheels: 5′ $1\frac{1}{4}$″ T.E.: 23,830 lb.
P.V.

69791	69793	69794*

69796 | 69797   **Total 5**

4-6-2T   4P   Class A5

A5/1 Introduced 1911. Robinson G.C. design.
A5/2* Introduced 1925. Post-grouping development of A5/1 with reduced boiler mountings and detail differences.

Weights: { 85 tons 18 cwt. / 90 tons 11 cwt.*
Pressure : 180 lb. Su.   Cyls.: 20″ × 26″
Driving Wheels : 5′ 7″   T.E. : 23,750 lb. P.V.

69800	69811	69822	69833*
69801	69812	69823	69834*
69802	69813	69824	69835*
69803	69814	69825	69836*
69804	69815	69826	69837*
69805	69816	69827	69838*
69806	69817	69828	69839*
69807	69818	69829	69840*
69808	69819	69830*	69841*
69809	69820	69831*	69842*
69810	69821	69832*	

Totals : Class A5/1   30
           Class A5/2   13

4-6-2T   4P   Class A8

Introduced 1931. Gresley rebuild of Raven Class "D" 4-4-4T (introduced 1913.)
Weight : 86 tons 18 cwt.
Pressure : 175 lb. Su.
Cyls : (3) 16½″ × 26″
Driving Wheels : 5′ 9″   T.E. : 22,940 lb. P.V.

69850	69862	69874	69885
69851	69863	69875	69886
69852	69864	69876	69887
69853	69865	69877	69888
69854	69866	69878	69889
69855	69867	69879	69890
69856	69868	69880	69891
69857	69869	69881	69892
69858	69870	69882	69893
69859	69871	69883	69894
69860	69872	69884	
69861	69873		

                      Total 45

0-8-4T   7F   Class S1

S1/1* Introduced 1907. Robinson G.C. design, since rebuilt with super-heater.
S1/2† Introduced 1932. S1/1 rebuilt with booster and superheater, booster since removed.
S1/3‡ Introduced 1932. New locos built with booster, booster later removed.

Weights: { 99 tons 6 cwt.* / 99 tons 2 cwt.† / 99 tons 1 cwt.‡
Pressure : 180 lb. Su.
Cyls.: (3) 18″ × 26″
Driving Wheels : 4′ 8″   T.E. : 34,525 lb.

| 69900* | 69902* | 69904‡ | 69905‡ |
| 69901† | 69903* | | |

Totals :   Class S1/1   3
                Class S1/2   1
                Class S1/3   2

4-8-0T   7F   Class T1

Introduced 1909. W. Worsdell N.E. design.
* Rebuilt with superheater.
Weight : 85 tons 8 cwt.
Pressure : 175 lb. SS.
Cyls.: (3) 18″ × 26″
Driving Wheels : 4′ 7½″   T.E. : 34,080 lb. P.V.

69910	69914*	69917	69920
69911	69915	69918	69921
69912	69916	69919	69922
69913			

                      Total 13

0-8-0T   5F   Class Q1

Thompson rebuild of Q4 0-8-0, introduced 1902.
Q1/1* Introduced 1942. 1,500 gallon tanks.
Q1/2 Introduced 1943. 2,000 gallon tanks.

Weights: { 69 tons 18 cwt.* / 73 tons 13 cwt.
Pressure : 180 lb. Cyls.: (O) 19″ × 26″
Driving Wheels : 4′ 8″   T.E. : 25,645 lb.

69925*	69929	69932	69935
69926*	69930	69933	69936
69927*	69931	69934	69937
69928*			**Total 13**

2-8-8-2T Unclass **Class UI**
(Beyer-Garratt loco)
Introduced 1925. Gresley/Beyer Peacock design.
Weight : 178 tons 1 cwt.

Pressure : 180 lb. Su.
Cyls.: (6) $18\frac{1}{2}'' \times 26''$
Driving Wheels : 4' 8" T.E.: 72,940 lb.
Walschaerts gear, derived motion, P.V.

69999   **Total 1**

BRITISH RAILWAYS STANDARD LOCOMOTIVES
Railway Executive member for Mechanical Engineering :
R. A. RIDDLES, C.B.E.

4-6-2   **Class 7MT**
Introduced 1951. Designed at Derby.
Weights : Loco.   94 tons 0 cwt.
           Tender 47 tons 4 cwt.
Pressure : 250 lb.
Cyls.· (O) $20'' \times 28''$
Driving Wheels : 6' 2" T.E.: 32,150 lb.
Walschaerts gear, P.V.

70000	Britannia
70001	Lord Hurcomb
70002	Geoffrey Chaucer
70003	John Bunyan
70004	William Shakespeare
70005	John Milton
70006	Robert Burns
70007	Coeur-de-Lion
70008	Black Prince
70009	Alfred the Great
70010	Owen Glendower
70011	Hotspur
70012	John o' Gaunt
70013	Oliver Cromwell
70014	Iron Duke
70015	Apollo
70016	Ariel
70017	Arrow
70018	Flying Dutchman
70019	Lightning
70020	Mercury
70021	Morning Star
70022	Tornado
70023	Venus
70024	Vulcan

4-6-2   **Class 6MT**
To be introduced 1951. Designed at Derby.
Weights : Loco.   86 tons 19 cwt
           Tender 47 tons 4 cwt.
Pressure : 225 lb.
Cyls.: (O) $19\frac{1}{2}'' \times 28''$
Driving Wheels : 6' 2" T.E.: 27,520 lb.

72000	Clan Buchanan
72001	Clan Cameron
72002	Clan Campbell
72003	Clan Fraser
72004	Clan Macdonald
72005	Clan Macgregor
72006	Clan Mackenzie
72007	Clan Mackintosh
72008	Clan Macleod
72009	Clan Stewart

4-6-0   **Class 5MT**
Introduced 1951. Designed at Doncaster.
Weights : Loco.   76 tons 4 cwt.
           Tender 47 tons 4 cwt.
Pressure : 225 lb.
Cyls.: (O) $19'' \times 28''$
Driving Wheels : 6' 2" T.E.: 26,120 lb.

73000	73008	73016	73024
73001	73009	73017	73025
73002	73010	73018	73026
73003	73011	73019	73027
73004	73012	73020	73028
73005	73013	73021	73029
73006	73014	73022	
73007	73015	73023	

4-6-0   Class 4MT

To be introduced 1951. Designed at
  Brighton.
Weights : Loco.   69 tons 0 cwt.
            Tender 43 tons 3 cwt.
Pressure : 225 ib.
Cyls.: (O) 18″ × 28″
Driving Wheels : 5′ 8″   T.E.: 25,100 lb.

75000	75005	75010	75015
75001	75006	75011	75016
75002	75007	75012	75017
75003	75008	75013	75018
75004	75009	75014	75019

2-6-4T   Class 4MT

To be introduced 1951. Designed at
  Brighton.
Weight : 88 tons 10 cwt.
Pressure : 225 lb.
Cyls.: 18″ × 28″
Driving Wheels : 5′ 8″   T.E.: 25,100 lb.

80000	80014	80028	80042
80001	80015	80029	80043
80002	80016	80030	80044
80003	80017	80031	80045
80004	80018	80032	80046
80005	80019	80033	80047
80006	80020	80034	80048
80007	80021	80035	80049
80008	80022	80036	80050
80009	80023	80037	80051
80010	80024	80038	80052
80011	80025	80039	80053
80012	80026	80040	
80013	80027	80041	

2-6-2T   Class 3MT

To be introduced 1951. Designed at
  Swindon.
Weight : 73 tons 10 cwt.
Pressure : 200 lb.
Cyls.: 17½″ × 26″
Driving Wheels : 5′ 3″   T.E.: 21,490 lb.

82000	82005	82010	82015
82001	82006	82011	82016
82002	82007	82012	82017
82003	82008	82013	82018
82004	82009	82014	82019

2-8-0   8F   Class WD

Ministry of Supply " Austerity "
  2-8-0 locomotives purchased by
  British Railways, 1948.
Introduced 1943. Riddles M.o.S. design.
Weights : Loco.   70 tons 5 cwt.
            Tender 55 tons 10 cwt.
Pressure : 225 lb.   Cyls.: (O) 19″ × 28″
Driving Wheels : 4′ 8½″   T.E.: 34,215 lb.
Walschaerts gear, P.V.

90000	90039	90078	90117
90001	90040	90079	90118
90002	90041	90080	90119
90003	90042	90081	90120
90004	90043	90082	90121
90005	90044	90083	90122
90006	90045	90084	90123
90007	90046	90085	90124
90008	90047	90086	90125
90009	90048	90087	90126
90010	90049	90088	90127
90011	90050	90089	90128
90012	90051	90090	90129
90013	90052	90091	90130
90014	90053	90092	90131
90015	90054	90093	90132
90016	90055	90094	90133
90017	90056	90095	90134
90018	90057	90096	90135
90019	90058	90097	90136
90020	90059	90098	90137
90021	90060	90099	90138
90022	90061	90100	90139
90023	90062	90101	90140
90024	90063	90102	90141
90025	90064	90103	90142
90026	90065	90104	90143
90027	90066	90105	90144
90028	90067	90106	90145
90029	90068	90107	90146
90030	90069	90108	90147
90031	90070	90109	90148
90032	90071	90110	90149
90033	90072	90111	90150
90034	90073	90112	90151
90035	90074	90113	90152
90036	90075	90114	90153
90037	90076	90115	90154
90038	90077	90116	90155

90156	90204	90252	90300	90348	90396	90444	90492
90157	90205	90253	90301	90349	90397	90445	90493
90158	90206	90254	90302	90350	90398	90446	90494
90159	90207	90255	90303	90351	90399	90447	90495
90160	90208	90256	90304	90352	90400	90448	90496
90161	90209	90257	90305	90353	90401	90449	90497
90162	90210	90258	90306	90354	90402	90450	90498
90163	90211	90259	90307	90355	90403	90451	90499
90164	90212	90260	90308	90356	90404	90452	90500
90165	90213	90261	90309	90357	90405	90453	90501
90166	90214	90262	90310	90358	90406	90454	90502
90167	90215	90263	90311	90359	90407	90455	90503
90168	90216	90264	90312	90360	90408	90456	90504
90169	90217	90265	90313	90361	90409	90457	90505
90170	90218	90266	90314	90362	90410	90458	90506
90171	90219	90267	90315	90363	90411	90459	90507
90172	90220	90268	90316	90364	90412	90460	90508
90173	90221	90269	90317	90365	90413	90461	90509
90174	90222	90270	90318	90366	90414	90462	90510
90175	90223	90271	90319	90367	90415	90463	90511
90176	90224	90272	90320	90368	90416	90464	90512
90177	90225	90273	90321	90369	90417	90465	90513
90178	90226	90274	90322	90370	90418	90466	90514
90179	90227	90275	90323	90371	90419	90467	90515
90180	90228	90276	90324	90372	90420	90468	90516
90181	90229	90277	90325	90373	90421	90469	90517
90182	90230	90278	90326	90374	90422	90470	90518
90183	90231	90279	90327	90375	90423	90471	90519
90184	90232	90280	90328	90376	90424	90472	90520
90185	90233	90281	90329	90377	90425	90473	90521
90186	90234	90282	90330	90378	90426	90474	90522
90187	90235	90283	90331	90379	90427	90475	90523
90188	90236	90284	90332	90380	90428	90476	90524
90189	90237	90285	90333	90381	90429	90477	90525
90190	90238	90286	90334	90382	90430	90478	90526
90191	90239	90287	90335	90383	90431	90479	90527
90192	90240	90288	90336	90384	90432	90480	90528
90193	90241	90289	90337	90385	90433	90481	90529
90194	90242	90290	90338	90386	90434	90482	90530
90195	90243	90291	90339	90387	90435	90483	90531
90196	90244	90292	90340	90388	90436	90484	90532
90197	90245	90293	90341	90389	90437	90485	90533
90198	90246	90294	90342	90390	90438	90486	90534
90199	90247	90295	90343	90391	90439	90487	90535
90200	90248	90296	90344	90392	90440	90488	90536
90201	90249	90297	90345	90393	90441	90489	90537
90202	90250	90298	90346	90394	90442	90490	90538
90203	90251	90299	90347	90395	90443	90491	90539

90540	90574	90608	90642
90541	90575	90609	90643
90542	90576	90610	90644
90543	90577	90611	90645
90544	90578	90612	90646
90545	90579	90613	90647
90546	90580	90614	90648
90547	90581	90615	90649
90548	90582	90616	90650
90549	90583	90617	90651
90550	90584	90618	90652
90551	90585	90619	90653
90552	90586	90620	90654
90553	90587	90621	90655
90554	90588	90622	90656
90555	90589	90623	90657
90556	90590	90624	90658
90557	90591	90625	90659
90558	90592	90626	90660
90559	90593	90627	90661
90560	90594	90628	90662
90561	90595	90629	90663
90562	90596	90630	90664
90563	90597	90631	90665
90564	90598	90632	90666
90565	90599	90633	90667
90566	90600	90634	90668
90567	90601	90635	90669
90568	90602	90636	90670
90569	90603	90637	90671
90570	90604	90638	90672
90571	90605	90639	90673
90572	90606	90640	90674
90573	90607	90641	90675

90676	90691	90706	90721
90677	90692	90707	90722
90678	90693	90708	90723
90679	90694	90709	90724
90680	90695	90710	90725
90681	90696	90711	90726
90682	90697	90712	90727
90683	90698	90713	90728
90684	90699	90714	90729
90685	90700	90715	90730
90686	90701	90816	90731
90687	90702	90717	90732
90688	90703	90718	Vulcan
90689	90704	90719	
90690	90705	90720	

2-10-0   8F   Class WD

**Ministry of Supply " Austerity "
2-10-0 locomotives purchased by
British Railways, 1948.**
Introduced 1943. Riddles M.o.S. design.
Weights : Loco. 78 tons 6 cwt.
　　　　　　Tender 55 tons 10 cwt.
Pressure : 225 lb. Cyls.: (O) 19″ × 28″.
Driving Wheels: 4′ 8¼″ T.E.: 34,215 lb.
Walschaerts gear, P.V.

90750	90758	90766	90773
90751	90759	90767	North
90752	90760	90768	British
90753	90761	90769	
90754	90762	90770	90774
90755	90763	90771	North
90756	90764	90772	British
90757	90765		

PRINCIPAL LOCOMOTIVE RUNNING DEPOTS

EASTERN REGION

Stratford	...	...	30A	**Norwich**	...	...	...	32A
Hertford East	...	...	30B	Ipswich	...	...	...	32B
Bishops Stortford	...	...	30C	Lowestoft	...	...	...	32C
Southend Victoria	...	...	30D	Yarmouth (South Town)	...	32D
Colchester	...	...	30E	Yarmouth (Vauxhall)	...	32E
Parkeston	...	...	30F	Yarmouth (Beach)	...	32F
Cambridge	...	...	31A	Melton Constable	...	32G
March	...	...	31B		
King's Lynn	...	...	31C	**Plaistow**	...	...	...	33A
South Lynn	...	...	31D	Tilbury	...	...	...	33B
Bury St. Edmunds	...	...	31E	Shoeburyness	...	...	...	33C

King's Cross	...	...	...	34A
Hornsey	...	...	...	34B
Hatfield	...	...	...	34C
Hitchin	...	...	...	34D
Neasden	...	...	...	34E
New England	...	...	...	35A
Grantham	...	...	...	35B
Peterborough (Spital)	...	...	35C
Doncaster	...	...	...	36A
Mexborough	...	...	...	36B
Frodingham	...	...	...	36C
Barnsley	...	...	...	36D
Retford	...	...	...	36E
Ardsley	...	...	...	37A
Copley Hill	...	...	...	37B

Bradford	...	...	...	37C
Colwick	...	...	...	38A
Annesley	...	...	...	38B
Leicester	...	...	...	38C
Staveley	...	...	...	38D
Woodford Halse	...	...	38E
Gorton	...	...	...	39A
Sheffield	...	...	...	39B
Lincoln	...	...	...	40A
Immingham	...	...	...	40B
Louth	...	...	...	40C
Tuxford	...	...	...	40D
Langwith	...	...	...	40E
Boston	...	...	...	40F

NORTH EASTERN REGION

York	...	...	...	50A
Leeds (Neville Hill)	...	...	50B
Selby	...	...	...	50C
Starbeck	...	...	...	50D
Scarborough	...	...	...	50E
Malton	...	...	...	50F
Whitby	...	...	...	50G
Darlington	...	...	...	51A
Newport	...	...	...	51B
West Hartlepool	...	...	51C
Middlesbrough	...	...	...	51D
Stockton	...	...	...	51E
West Auckland	...	...	51F
Haverton Hill	...	...	...	51G
Kirkby Stephen	...	...	51H
Northallerton	...	...	...	51J
Saltburn	...	...	...	51K

Gateshead	...	...	...	52A
Heaton	...	...	...	52B
Blaydon	...	...	...	52C
Tweedmouth	...	...	...	52D
Percy Main	...	...	...	52E
North Blyth	...	...	...	52F
Hull (Dairycoates)	...	...	53A
Hull (Botanic Gardens)	...	53B
Hull (Springhead)	...	...	53C
Bridlington	...	...	...	53D
Cudworth	...	...	...	53E
Sunderland	...	...	...	54A
Tyne Dock	...	...	...	54B
Borough Gardens	...	...	54C
Consett	...	...	...	54D

SCOTTISH REGION

Inverness	...	...	...	60A
Aviemore	...	...	...	60B
Helmsdale	...	...	...	60C
Wick	...	...	...	60D
Forres	...	...	...	60E
Kittybrewster	...	...	...	61A
Ferryhill	...	...	...	61B
Keith	...	...	...	61C
Thornton	...	...	...	62A
Dundee (Tay Bridge)	...	...	62B
Dunfermline	...	...	...	62C
Perth South	...	...	...	63A
Stirling	...	...	...	63B
Forfar	...	...	...	63C
Fort William	...	...	...	63D
Oban	...	...	...	63E
St. Margarets	...	...	...	64A
Haymarket	...	...	...	64B
Dalry Road	...	...	...	64C
Carstairs	...	...	...	64D
Polmont	...	...	...	64E
Bathgate	...	...	...	64F

Hawick	...	...	...	64G
Eastfield	...	...	...	65A
St. Rollox	...	...	...	65B
Parkhead	...	...	...	65C
Dawsholm	...	...	...	65D
Kipps	...	...	...	65E
Grangemouth	...	...	...	65F
Yoker	...	...	...	65G
Helensburgh	...	...	...	65H
Balloch	...	...	...	65J
Polmadie	...	...	...	66A
Motherwell	...	...	...	66B
Hamilton	...	...	...	66C
Greenock	...	...	...	66D
Corkerhill	...	...	...	67A
Hurlford	...	...	...	67B
Ayr	...	...	...	67C
Ardrossan	...	...	...	67D
Carlisle (Kingmoor)	...	...	68A
Dumfries	...	...	...	68B
Stranraer	...	...	...	68C
Beattock	...	...	...	68D

BRITISH RAILWAYS
EASTERN & NORTH EASTERN REGION

Chief Mechanical Engineer
A. H. Peppercorn   -   -   1948-1949
(*post abolished*)

LOCOMOTIVE SUPERINTENDENTS AND CHIEF MECHANICAL ENGINEERS OF THE L.N.E.R.

Sir Nigel Gresley   1923—1941

E. Thompson   -   1941—1946

A. H. Peppercorn   1946—1947

Great Northern Railway
A. Sturrock	..	1850—1866
P. Stirling	..	1866—1895
H. A. Ivatt	..	1896—1911
H. N. Gresley	..	1911—1922

North Eastern Railway
E. Fletcher	..	1854—1883
A. McDonnell*	..	1883—1884
T. W. Worsdell	..	1885—1890
W. Worsdell	..	1890—1910
Sir Vincent Raven		1910—1922

Great Eastern Railway
R. Sinclair	..	1862—1866
S. W. Johnson	..	1866—1873
W. Adams	..	1873—1878
M. Bromley	..	1878—1881
T. W. Worsdell	..	1881—1885
J. Holden	..	1885—1907
S. D. Holden	..	1908—1912
A. J. Hill	..	1912—1922

Lancashire, Derbyshire and East Coast Railway
R. A. Thom	..	1902—1907

Manchester, Sheffield and Lincolnshire Railway
Richard Peacock		—1854
W. G. Craig	..	1854—1859
Charles Sacré	..	1859—1886
T. Parker		1886—1893
H. Pollitt	..	1893—1897

Great Central Railway
H. Pollitt	..	1897—1900
J. G. Robinson	..	1900—1922

Hull and Barnsley Railway
M. Stirling	..	1885—1922

Midland and Great Northern Joint Railway
W. Marriott	..	1884—1924

North British Railway
T. Wheatley†	..	1867—1874
D. Drummond	..	1875—1882
M. Holmes	..	1882—1903
W. P. Reid	..	1903—1919
W. Chalmers	..	1919—1922

* Between McDonnell and T. W. Worsdell there was an interval during which the office was covered by a Locomotive committee.

† Previous to whom, the records are indeterminate.

ROUTE AVAILABILITY OF LOCOMOTIVES

Restrictions on the working of locomotives over the routes of the former L.N.E.R. are denoted by Route Availability numbers. In general a locomotive is not permitted to work over a line of lower R.A. number than itself. The scheme is as follows :

R.A.1 : J15, J62, J63, J65, J71, Y1, Y3, Y6, Y7, Y8, Y10, Y11, Z4.

R.A.2 : E4, J24, J67/1, J70, J72, J77, Y9, Z5.

R.A.3 : B12/1, D3, D41, F3, F4, F5, J3, J4, J10, J21, J25, J36, J66, J67/2, J68, J69, J88, J92, N9, N10.

R.A.4 : A6, B12/3, D2, D31, D40, F6, G5, J1, J5, J17, J26, J55, J83, N4, N5/2, N8, N13, N14, Q5, V4.

R.A.5 : A5, A8, B1, B2, B6, B17/1, B17/4, C12, C13, C14, D15, D16, F2, J2, J6, J11, J19, J20, J27, J52, J73, J94, K2, N1, N5/3, N7.

R.A.6 : C15, C16, D10, D11, D20, D29, D30, D32, D33, D34, J35, J39, J50, K1, K4, N2, N15, O1, O2, O3, O4, O7, Q6, V1, Y4.

R.A.7 : A7, B16/1, B17/5, L1, L3, Q7, U1, V3.

R.A.8 : B16/2, B16/3, D49, J37, J38, K3, K5, Q1, S1, T1.

R.A.9 : A1, A2, A3, A4, V2, W1.

———

CLASSIFICATION OF L.N.E.R. LOCOMOTIVES

The L.N.E.R. locomotive classification scheme was based on that used on the former G.N.R. Each wheel arrangement was allotted a letter, and the classes of that arrangement were numbered in groups according to the pre-grouping ownership, in the order G.N., G.C., G.E., N.E., N.B., G.N.S. L.N.E.R. classes were at first usually added at the end of the list, but later standard locomotives have been given the lowest number. Many classes are sub-divided into " parts," denoted thus : " D16/3." This division is not entirely consistent, as some classes with comparatively wide variations, such as " A4," are not sub-divided, but others, such as " O4," have some divisions dependent only on details such as brakes and whether or not the tender has a water scoop. In these lists, sub-divisions are denoted by " parts " where these exist, but elsewhere it is to be assumed that any variations between the locomotives in the class are not covered by the classification (e.g. " A4 ").

First published 1951
Reprinted 2002

ISBN 0 7110 2874 5

© Ian Allan Publishing Ltd 1951 / 2002

Published by Ian Allan Publishing

an imprint of Ian Allan Publishing Ltd, Hersham, Surrey, KT12 4RG.

Printed by Ian Allan Printing Ltd, Hersham, Surrey, KT12 4RG.

Code: 0201/C

This is a facsimile reprint of an original edition first published in 1951,
and as such, all advertisements are no longer valid.

Front cover:
BR Standard Class 7MT No 70004 *William Shakespeare* at the head of the
Southern Region's 'Golden Arrow' Pullman service. *Ian Allan Library*

Back cover, top:
Built by BR to a GWR design was 'Castle' No 7028 *Cadbury Castle*.
Ian Allan Library

Back cover, bottom:
The standard LMS 0-6-0DE shunter was the forerunner to the BR-built
Class 08. No 12082 was later designated Class 11.
H. C. Casserley